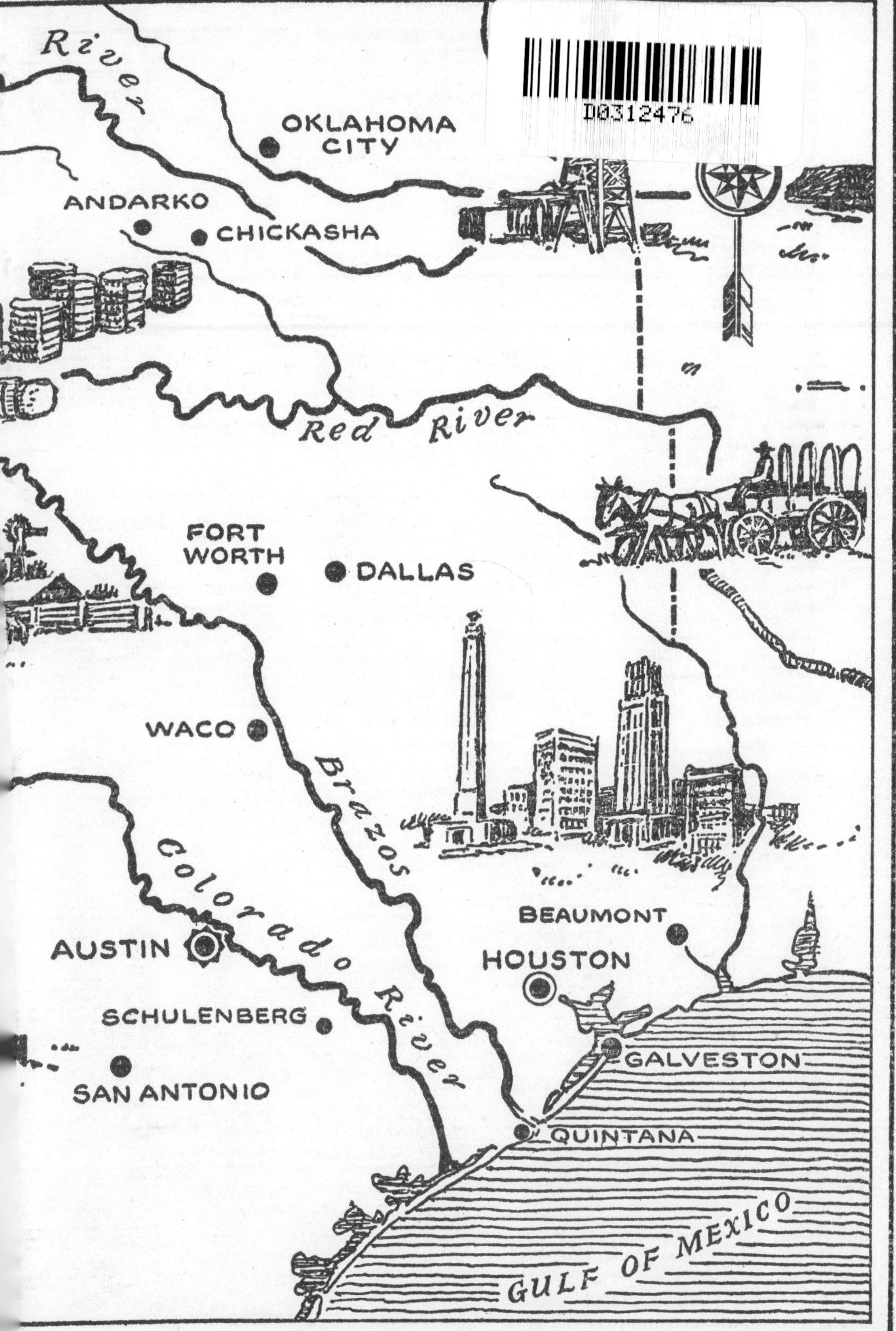
River
OKLAHOMA CITY
ANDARKO
CHICKASHA
Red River
FORT WORTH
DALLAS
WACO
Brazos
Colorado River
AUSTIN
BEAUMONT
HOUSTON
SCHULENBERG
GALVESTON
SAN ANTONIO
QUINTANA
GULF OF MEXICO

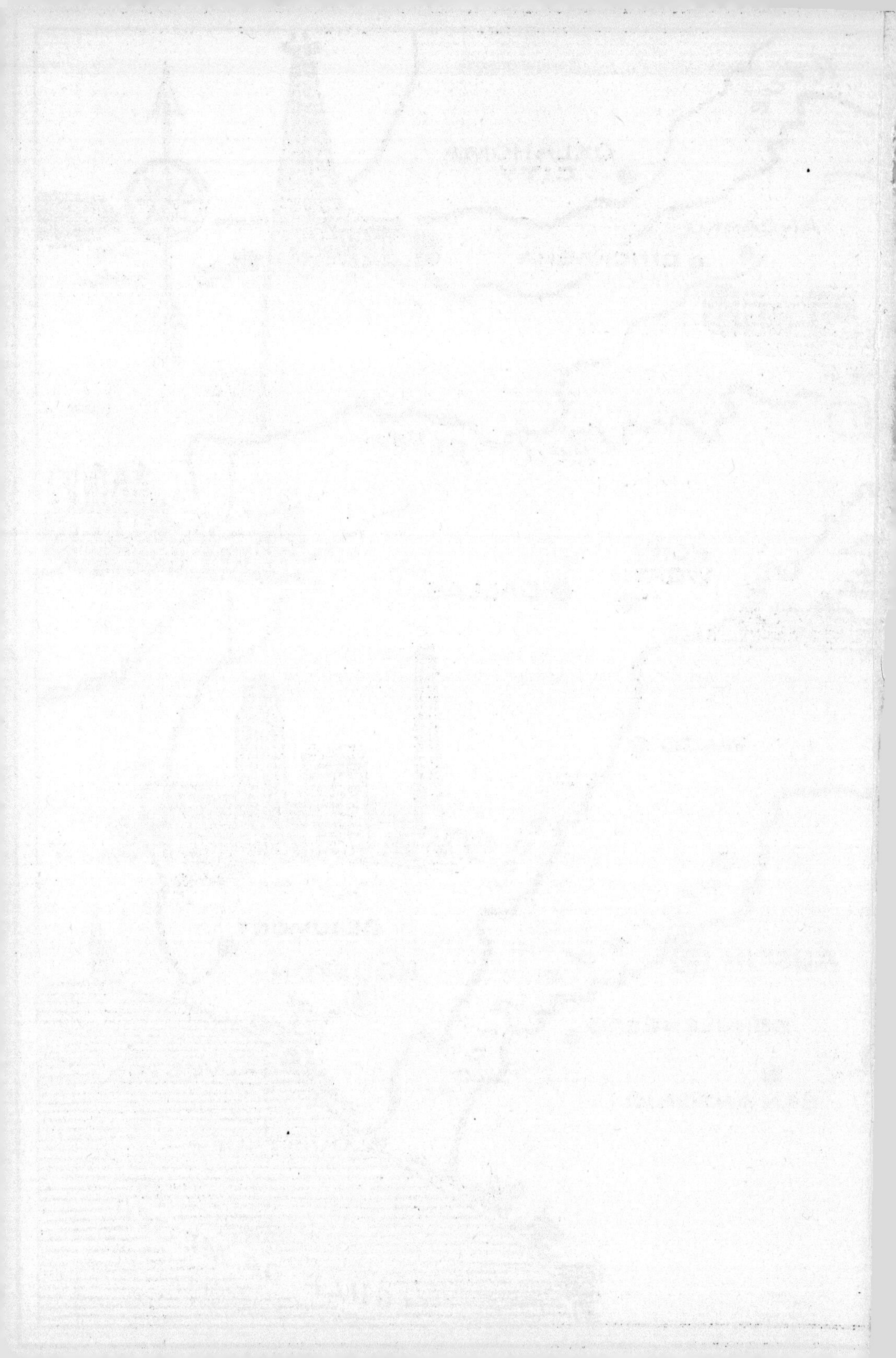

HUGH ROY CULLEN

A STORY OF AMERICAN OPPORTUNITY

HUGH ROY

CULLEN

A STORY OF AMERICAN OPPORTUNITY

By Ed Kilman
and Theon Wright

ILLUSTRATED BY
Nick Eggenhoffer

PRENTICE-HALL, INC. · NEW YORK

Library of Congress Catalog Card Number: 54-8482

Printed in the United States of America

Publisher's Note

The story of Hugh Roy Cullen and Mrs. Cullen, and their family, is one of the most inspiring we have had the privilege of publishing. We believe it should have a wide distribution and should serve as an inspiration to every American.

This is not because Mr. Cullen became one of the world's richest men. He is not so rich now, because he has given most of his wealth away. Nor was he always rich—he began life a comparatively poor boy, who went to work in his early teens.

In our opinion, this story is significant and inspiring for three reasons: First, finding oil was not a matter of luck with Hugh Roy Cullen. It was the result of study and creative thinking, of sound judgment exercised to overcome great risks.

Second, Mr. Cullen was able to undertake and carry out the hazardous and complex operation of drilling for oil because in earlier careers as cotton broker and real estate operator, he had established a reputation which earned him the respect of every man who knew him. Third, Mr. and Mrs. Cullen have chosen to enjoy the greatest happiness their money can give, the pleasure of seeing it used for the benefit of others.

Here is the story of a pioneer in American industry, who by working in the oil fields uncovered wealth hidden in the earth. He brought it forth for the benefit of his fellow man by giving them oil to produce power and improve their standard of living, and by dedicating the direct wealth thereby created to educational, religious, medical, and other social benefits for the community.

HUGH ROY CULLEN: *A Story of American Opportunity* will show democratic thinking people everywhere that frontiers are never closed, that opportunities are always open to those willing to work for them, and that the American way of life has much for all the world to admire.

Contents

CONTENTS

HUGH ROY CULLEN

A STORY OF AMERICAN OPPORTUNITY

CHAPTER 1

"I never tried to out-trade a man—and I never let a man out-trade me"

On a hot, sticky night in July, in the year 1930, Roy Cullen was awakened by the sharp ringing of the telephone in the upstairs bedroom of his home in Houston. He picked up the phone quickly, and said, "Yes," very quietly to avoid awakening his wife. But she turned over at the sound of his voice, and said: "What is it, Roy—is something wrong at the well?"

Roy Cullen listened for a short time, and then spoke a few words. Then he turned to his wife, Lillie, who was watching him anxiously:

"We've reached oil sand, honey—I've got to get out there quickly."

He slipped out of bed and took his khaki field clothes from the closet. In a few minutes he had dressed, and pulled on his white "witch elk" boots—a Roy Cullen trade-mark in the oil fields. He went downstairs softly, to avoid awakening the children, Margaret and Wilhelmina, and walked quickly to the garage. A quarter of an hour after the phone call, his car was humming through the silent streets of Houston toward Rabb's Ridge, fifty miles southwest.

The phone call had been from the night driller at Rabb's Ridge. He had said:

"Mr. Cullen, we've hit salt water sand."

Roy had told the driller to "drill through the sand—there may be a break below the sand." But he and the driller both knew the conversation was a cover-up. "Salt water sand" is usually the dead-end of oil-well drilling. It means that the drill, boring into the earth in search of subterranean deposits of oil, has struck a layer of salt water. The water will gush into the pipe instead of oil, and there is nothing to do but close up the hole and try somewhere else. But in this case it was a code phrase arranged with the driller on Rabb's Ridge. It meant the drill had struck oil.

Roy Cullen was what is known as a "wildcatter," one of those hardy pioneers of the oil business, who range far and wide over the land like prospectors looking for gold—except that their grubstake is not a sack of food and a prospector's pick, but a hundred thousand dollars worth of tools and labor. They are also the gamblers of the oil business, who back their judgment and instinct against the parsimony of Nature, who yields her great stores of wealth grudgingly, and only to a chosen few.

For a dozen years Roy Cullen had roved over Texas from the New Mexican border to the Gulf of Mexico, hunting on the earth's surface for signs of oil, often crawling through underbrush and scaling rocky ledges, to find visible indications of the stores of liquid wealth that might lie far below. His luck had gone up and down with his drills, and Dame Fortune had smiled fleetingly at him several times; but on this sultry July night she grinned, almost wantonly.

A Story of American Opportunity

It was a smile that opened the way to one of the most fabulous stories in the altogether fabulous history of Texas—the story of the "King of the Texas Wildcatters" and a billion-dollar fortune in oil!

Rabb's Ridge a quarter of a century ago was a tangled mass of brush and scrub oak, pecan and ash trees, rearing its thorny shoulders above the swampy lowlands of the Brazos River bottoms in Southeast Texas. The soggy marshes around the ridge were alive with rattlesnakes and copperheads.

Several oil companies had explored Rabb's Ridge, but the reports of the geologists had been negative. Roy Cullen had several assets in oil hunting, however, that were—if not different—at least in greater measure than those of most wildcatters of his day. One was a kind of horse-sense judgment about finding oil. He sometimes ignored the conclusions of geologists in favor of what he called "creekology"—an indefinable sense of the meaning of down-to-earth clues, such as the course of rivers and creek-beds and dry streams, which he patched together with geological data until the formations of earth far below seemed to be spread out like a map in his mind.

As he drove along the winding road toward the sandy ridge of land, rising a few feet above the swamps, he knew his judgment had been vindicated. A lot of people had called it "Cullen luck" when he brought in wells where many of the big companies had given up hope; but Roy Cullen knew his "creekology" and the other things which made up his judgment were not just luck.

Twenty years before he had come to Houston on what might have been regarded as a "gamble." But to him it wasn't a gamble. It was a plan. He had looked over the map of the United States and seen where the natural flow of wealth from the Southwest had to go—and so he had picked up his family and belongings, left a good business in Oklahoma, and had come down to Houston.

It was the same with wildcatting for oil: He had gone out into West Texas a dozen years before—not on a gamble, but on a plan. He had spent three years and had nearly gone broke; but he had come back with a store of knowledge about oil geology which he had learned in the rough-and-ready school of oil hunting, and this was locked safely in his mind.

The first streaks of dawn colored the sky to his left with a faint wash of slate gray as he turned off the highway to a side road which led to the drilling location on the ridge. He could see the derrick looming like a ghostly ship against the lightening sky. A man was walking down the corduroy road, and Roy stopped his car, got out and stood in the road, grimly waiting.

"Get in the car," he said shortly. "I'll drive you back up to the rig . . . Nobody leaves this oil field tonight."

The man said nothing, but climbed in. When Roy drove up to the drilling area, he motioned toward the man in the car, "See that he doesn't leave." Then he walked up and looked into a bucket on the derrick floor. In the bottom was a cylinder of hard-packed, bluish sand. It was a "core," or sample, taken from the bottom of the well.

He reached down and pinched off some sand, rubbing it between his thumb and forefinger. Then he sniffed it, the deep lines of his face tightening with concentration.

"It looks like a good one," he said.

The bucket was placed in the back of his car; and after a few words of instruction to the night crew, he headed back for Houston. There were several things that had to be done quickly; additional pipe and equipment had to be ordered, to get ready to test the well. But most important of all, he had to get to Hiland P. Lockwood as soon as possible.

The land on which the well had been drilled had been leased from Lockwood, a land operator in South Texas; and he had an additional fifteen hundred acres adjoining. Roy Cullen knew how swiftly information on a new "discovery well" would spread through the mysterious grapevine of the oil business. Secrecy during the first few hours of the discovery was vital to protect drilling rights on adjoining land; and that had been Roy Cullen's reason for stopping the man who was leaving the field when he drove up.

The blazing summer sun was already slanting across Houston's rooftops when he drove up to his house at Austin Street and Alabama Avenue. A slender woman with graying hair and blue eyes was standing at the door of the back veranda, leading to the garage.

Roy took off his hat, exposing a shock of black hair, and kissed his wife. Then he put his big arm around her shoulder, and they went into the house.

"Something has sure happened at the well, Lillie. We've hit oil—and it looks like a big one!" He sat down and pulled off his white boots. He was a big man, slightly under six feet, with broad shoulders and big, powerful hands. Roy Cullen was then in his late forties, and his face was deeply seamed, rugged and leathery from many years in the open.

"I've got to talk to Lockwood, Lillie—before anyone else talks to him. The well's on his land, and I want to see about the other lease."

Lockwood owned three thousand acres of land around a small railroad siding called Thompson. The Gulf Oil Company also owned land in the area, and they had asked Lockwood to lease his land to them for exploratory drilling. Lockwood agreed, on condition that Roy Cullen do the drilling.

Cullen had refused to drill under contract, but agreed to work on a "fifty-fifty" arrangement, if he could lease fifteen hundred acres of Lockwood's land to match the Gulf holdings. He had gotten the lease, and was about to strike oil. Now he needed the rest of the land, and he wanted to talk with Lockwood as soon as possible.

He put in a phone call to Lockwood at the Rice Hotel. It was about seven o'clock, and Lockwood's deep voice answered.

"Are you up, Hiland?" Cullen asked. "I wouldn't have called this early—but this is pretty important."

"Just getting ready to go down for some breakfast," Lockwood said. "What's happened, Roy?"

"Forget the breakfast," Cullen said. "Get a cab and get out to my house and I'll show you something a lot prettier than ham and eggs."

Lockwood laughed.

"There isn't much that's prettier than that. What is it, Roy?"

"A bucket of oil sand."

"I'll be right out," Lockwood said. In a few minutes he rang the doorbell, and Cullen led him around to the garage, and pointed to the bucket of sand. Lockwood pinched off some of the sand and did exactly as Cullen had done a few hours earlier—rubbed it between his thumb and forefinger, and then he sniffed it.

While Lockwood was examining the sand, Cullen watched him intently. The latter looked up.

"Out of our well?" he asked.

Cullen nodded. "It will make you rich, Hiland. I think it's a big field, and I'd like to lease the adjoining land. Still want to lease it to me?"

Cullen's question was loaded with importance, because the value of land after a discovery well has been drilled increases astronomically.

Lockwood nodded.

"Sure," he said.

"For how much?"

"Same as before—forty dollars an acre, plus the usual royalty."

Cullen's face showed his surprise.

"After seeing this sand?"

Lockwood nodded.

"Why not, Roy? You showed me the sand first. Most men would have made the deal first—and then showed the sand."

Cullen's seamed face softened into a smile. He held out his hand.

"We'll both make some money out of this, Hiland, but I guess neither of us will die with all of it in our pockets," he said, with a grin.

That morning Cullen took the bucket of sand down to his office and showed it to his partner, Jim West, a big, bluff East Texan who had made a fortune in cattle and lumber before he joined Cullen in the oil business.

West looked at the oil sand, leaned down and went through the routine of pinching off a bit of sand and rubbing it with his fingers. He grunted and looked up sharply at Cullen.

"Where did that stuff come from, Roy?"

"From the bottom of our hole at Thompson."

West stood up.

"The hell you say!" He examined the sand more carefully. "It looks like good oil sand, Roy."

"It is good," Cullen said quietly. "Jim, that is a real oil

field. Judging from our ground reports, it will run well over a hundred million barrels."

West stared again at the sand. Then he said suddenly: "My God—we didn't get the adjoining land from Lockwood! Does anybody know about this?"

Cullen nodded.

"Lockwood knows about it."

West's face sagged.

"How'd he find out about it?"

"I showed him the sand—this morning."

West looked at his partner and scowled. After a few seconds, he said:

"Why in hell did you do that, Roy? It'll cost us a million dollars to get that land—and we could have leased it for the same price as the land we already have."

Cullen laughed shortly.

"Lockwood let us have that land because he trusted me, Jim. Do you think I'd try to slick him now?"

West shrugged. "I guess you're right, Roy. But you found the oil—he didn't. And the difference is almost a million dollars. I think you might have traded with him for the other tract."

"I have, Jim. We've got it."

West's expression tightened. He asked:

"For how much, Roy?"

"Forty dollars an acre—plus royalties."

This time the big cattleman's jaw dropped. He stared unbelievingly at his partner.

"Did you get it in writing?" he finally asked. Cullen shook his head.

"I don't think I'd want to ask Lockwood to put it in writing, Jim—after he agreed to lease it for forty-plus."

West nodded. He was still a bit skeptical, however.

"We'll probably never get it at that figure—after Lockwood finds out how much it will be worth."

Cullen laughed, and dropped his big hand on West's shoulder.

"I've never tried to out-trade a man in my life, Jim—and I never let a man out-trade me if I can help it. I think we'll get the land."

Later that day West told Ben Belt, assistant to L. P. Garrett of the Gulf Company, which was half owner of the new well, about the strike. He showed him the "core" of oil sand. Belt showed the same skepticism that West had displayed earlier about leasing the additional land at forty dollars an acre.

"How do you know we can lease for that—if Lockwood knows about the oil?"

This time West grinned.

"Cullen says he can get it—and that means he can."

By the end of the day, when Roy trudged up the back steps of his home at Alabama and Austin, a check for sixty thousand dollars for the remainder of the Lockwood tract was in Hiland Lockwood's hands; and Cullen and West had a lease on 3,000 acres around the new well.

Lillie was at the door again when Roy came in. He put his arm around her shoulders, and kissed her. Then he pulled two chairs together and said, "Let's sit a while, Lillie."

He had often done that when he came in from the fields. On some days his clothes were covered almost to his neck with blue gumbo mud from days and nights of slogging through the mud which is always around a drilling well. On many of these evenings, Roy had stretched out in the same chair and Lillie had helped him pull off his white "witch elk" boots; and he had patted her on the shoulder and said, "Let me go upstairs, Lillie, and take a bath and a shave—and tomorrow will be another day."

And this was "tomorrow." The other wells he had brought in had been fair to middling—and some were good. He could look off across the rooftops toward the southwest, where the sun was sinking in a haze of fire and gold. Out there lay Rabb's Ridge . . . and Pierce Junction, a few miles to the east, where he had brought in his first well ten years ago. It was a "twenty-five-hundred-barrel" gusher, but it went to water in less than two years.

He remembered how the men who had put money into that venture with him—Judge Brooks, Captain Jim Baker, Abe Levy the merchant, Joe and Will Rice, Sam Streetman and others—had gathered at the well, jubilantly waiting for it to "come in." He also remembered how the wife of one of the men had turned to her husband, after the well came in, blowing off the rig of valves called a "Christmas tree" that capped the well pipe, and had said: "Now we're fixed for life—we'll never have to worry any more!"

But Roy Cullen had not been willing to settle for the Pierce Junction well, and he had kept on drilling. One dry hole followed another. He had struck oil later at Humble, and at Blue Ridge—enough to put him on "easy street" if he had wanted to quit; but they were not bonanzas.

Now he had struck the bonanza. He knew from geological reports that there was a great pool of oil under Rabb's Ridge that would probably pour out "black gold" for a hundred years or more; and his share of that reservoir of underground wealth would take care of his family—his children and his children's children—for as far ahead as he cared to think into the future.

He turned to Lillie, and smiled, patting her hand.

A Story of American Opportunity

"It's been a long trail, Lillie—and pretty rough at times. But this one ought to make up for everything . . ."

His wife looked at him, her eyes full of concern.

"This is the last one you'll have to drill—isn't it, Roy? You can stay home now . . . and spend more time with me and the children?"

Roy Cullen smiled. His face was deeply lined, and when he smiled it transformed his features from a set, almost expressionless mask into a boyish grin.

"You better worry about the children staying home with us, Lillie. Roy is married, and Lillie Cranz is married . . . and Agnes and Ike are getting married. Pretty soon Margaret and Wilhelmina will be getting married."

Margaret and Wilhelmina were the two youngest of the big Cullen family; and both were in grammar school. Margaret, the elder of the two, had arrived sixteen years after the oldest of the Cullen children, Roy Gustave, had been born; and the laughter of children had been ringing in the Cullen household for almost two decades.

Roy Cullen closed his eyes, against the glare of the sinking sun. Out where the sun was setting were the flat streets of San Antonio and the rolling plains of Texas. It was out there, halfway to "San Antone," that Lillie had been born, in the little town of Schulenberg . . . and out there in the streets of San Antonio Roy Cullen had played as a boy, swimming in the San Antonio River.

In Roy Cullen's closed vision he might have seen a slim, sun-tanned boy, with a shock of black hair, crouching on the river bank, where a bend in the river created a dangerous whirlpool into which driftwood was sucked by the swirling current. The boy was watching the driftwood, as it glided downstream and suddenly plunged out of sight into the vortex of the whirpool; and then, a few seconds later, popped to the surface again below the whirlpool, floating in the quiet waters.

In his vision he might also have seen the black hair of the boy, who had been crouching on the bank, suddenly appear in the water, bobbing along on the gathering ripples, until it sank out of sight . . . and several seconds later reappeared on the surface of the calm water below the whirlpool, from where the boy struck out strongly for the shore . . .

CHAPTER 2

"Anybody can swim into a whirlpool—it's coming out of it that counts"

THE STORY of the boy on the bank of the San Antonio River was not imagination. Roy Cullen had often told the story, because it embodied some of his own philosophy of life. Discovering an oil well was something like plunging into that whirlpool: Anybody can swim into a whirlpool—just as anyone can drill for oil. It is coming out of it that counts.

"If you plan anything before you do it," he often said, "you will usually come out all right. When you jump into anything without thinking about it ahead of time, you've got to trust to luck."

That was the way it was with the whirlpool in the San Antonio River. Roy had been a boy when it happened—some thirty-five years before. He used to swim in the river when he was a youngster, even when it was a swollen flood. When Roy was three years old one of his older brothers had tossed him into a swimming hole, and he had thrashed his way to the bank. After that swimming was as natural as walking.

He was a slim, wiry boy, and one day he sat on the river bank, near a bend in the San Antonio about a quarter of a mile from the famous Concepción Mission. His tangle of black hair fell down the sides of his face as his gray eyes stared seriously at the swirling water. The river at this point was full of whirlpools, and many strong swimmers had been sucked into them and drowned. A brother of Oscar F. Holcombe, later the perennial mayor of Houston, had been one of the river's victims.

Young Roy watched the eddies as they gathered speed, racing toward the whirlpools. Somehow the treacherous currents fascinated him with their lurking danger. They offered a kind of challenge.

He began to study the way pieces of driftwood were drawn toward the whirlpool. They would glide faster and faster, until suddenly they would disappear into the whirling water; and then a few seconds later the pieces of wood would bob to the surface a few feet beyond the whirlpool and float freely downstream.

Roy knew that wood floated more naturally than the human body; yet a person could remain afloat in the water if he lay semi-rigid and motionless. It seemed impossible that no one could swim through these whirlpools . . . if a bit of driftwood came through all right.

He watched the way the wood went under; and then he tried an experiment. He tossed a log, about his own weight, into the water and watched it disappear as it reached the whirling eddies over the deep bottom of the river. He counted the seconds before the log came up. He had no watch to measure time, but he worked out a counting rhythm.

Then he began to hold his breath while he counted, and continued to hold his breath twice as long as the logs remained under.

The San Antonio, at this point, was a swift-flowing current. This was long before the drilling of water wells at the source of the river had lowered the volume of water; and while Roy had no fear of water, no matter how swift or swollen the current, he knew that many who were as strong swimmers as he had been unable to fight their way through the whirlpool and come out alive.

He decided it must be the fact of fighting the water that prevented the swimmers from being thrust to the surface again, the way the logs came out. And so he began carefully to plan a way to beat the river . . .

Finally he was satisfied that he had worked out the plan perfectly in his mind. When there were no other boys around to stop him, he dove into the river and swam toward the whirlpool. This was the moment when fear would come—if it came at all; but he had determined in advance to think only about holding his breath and remaining still and rigid—like a log—when he was sucked under.

As the current dragged him swiftly toward the churning trap, young Roy closed his eyes and held his breath. He tried to relax his arms and legs. Suddenly it was as if a smooth hand caught his legs and jerked him down toward the bottom of the river bed. He began counting mechanically and tried to think only of that. The roaring water closed on him like a vice, dragging him down, and his ears seemed about to burst . . . Then suddenly he was floating on the surface again, in quiet water.

This was the first time in Roy Cullen's life—although not the last time—that he had staked everything on his own judgment, and won.

In this case, he had risked his life. And yet when the black-haired, sun-browned boy of twelve climbed out on the bank below the whirlpool, dripping and happy at the success of his experiment, he was hardly aware that he had run a close race with death.

"The only thing I had to worry about," he said later, "was what might have been at the bottom of the whirlpool. A tangle of wire could have caught me . . ."

Roy was one of a family of seven children—five of whom were half-brothers and half-sisters. His mother, Louise Cullen, had been widowed by the death of her first husband. She brought her family down to San Antonio from a farm in Denton County, Texas, where she had gone to live with her second husband, Cicero Cullen.

A quarter of a century before Roy was born, his mother had lived in Florida where her family, who had founded the great Retrive Plantation in South Carolina, had migrated. It was here that she met Cicero Cullen, when she was a girl of fourteen and Cicero was ten years older. Cicero was a studious young man, the son of one of the most illustrious sons of Texas—Ezekiel Cullen—and he fell deeply in love with the slim, brown-eyed girl. However, Louise Beck married her cousin, James Beck, and they moved out to Texas during the stormy period of Reconstruction after the Civil War; and it was not until a quarter of a century later that Cicero, then living in Dallas, heard that James Beck had died, and he hastened down to San Antonio where Louise was living, to renew his suit.

They were married and moved into a farm in Denton County, northwest of Dallas, where Roy Cullen was born on July 3, 1881—a year before his famous grandfather, Ezekiel Cullen, died.

Young Roy, in swaddling clothes at the time, had no personal recollection of his illustrious grandfather, but in his early boyhood days in San Antonio he had many reasons to remember him.

A Story of American Opportunity

Ezekiel Cullen was a tradition in Texas—one of the men who had come out of Georgia to Texas in 1835 with a burning desire for adventure and hopes of finding fortune in Texas land, which sold then for about twelve cents an acre. He had fought with Ben Milam's "Texas Raiders" in the Battle of San Antonio a half century before Roy was born. And he had founded the public school system of Texas.

Roy's mother had told him how his grandfather had ridden into San Augustine, the seat of the new revolutionary government of Texas, on a spring day in 1835 just as the rebellion against Mexico was about to burst into flame. Young Cullen was a dashing youth, with a ferocious moustache and a bristling beard that encircled the lower half of his face. He had one personal slave and about ten thousand dollars in cash.

Roy knew the story of how young Ezekiel Cullen, in a crowd in front of General Burleson's headquarters at San Augustine, had heard old Ben Milam, a famous frontiersman of early Texas days, shout his historic challenge: "Who will go with old Ben Milam into San Antonio?"

Young Cullen had been among the first to join, turning his slave and money over to a friend. With Milam's band of about three hundred Texans, he had ridden into San Antonio on the night of December 6, 1835. Milam assigned him to a battering ram—a twelve-foot log which he and several others of the band carried through the streets, knocking down Mexican fortifications.

Within five days Ben Milam's raiders had driven the Mexican Army out of San Antonio in the first big victory of the Texas Revolt, and Ezekiel Cullen had ridden back to San Augustine—a Texas hero!

All these things had happened fifty years before Roy was born; but the tales of his grandfather's exploits in the young days of Texas were the legends of his younger days; and his mother, proud of her sons' forebears, told him many of these stories which became engraved in his memory.

The stories of his grandfather were more vivid in young Roy's recollection than the memories of his father. Cicero Cullen was past fifty when Roy was born, and he had never adjusted himself to the life of the Beck household; and shortly after Dick, the second son, was born, he and Roy's mother agreed to live separately.

Cicero Cullen had been in the cattle-buying business in San Antonio, and was moderately successful; but after his separation from his family, he returned to Dallas where he entered the real-estate business. Louise Cullen remained in San Antonio, in the big frame house built of lumber that James Beck had hauled up in wagons from the Gulf Coast, and which he had left her when he died.

Roy was a baby when this happened, and except for one swift burst of excitement—when the usually placid Cicero came down from Dallas and "kidnaped" his two sons, taking them back to Dallas with him—Roy saw little of his father until he had grown almost to manhood.

Meanwhile the Cullen home in San Antonio was a pleasant and interesting place, full of fun and merriment, and presided over by Louise Cullen. Roy was two years older than Dick, and much younger than the older of the Beck children—Lucien, the oldest, who was studying medicine; and Joe; Jim; Louise and Daisy. Possibly as a result of this difference in ages, almost a generation separating Louise Cullen's oldest son from her youngest, Roy spent much of his boyhood either chasing after Joe, who hardly wanted him around, or fighting off boys in the neighborhood who picked on his younger brother, Dick.

Louise Cullen cared for her family with the income from

James Beck's estate, and the help she received from Cicero Cullen, who was engaged in real-estate and insurance business in Dallas.

In spite of constant financial worries, she was a wise and cheerful mother, and the house was full of laughter. She taught her children at an early age that being honest and courageous and generous was better than being wealthy. She was a beautiful woman, in her middle forties now, with soft brown eyes and a crown of lovely brown hair. Roy Cullen's earliest memories were of his mother, and the stories she told him as a child.

During the evenings she read stories to Roy and Dick about King Arthur and Lancelot and Guinevere, and the Knights of the Round Table; and in her gentle way she introduced Roy to many of the fine characters of literature that he remembered in the later years of his life.

"Don't ever lie, Roy," she told him. "The Knights of the Round Table were fine men because they were brave and honest." Many times, when Roy had grown to boyhood, she told him: "You can lock your house against a thief, but you have no protection against anyone who lies."

He learned from her in his early childhood the value of giving; and on Christmas, although she had little to give to her own children, she always took a few packages to other families in the neighborhood who were even needier. As a little boy, Roy could remember these excursions, with a little bundle of gifts tucked under his mother's arm. Most of these she left on doorsteps, and the neighbors' children never knew where they came from.

CHAPTER 3

"Some day we'll have a big white house to live in"

SAN ANTONIO in the 1880's was a sprawling frontier town, spread along the banks of the San Antonio River, with stockyards on the south side and a population that was predominantly Mexican. On the streets of this city young Roy Cullen first learned to take care of himself.

His elder half-brothers—Joe and Jim—paid little attention to him. When he tried to follow Joe, he cuffed him and sent him home. His activities centered largely around his young brother, Dick. He had assumed the role of protector of his brother, and most of his early experiences fighting with other boys in the neighborhood were in defense of Dick.

Roy was six years old when his father—who had been away in Dallas for two years—drove into San Antonio one day. He wanted to take pictures of his two sons, and Louise let them go with him. That night they did not return, and the mother frantically tried to find them. By morning she knew her husband had taken the boys north, and she arranged for neighbors to care for the other children and set out for Dallas. She found Cicero; he had his two sons—and was determined to keep them!

She retained a lawyer in Dallas, who demanded the return of the boys; but before legal action could be started, Cicero Cullen and the two boys had disappeared.

It was several weeks before Louise Cullen saw her two youngest children again—and it was Cicero who brought them back.

"I made a mistake, Louise," he told her. "Take the boys—they are yours and they want to be with you."

He had taken Roy and Dick all the way to Phoenix, Arizona; and on one occasion young Roy had fallen off the seat of a stagecoach and had been run over—and that was enough for Cicero.

Back in San Antonio, the tousle-haired boy began to understand at an early age the burdens that had been laid upon the shoulders of his mother. Louise Cullen, nearing fifty, was still a beautiful woman; and on Saturdays, when he worked with her in the flower garden, Roy watched with fascination as she moved gracefully among the plants.

His oldest half-brother, Lucien, had left home to study medicine at Sewanee; and Jim, the "Beau Brummell" of the family, had gone to El Paso to work in a printing shop. Joe, the more restless of the trio, finally joined the Army and later fought with Colonel Theodore Roosevelt's "Rough Riders" in the Battle of San Juan Hill in the Spanish-American War, and finally died of tropical dysentery.

The financial panic of 1893 had bitten deeply into the economy of Texas. Cotton markets were low, and the price of beef had fallen off so badly it hardly paid to drive stock to the shipping pens. San Antonio itself suffered its worst depression since Texas became a part of the Union. Louise Cullen found the problems of her family increasingly hard, with little help from any source.

As Roy passed from childhood into boyhood, he saw the increasing burden of worry and anxiety growing in his mother's eyes; and with his elder brothers away a good deal of the time, he began to feel the responsibilities of manhood long before his age should have required it. He loved to listen to his mother talk and read, and from her he drew a wealth of interest in books. She read the Bible to him when he was a boy; and as he grew older, she introduced him to Dickens, Irving, Cooper and Scott. Louise Cullen awakened in him a pride in the accomplishments of great men; she told him of his Scottish forebears, and the Wimberlys of Cheshire and Lancaster, in England; and of the first John Wimberly, one of Ezekiel Cullen's ancestors, who came to Virginia in 1670, and whose people migrated to the Carolinas and to Georgia, and finally—through the Cullen branch—to Texas.

Roy's fights with the other boys in the neighborhood—usually fending off an attack on his brother Dick—worried his mother; yet she never forbade him to fight. At times, when he would come home bloody and bruised from his skirmishes, she would help him swab off his face, and then would say seriously:

"Remember what I've always told you, Roy—don't ever pick a fight, and don't ever run away from one."

Roy was proud of his mother; she seemed to grow more beautiful with the years, and she possessed a mixture of tenderness and wisdom that was needed to guide a boy, without his father, through the rugged life of a frontier town.

On one occasion, while Roy was at the Pecos Street School, the principal, Mr. Lukin—a towering man, with near-sighted blue eyes and thick-lensed spectacles—threatened to whip Roy for fighting in the schoolyard. When Roy came into the principal's office, he stood with his legs braced and the toes of his bare feet curled against the floor. Mr. Lukin took down a pomegranate switch, which was the feared and respected symbol of authority in the school.

"You aren't going to whip me, Mr. Lukin," Roy said. It was more of a statement than a protest.

The principal swished the switch suggestively.

"Why not, Roy?"

"Because they hit Dick—that's why I hit them," the boy said. His mouth was tight and his eyes were blazing.

Mr. Lukin shook his head slowly.

"I am going to whip you, Roy."

Roy set his feet farther apart, and looked around. There was a row of jars on the window sill, containing butterflies, frogs and all manner of small insects, pickled in alcohol. Suddenly he reached over and picked up two jars.

"Why, Roy!" the principal exclaimed. "What do you mean?"

Roy shook his head stubbornly.

"My mother told me it was right to keep the bigger boys from hitting Dick. She said it was right—and you aren't going to whip me for it!"

Mr.Lukin slowly lowered the switch. His eyes studied the tense little face for a moment; then he sat down. He laid the switch on his desk.

"Come here, Roy," he said, finally. "I'm not going to whip you—now. I'm going to write a note to your mother—and if she says the same thing you have told me, I won't punish you—for something your mother told you was right. But, Roy—"

He leaned forward, and put his big hand on Roy's shoulder.

"Don't fight in the schoolyard again. I am telling you this, Roy—and the next time I will punish you for it."

Roy was twelve at this time—but only in the fifth grade.

That was because Mrs. Cullen had kept him out of school until he was eight, fearing that Cicero Cullen might make another attempt to kidnap him. One evening, after school, Roy found his mother working in the flower garden in the yard behind the house.

Roy looked seriously at his mother, and then said:

"Mother, I'm quitting school."

Mrs. Cullen's dark eyes widened. She took Roy's hands and drew him close to her.

"Whatever has come over you, Roy? You're just a boy, honey, you must keep on with your school!"

Roy shook his head stubbornly.

"That's what I'm going to do—no matter what you say, Mother. I've thought it over, and . . . anyway—that's what I'm going to do! I'm going to get a job—and nothing you say will change me."

Louise Cullen spoke to him quietly, her soft eyes watching the face of the boy anxiously. She explained that, although times were hard, she had enough money to live on. She also told him about Grandfather Ezekiel Cullen, who had established the school system in Texas . . . and how much he owed it to the memory of his grandfather to take advantage of the schools. Roy merely shook his head.

"My mind's made up, Mother. I've thought about it, and I know what I'm going to do—so there's no use talking about it."

A few days later he got a job—sacking candy at Dueler's Candy Factory, for three dollars a week. Each Saturday he would hand the three dollars to his mother.

After the first efforts to dissuade him, Louise Cullen gave up her objections. Young Roy, in spite of his years, was given to firm decisions—once he had made up his mind. And she knew that one of the things that governed his decision was an underlying pride—a kind of fierce, boyish desire to hold his own life. He was older than other boys in his class at school, because of his late start; and he undoubtedly felt the sharp cleavage in thinking and in learning habits between himself and those in his classes.

His life had been more lonely than it normally would have been, for many reasons. His brothers were much older than he; and the difference in their ages divided them, no matter how much Louise Cullen sought, by her love and deep affection for all her children, to bridge that natural gap. Added to this was the realization on Roy's part that he was now, by a process of elimination, the "man of the house."

Although only twelve, he was the oldest boy at home. Lucien had left for college; and Joe, adventurous and rather wild, had left home; and so had Jim, the fashion plate of the family. At times they sent home some money, but they were not regular supporters of the family; and Roy felt that he must now take his part, accepting the responsibilities they had left him.

At the same time, he had determined that his decision to "go to work" would not leave him without schooling. During the evening hours when the rest of the family were in the "living room," listening to his mother and sister Louise playing the piano, or singing with young men who visited the Beck girls, Roy would remain upstairs in his room, reading and studying maps. He had hung a blanket across his bed, so the light would not shine in the hallway or downstairs; and he had pasted charts and maps on the walls of his room. On these he wrote notes recording the incidents that had taken place in history—names, places, dates of battles.

There must have been wistfulness in Louise Cullen's eyes when she looked upstairs and saw the dim light from Roy's room. Each evening, after dinner, he would climb the stairs to his room, where he had stacked all the books he could lay his hands on, and he would pursue his self-imposed studies.

It was a strange fare: history books, the Waverly novels of Sir Walter Scott, which he read from cover to cover; translations of Greek myths; the philosophy of Thomas Carlyle; Shakespeare's plays; Dickens, of course; and oddly enough, Blackstone, on English common law. He read all the history books he could find, and plotted the history of the world on the charts pasted on the walls—marking off events and dates on the maps.

During the hours at night, poring over books and charts, Roy began to "dream out" his future. He would close his eyes at times, and think of what he wanted . . . far in the future. He knew he wanted his mother to be happy and to have less work and care; and he knew he wanted to move out into the world, to travel places, and have his own business. Perhaps the most real of all his dreams was the "big white house"—a great, spreading mansion, with white porticoes and columns along the front.

"Some day," he told his mother, "we'll have a big white house to live in—and you won't have to work. And we'll have a garden like ours . . . only bigger."

Louise Cullen always listened quietly while Roy told of his dreams; and she would smile and nod while he explained what he planned to do.

Life at the candy factory was not particularly stimulating to Roy's imagination. He learned the first day he went to work a stern lesson in tact. Arriving at the plant in his Sunday suit, he quickly found that the Poles and Germans who worked there had little taste for the "young student." After a few days of arriving in his best clothes, he changed to working clothes and gradually he found himself "accepted" by the candy factory crew.

After his first few weeks as a packer, working ten hours a day wrapping up candy in packages and binding the packages into bales, his employer, Gus Dueler, called him into his office.

"You are a hard worker, Roy," he began, ponderously. "You have done your job well—and now you are promoted. You have a raise of fifty cents a week."

Roy's new job was far more interesting. It involved figures: keeping records of the amounts of sugar, syrup and other ingredients brought into the factory; and the pails and boxes of candy turned out for shipment. He began to feel a new kind of responsibility—and to study each phase of the work: the input of raw materials, and the output of finished products. He used the simple arithmetic he had learned in school to keep track of these, even to fractional quantities.

One evening he sat in his room, staring at the open pages of a book but reading nothing. He was listening to the music downstairs. His sister Louise was playing the piano, and someone was singing. Roy was sixteen—and the other boys of sixteen he had known in school were not spending their evenings reading Blackstone and Chaucer. He listened for a while; then he shook his head slightly, and went back to work.

The next afternoon on his way home from Dueler's factory, Roy met a boy he had known in school—Bob Aiken. They talked a minute; and then Bob asked:

"Are you doing anything tonight, Roy?"

Roy shrugged.

"Got a little work to do at home," he said, and hurried on home. After supper he climbed the stairs, lighted the kerosene lamp, and got out his books. The open pages stared back at him without meaning. Suddenly Roy wanted to bury his face in his arms and cry. He could hear the sound of the piano downstairs. "Everybody is doing something tonight," he thought . . . "except me."

Suddenly he slapped shut the book he had been studying. He put on his hat and went downstairs; and without speaking to his sisters or his mother, he walked out and started up the street toward Bob Aiken's house.

Bob was sitting on the front porch when Roy walked up.

"Doing anything tonight, Bob?" Roy asked cautiously.

Bob Aiken came down the steps.

"Sure . . . I've got a date."

Roy hesitated a moment, then asked:

"Has she got a friend, Bob?"

Aiken laughed. "Sure she has," he said. "I'll ask her to bring along her friend."

Roy's date was a pretty, redheaded girl, quite friendly, and curious about the slim boy with the gray eyes. She greeted Roy with a warm handclasp, and quickly began to chatter gaily. Why hadn't she met Roy before, she wanted to know . . . and who else did he know among the girls in San Antonio? Roy shrugged. He was pretty busy most of the time, he explained, and told her about his job in Gus Dueler's candy factory. This impressed her, since Roy was doubtless a boy with an independent income.

The four started down the street, walking in pairs, and finally reached Travis Park, a public park near the center of town. It was cool and pleasant, and Roy listened to the girl's aimless chatter, wondering nervously what might be expected of him . . . But it was nice having a girl to talk to, and as they walked along, he began to talk more freely.

After a few steps into the park, Roy realized that he and the girl were alone. Bob Aiken and his companion had disappeared.

The sudden realization that he was alone with this girl startled Roy, and he became even more nervous.

"Let's sit on a bench and talk," the girl suggested, and Roy nodded. They found a bench along one of the walks, under a spreading tree, and for the next few minutes Roy found his tongue unaccountably frozen. He had no idea what young people talked about, sitting on a bench under a tree in a park.

It had turned mildly chilly, and he wondered if he should put his arm around her shoulder . . . but even as the notion struck him, he found himself squirming a little farther away on the bench. The girl had stopped talking; and after a few minutes she looked around nervously, and said:

"It's getting late—I guess I'd better get home, don't you think?"

Roy felt a flood of relief. He nodded, and helped the girl to her feet. They walked home, rather solemnly; and when they reached the girl's home, Roy said, "Good night," and held out his hand awkwardly.

The girl smiled.

"I had a wonderful time," she said.

Roy nodded stiffly, and strode off quickly toward his home, with a vague sense of relief that the evening was over. He went directly to his room, although his sisters were in the downstairs parlor with some friends, and got out his books and tried to study. But the pages of the book seemed dim, and he found himself thinking of the redheaded girl. He wondered what she thought of him . . . Probably she thought he was a fool for not putting his arm around her. He shook his head. This was something new, and vaguely interesting . . . He decided he would see Bob Aiken more often, and perhaps some of the other boys he knew, who had dates with girls.

It was not long afterwards that Roy, quite unexpectedly,

had another adventure, more lasting in its effect. He had his first long trip away from home.

Shortly after Roy's date with the redhead, Mrs. Cullen received word from Daisy, who had married and gone to live in Dallas, that Cicero Cullen was ill. Roy knew his father was living alone; and so he asked his mother if he might go to Dallas to visit him.

Louise Cullen looked at her son. He was a strong, well filled-out boy by this time. His shoulders had widened, and his legs were long, giving him a rangy awkwardness peculiar to boys of his age. In the four years since he had left school his face had become more firm and his expression defined, like the lines of a map gradually deepening and taking shape.

It was a self-reliant face; more than might have been expected of a boy in his teens. His eyes were serious.

She suddenly smiled. Perhaps the notion of young Roy returning to his father brought a quick memory of the day ten years before when she had discovered that her husband had kidnaped him. But Roy was older now, and he seemed quite capable of taking care of himself.

"Of course you can go, Roy," she said. "Your father is a fine man, and if he is ill, you will want to see him. I've got some things I want you to take for Daisy."

And so it was settled that he was to go to Dallas. His mother carefully packed his bag. She looked at him with her soft brown eyes after he had kissed her goodbye at the door; and Roy turned quickly and walked down the street, with a long, swinging stride.

He turned back once and waved, and his mother smiled and waved back. It was the last time Roy would be home as a boy; when he came back, he would be a man.

CHAPTER 4

"Don't give anyone reason to feel insulted—and don't ever take an insult"

THE SPANISH-AMERICAN WAR, sweeping over the embryonic Southwest during its period of fiercest growing pains, stirred Texas with a martial enthusiasm that had not been experienced since the beginning of the War between the States.

Dallas was the new and growing hub of the Southwest, bustling with a population of drummers from St. Louis and Kansas City, cattlemen and merchants, including many cotton men. It had become the largest city in Texas, exceeding Waco and San Antonio; and its thriving markets were a magnet for buyers and businessmen from the East, South and Middle West.

When Roy arrived in Dallas, the battleship *Maine* had been blown up in Havana Harbor, and the nation was seething with demands for war against Spain. The streets rattled with the guns of national guardsmen, drilling and shouting orders. There was more patriotic fervor than military science in the drilling maneuvers, and few of the troops ever saw combat; but every young man in Dallas was alive with war fever—and Roy Cullen was no exception.

His father was in poor health, although not seriously ill. He had given up a prosperous real-estate business and was making a rather meager living in the grain business. Daisy and Frank Knight, her husband, were living in Dallas; and Roy decided to remain a while, attracted as much by the spirit of patriotic excitement as anything else. He quickly enrolled in one of the amateur military organizations, known as "Dallas Defenders," and began drilling in the evenings on the downtown streets of Dallas.

The "Defenders" were only semi-military in character, drilled by a young instructor in military training from the Oak Cliff Military Academy; and although there were many rumors of activating the organization as a Regular Army unit, it soon began to appear that the "Defenders" would have to confine their belligerent activities to marching on the streets of Dallas.

Roy finally decided to enlist in a Regular Army unit. His brother Joe had gone off to war with Colonel Roosevelt's "Rough Riders"; and Roy had no intention of remaining in Dallas waiting for the War Department to recognize the military value of the "Dallas Defenders" when there was fighting going on in Cuba. So he applied for enlistment in the "Dallas Zouaves," a recognized Army organization.

His first application was rejected. Although sufficiently tall, he was underweight for his height. He said nothing about his age, which was two years under the required age for enlistment. After the first rejection, he went home and drank water and stuffed himself with food for two days; then he went back to the enlistment office and re-applied. This time he was accepted, and assigned to quarters at the St. George Hotel on Elm Street. The hotel was as far as he got in military service.

Cicero Cullen, having found out about his son's enlistment, promptly advised the military authorities of Roy's age, and the authorities with equal promptness discharged Roy honorably from the service.

Daisy Knight had moved with her husband, who was in the cotton-compress business, to Schulenberg, Texas, a prosperous German community about a hundred miles east of San Antonio. Roy received word from his mother that his grandmother had died, and he hurried back to San Antonio. After a short time there, he wrote his brother-in-law, Frank Knight, to see if he could find a job for him in Schulenberg; and as a result, he went to work for a cotton-buying firm—the Ralli Brothers—one of the largest in the world, with an office in Schulenberg.

A friend of Roy's, Alma Wurzbach, who lived across the street from the Cullen home in San Antonio, was visiting the Perlitz family in Schulenberg during the summer of 1899; and Roy was often invited to the Perlitz home.

Fayette County had been settled by German families in the years before the Civil War; and in the half century afterwards many of these families had prospered and acquired large landholdings. Among these was the Kessler family, which included five daughters and one son of Charles Kessler and his wife, Wilhelmina. The five girls had married young men of prominent families in Schulenberg—Gustave Cranz, Robert Boettcher, W. O. Neuhaus, Charles Krook, and Adolph Wangemann, who lived in Yoakum, Texas. The only son, Edmund, had married a Schulenberg girl, Mary Wolters.

As the years passed, the Kessler family prospered, and their sons-in-law became important citizens of Schulenberg, with beautiful homes in the residential district of the little Texas town.

It was in this clannish social circle that Roy Cullen moved. It was pleasant, and quite in contrast to the lonesome nights Roy had spent in the seclusion of his upstairs bedroom in San Antonio, poring over books and charts while the singing went on down in the parlor below.

A friend of young Charlie Perlitz, Annie Schuhmacher—whose father, John Schuhmacher, was a banker and merchant in nearby La Grange—one day introduced Roy to a beautiful blue-eyed girl named Lillie Cranz, the daughter of Gustave Cranz, who had married one of the Kessler girls and had become the most prominent merchant in Schulenberg.

The next day Roy sent a note to Miss Cranz at her home, asking if he might call on her. This was the usual custom in days when telephones were rarely used. Miss Cranz replied to the note, inviting Roy to call at her home.

The Cranz home was a spacious house, with wide verandas, covered with ornamental woodwork characteristic of the better homes of that period; and when Roy called that evening, he was met by Lillie at the door. She was a shy, beautiful girl, with the bluest eyes he had ever seen.

She introduced him to her father, a scholarly-looking man who had studied in Germany for the Lutheran ministry; and later he met her mother, a charming woman, who made him feel quickly at ease in the warm family atmosphere.

Roy was in love for the first time in his life. A few days later he called on Lillie and asked her to join him in an afternoon gathering at the local ice-cream parlor. Later they walked together in the park, and that evening he sat with Lillie in the parlor of the Cranz home and told her, quite simply, that he was in love with her and some day he would like to marry her.

Lillie accepted the declaration with equal simplicity. She said she would marry Roy whenever he thought best. Nothing more was said . . . The engagement remained a personal matter between them. But Roy had made up his mind that he would build his own business, and marry Lillie Cranz.

This was in July of 1899. During the summer Roy began to plan his future career. His work with Ralli Brothers had already taught him a great deal about the cotton business, and he determined that he would learn all he could and then go into business for himself.

During the fall cotton season, he learned about classing cotton from an Irishman named Rollins, who was a classer for the Ralli Brothers. He taught Roy how to "sample" and "class" cotton—that is, to take a handful of cotton from a bale and determine what grade it was.

"Classing cotton is like recognizing a man," Rollins told him. "If you meet a man you know, you recognize him the minute you see him, don't you? Well, it's the same classing cotton. You don't have to look it over carefully to see what class it is. If you don't know it the minute you lay eyes on it, you're not a good cotton classer."

The work with Ralli Brothers opened Roy's eyes to a new and decidedly interesting prospect. It was the kind of business that interested him. The work involved knowledge—the things he had learned in school, and in his own studying alone; and it offered the possibility of a good income.

He decided to learn all he could about the cotton-buying business, asking questions of Rollins and others, and observing the ways in which business was done. Then he could apply for a job as a cotton buyer.

He worked industriously for Ralli Brothers; and at the same time he continued to see Lillie Cranz as frequently as possible. It became a more or less accepted social practice in

Schulenberg that when there was a party, Roy and Lillie would be invited together.

Roy's mind was never still, however. He knew that he did not intend to continue working indefinitely for Ralli Brothers, even though he was being paid a fair salary for a young man of little experience. But the firm was too large; he wanted to work for a company in which the job and the size of the company would contribute to his advancement. And so he began to inquire among the cotton people about the different companies; and he found that the Clarkson Company of Houston probably fitted his requirements better than any others.

Cotton buyers were the itinerant nomads of the cotton business. They roamed from one place to another—Schulenberg, Weimar, westward to Seguin; and as far north as Oklahoma. It offered not only the prospect of an exciting life, but a fairly lucrative business. Roy decided to embark on a career as a cotton buyer, even if it meant leaving Schulenberg temporarily. He wrote to the Clarkson cotton firm of Houston, and received a reply from the head of the company, W. B. Clarkson, offering him a job with the company. It was a smaller concern than Ralli Brothers, but there was a better chance for advancement. Roy's temporary departure from Schulenberg was not too much of a wrench, because Lillie Cranz was preparing to leave for San Antonio at the end of the summer, to attend St. Mary's Hall, an Episcopal college in that city.

Although Roy previously had a job with responsibilities, he had always worked for someone who directed him, and told him what to do. Now he was on his own—a boy barely turned eighteen! He had to make business deals with men who were far older and more experienced . . . and he knew he must justify Mr. Clarkson's confidence in him.

He knew how to class cotton, but there were far more complicated responsibilities in his new job. He had to figure out the amounts of payments to make on the cotton purchased, calculating the price of each bale on the basis of the grade and classification. He knew buyers had a system, but he did not know what it was. Roy had taken the job with Clarkson as a full-fledged "cotton buyer," and he had no intention of asking anyone how to handle the work. He would have to figure it out for himself. He knew it would require an immense amount of calculating—but he had learned how to use figures when he was at Dueler's candy factory, and this would be no different, although it would probably be harder.

His first order was for two hundred bales of cotton to be purchased from a cotton seller at Weimar named Munn. Roy sat up all night in his room, figuring the price for each grade, and working out a system of payments according to the amounts in each grade, since he knew he would have no time to do the calculating at Weimar.

The following morning, sleepless as a result of the night's work, he set out for Weimar. He met Mr. Munn, classed the two hundred bales, and shipped them. When he finished checking, he compared his figures with those of the seller, and they agreed entirely.

He moved among the cotton merchants and "ginners," buying for Clarkson, until the season in South Texas ended. Then Clarkson decided to send him to Oklahoma.

He was first assigned to Ardmore, Oklahoma, one of the big cotton-buying centers; but Roy's father had retired from business in Dallas and moved to a small farm in Greer County, Oklahoma, near the town of Mangum; and Roy decided to make Mangum his headquarters.

He stopped to see his mother in San Antonio, and then headed into the new territory. He arrived in Mangum early in the year 1900, and found it a rough, boisterous frontier town, with a single two-story frame hotel in a cluster of buildings—chiefly saloons—fronting a sandy space called the "courthouse square," although there was no courthouse.

Roy had matured rapidly since he last saw his father. He was still lanky, but his body had filled out, and constant work in the open had toughened his arms and legs. His smooth, boyish face had begun to settle into firm lines, and he wore a bristling, close-cropped moustache which made him look several years older than his actual age.

He visited his father on the farm down in the Elm River country, and then returned to Mangum to set up his "office."

Western Oklahoma was still in the quivering aftermath of the "land rush" days, when a large part of the Indian Territory land had been thrown open to settlers. Homesteaders, gamblers and speculators milled in the towns—and not too far off in the hills were remnants of outlaw bands and rustlers who had terrorized that part of the Southwest during the turbulent 1890's.

Roy readily fitted himself into his new business routine. Mangum was a cotton-buying center, with cotton yards on the edge of town; and although he had been operating for Clarkson less than a year, he had little trouble fitting himself into the job of representing the big Houston firm in this new country. Within a short time he built up a reputation as a "good trader"—quite able to hold his own, and to deal shrewdly but fairly.

He got along well with the men in Mangum. His mother had told him years before: "Roy, don't ever give anyone reason to feel insulted by you—and don't ever take an insult from anybody else." It was a creed that fitted admirably into the hard life in Oklahoma.

He had a likeable personality, and he quickly learned that

honesty and integrity were better assets in business than anything else. They built confidence, and if men had confidence in those with whom they did business, there was no need for shrewdness or trickery.

One of Roy's first business problems occurred a few months after he came to Mangum. He had been unable to buy cotton at first, because buyers shipping to Eastern ports offered rebates, and he could not match the prices buying cotton for shipment through Houston. Finally, worried because he seemed unable to buy enough cotton to justify his salary and expense account, he bought a thousand bales and found he had exceeded the limits set by Clarkson.

Roy immediately wrote Clarkson, offering to pay out of his salary whatever loss might have been incurred. Clarkson was worried, too; but he assured Roy that he would not take the money out of Roy's pay. However, Nature intervened with some totally unexpected assistance. The cotton in Western Oklahoma was extremely dry, owing to the climate; and Houston was extremely wet. By the time the cotton reached the shipping point, it had picked up enough moisture to increase the weight enough to cover the loss, and provide a profit.

Clarkson wired Roy: "Use your own judgment after this."

The incident was a valuable lesson. Roy's frankness in reporting his mistake to Clarkson increased the latter's confidence in him; and he learned something about cotton shipments. After that he calculated the changes in weights due to weather on every shipment he made.

Roy's abortive service in the "Dallas Zouaves" had given him the right—as a veteran of the Spanish-American War—to settle on one hundred and sixty acres of homestead land in Western Oklahoma, so he decided to become a landowner. He chose a site more for its natural beauty than for fertility of the soil and filed his claim. The homestead was located in the "gypsum breaks," four miles west of Mangum, in Greer County, a few miles from his father's farm. Roy had no particular plans for the land, since he was getting well established in the cotton business, and he had no intention of becoming a farmer. But Oklahoma was a "land-crazy" country, and he thought everyone should have some land.

The settlers around Mangum were a varied lot—farmers from the Middle West, and some from as far east as Pennsylvania, who had been lured to Oklahoma and Indian Territory by the land rush to "the Strip country" in the early 1890's. Many of the farmers had come with only bare household possessions, and they had neither money nor materials to build a home. But they dug holes against river banks, cutting four poles as corner-posts and made "dugouts" of old planks and sheets of tin, often roofing the houses with sod.

Most of the farm tools were cheap and rudimentary—three-dollar plows, with which they cut furrows in the ground, tossing in corn or alfalfa seed at every pace, and waiting for the crops to come up. It was fairly fertile land, particularly near the river bottoms, and many of the farms had already begun to show signs of prosperity. But it was a far cry from the orderly German farming establishments of Fayette County.

Mangum was a booming little town, existing chiefly on the growth of a new and rapidly developing cotton-growing country. Outside the town, along the tracks of the Rock Island Railroad, were sheds in which bales of cotton were piled during the early winter and spring seasons; and this was where Roy Cullen's business was centered.

The town itself was composed of mercantile establishments, where the nearby farmers bought supplies and tools; and around the "town square"—an irregular area in the middle of town—were clustered the usual disproportionate number of saloons and honky-tonks. These ran full blast day and night; and while there were few refinements in Mangum, it was in the process of growing and this lent a constant air of excitement.

In spite of the influx of Easterners, Mangum was essentially a frontier town. Men wore guns, and quarrels were often settled in a quick, decisive way, in which the loser of the argument wound up on "Boot Hill." Many of the outlaws who had been driven into Western Oklahoma by sporadic forays of law and order in the eastern part of the state would "hole up" in the smaller towns, and were virtually immune from arrest—chiefly because of the unwillingness of the local law officers to risk their own lives making the arrest.

There was a tolerance for lawless men that was inherent in the restless exuberance of the Western Oklahoma people. Men who had business in the area—whether farming or cotton buying—stuck to their business and paid little attention to what was going on around them. Lawless men and lawful men mingled freely in the towns, yet each group kept to itself. Jail breaks were common, and seldom evoked much public protest—since a jailbreak usually rid the community of an unwanted resident.

Even the denizens of the prairie—the wild animals—enjoyed a kind of lawless tolerance; and it was not unusual to see a prairie dog and a snake and a rabbit—and even an owl—scurry down the same hole when a rider came by.

Most of Roy's business was done in Mangum and nearby railroad centers, where cotton traders representing the growers in the surrounding territory came to deal with the buyers. Clarkson was a big outfit; but there were other important buyers in the area, representing big cotton firms in Oklahoma City and Dallas. Young Cullen—or "Cully," as he was known—rapidly developed a reputation for honesty and straightforwardness, which drew many of the cotton sellers to him. His business increased; and as he began to deal directly with the banks, he developed a knowledge of business that gave him a maturity far beyond his years.

During this period of life, he traveled a great deal, buying cotton in Western Oklahoma during the spring months, and returning to South Texas for the fall buying season. On these trips he always stayed as long as possible in Schulenberg, which was one of the big cotton centers of South Texas. He saw Lillie often on these trips, and during the times he was in Oklahoma they kept up a constant correspondence.

For several months Lillie was away with her family on a trip to Europe; and during this period Roy spent most of his time working at the cotton business in Oklahoma and helping his father to improve the Elm River farm. Mangum was showing increasing signs of dependable growth, and Roy believed that he could establish himself in business there. New banks had been established to handle farm credit, and he knew most of the bankers personally.

He was now entering young manhood—twenty years old, and filled with growing responsibilities. He had worked since he was twelve; and for the past four years—since he was sixteen—had worked as a man, in competition with much older men. His understanding with Lillie that they would be married "as soon as they grew up" had not been revealed to members of either family; but Lillie's grandfather, Charles Kessler, knew about it, and had offered Roy an opportunity to take up some of his vast landholdings and become a rancher.

However, Roy had begun to see signs of increasing opportunity in the wild country of Western Oklahoma; and he wanted above everything else to establish a business for himself, so that he could support Lillie when they were married.

He knew cotton buying was a good business; but what future did it hold for him? Would he always be working for a firm like Clarkson? And if he did not want to work for someone else, how would he establish himself in business?

Part of the answer seemed to lie in owning land. Those who did, became prosperous and independent. Those who had no land worked for those who had it. Roy began to understand the "land-rush" craze which had driven men into this wild country to get a foothold in the earth—to own land and develop it. Even those who had been robbed by speculators still continued to seek more land.

So Roy Cullen began to study the possibilities of getting land. The area around Mangum was not promising. Although much of the river bottom land was good, the best acreage had been taken up. His homestead west of Mangum was rocky and not fertile.

About this time reports came in of a great "land rush" in the Texas Panhandle, near the town of Lubbock. This was a frontier country, high up on the "Caprock," a huge plateau formed by rising tableland and extending perhaps three hundred miles across the Panhandle from north to south.

Land near Lubbock had been offered by the state of Texas, with forty years in which to pay. The area was known to be rich country, and it was new. The prospect of getting in on the ground floor of a "land rush" excited Roy. It seemed to be the answer to his prayer. Here he could establish the kind of landholding he had dreamed of—and he would have a stake for a future home!

He wrote Clarkson, asking permission to leave Mangum for a couple of weeks; and then he rode down to his father's farm and prepared for the long trip across Southwest Oklahoma and the Red River, which was the southern boundary of Oklahoma Territory.

The only way to make the trip was by horse; and since there were stretches across the barren plains where only a few "nesters" and perhaps outlaws or rustlers were to be found, Roy for the first time armed himself with a Colt revolver.

He did not wait for a reply from Clarkson. The winter was moving down on Texas with full force, and unless he made the trip quickly, he felt he might be snowed in and held up indefinitely. He had a fair idea of the route, which descended to the Red River where the South Fork branched off, and then up across the sprawling ranges of the great Matador Ranch, one of the largest in Texas and notorious for its crew of rough-riding cowboys who made a practice of keeping strangers who might be "land settlers" away from their range. Their usual form of persuasion was a Colt forty-five.

It was a long, hard trip; and Roy knew that the winter weather could quickly become bitter and even dangerous if a sudden "norther" should blow up. However, he wanted the Texas land badly, and if he waited until spring it might all be taken up.

So on a cold winter morning, early in 1901, he rode out from his father's farm, heading across the open country toward the Red River.

CHAPTER 5

"The Caprock in a 'blue norther' is like Hell froze over!"

THE COUNTRY over which Roy Cullen rode down to the southwest corner of Oklahoma and the Red River was bleak and lonely; and as he rode through the brushy badlands, he felt the sharp bite of increasingly cold winds, blowing down from the north.

It was about one hundred and forty miles from Mangum to the Caprock and another sixty miles to Lubbock; and he knew he was in for a good week of travel. The prospect of a Texas "norther" was not inviting. There were few settlements between Mangum and Childress, the first town of any size on the way to Lubbock; and beyond that was even more sparsely settled country, belonging to the Matador Ranch which asserted its unofficial suzerainty over several hundred square miles of Texas.

Roy knew that most of the people he would meet between Mangum and Childress would be either "nesters"—small landowners, trying to grub a bare living from the ground, and fearful of being driven off by the big cattlemen whose ranges sprawled around them—or outlaws who had scattered when Oklahoma and Indian Territory began to fill up in the "land-rush" days, and now were hiding out in outlying ranch houses, or in dugouts in the hills between the Red River and the Caprock. The dugouts were small shacks, built into ledges of rock so that the ledge formed three sides of the wall sections. Most of them were one-room affairs, hardly visible from the trail, except for a corral and perhaps a lean-to shed, which formed the nucleus of the "ranch." Those who were honestly homesteading had small gardens, and ran a few head of cattle; but many of the denizens of the dugouts merely used them to hole up during the winter, and they offered little semblance of a home.

The first night he found shelter in one of these dugouts. There were a half-dozen rough men in the shack, and Roy slept with his hand closed around the handle of his Colt revolver—a piece of traveling equipment he had purchased just before he left Mangum. He shared his narrow bunk with a boy, several years younger than Roy. The boy was unkempt and dirty; and he accepted Roy as a bunkmate without either friendliness or protest.

The night passed without incident, and Roy was glad to be on his way early the next day. The wind had flattened out during the night, but an ominous haze in the north gave evidence that the storm had not blown itself out. The winding trail crossed the Red River, and threaded out over the barren plains toward the Matador Ranch. Roy crossed the shallow stream of the North Pease River the following morning and started a long climb toward the Caprock.

It was about noon that his horse, plodding slowly down the dry bed of a stream, pulled up suddenly in front of a dugout. Roy's hail brought out an old man, who invited him in for some food. He was a nester who had settled on the range land near the gate to the Matador Ranch, and he lost no time apprising Roy of the condition of the country ahead.

"They shoot first, and then ask who you are," he said. "There's only one place between here and Matador—and that's forty miles from here—where a fellow lives in a dugout, like me."

"A nester?" Roy asked.

The old man nodded. "Like me." He pointed to the north, where blue clouds were banking up across the sky. "You better stay here tonight, son," the old man advised. "That looks like a blue norther blowing off the Caprock—and the Caprock in a blue norther is like Hell froze over!"

The sun had come out during the morning, shedding a sallow light upon the bleak land. The ground was whitened with snows of several days, and the stretch of country between the dugout and the Matador Ranch, according to the old nester, was rougher than the country Roy had just crossed.

Roy was dressed warmly, with two flannel shirts, and a heavy coat, with a woolen cap drawn down over his head and ears. A bandana handkerchief was wrapped around his throat. The temperature was well below freezing, but the sun was still shining—in a rather sickly fashion—and he decided to push on.

Roy had gone only a few miles from the dugout when the old man's dire prediction began to come true. The sun disappeared completely, and the sleet, foreshadowed by the blue clouds to the north, began to whip across the open country. The temperature dropped sharply, and gusts of harsh wind drove the sleet in flurries across the flatlands.

An hour before sundown the sky became almost black; and the sleet, whipped against him by the bitterly cold wind, made progress difficult. Roy still felt warm within the folds of his heavy coat; but he knew the horse would soon be suffering. He still had a good twenty miles to cover, in order to reach the Matador Ranch that night; and the gathering darkness made it impossible to follow the trail with any certainty. Several times he found himself off the trail, and finally he had to admit to himself that he was lost.

The horse began to slip badly on the glazed rocks. He climbed off the horse, staggering under the impact of the fierce gusts of wind, and managed to cut hard-packed balls of snow away from the bottom of the animal's hoofs, where they had formed within the iron shoe.

Then he clutched the reins with one mittened fist, and followed the horse on foot, trusting to its instinct to lead him through the blinding storm. The wind rose to a howling fury as it tore through narrow gorges; and the night came on swiftly, blotting out the ground. The earth seemed to converge upon man and horse as they ploughed through the darkness, stumbling through thickets and the barren rock of dry creekbeds.

The horse plodded down through the creek bottoms—apparently sensing the direction, since not even a horse could see in the blackness—and Roy plodded blindly along beside it. As he pushed stubbornly through the night, his senses slowly became numb—partly from the cold, which had dropped constantly since nightfall, partly from the apparent hopelessness of their plight. It was senseless to think about it; all he could do was plod forward.

Roy followed the horse, holding the reins, for what seemed to be several hours. Both man and animal were almost exhausted, when he heard the faint sound of a dog barking. By this time he was hopelessly lost. The sound out of the night heartened Roy, and he thought the horse was moving faster. Then it stopped abruptly. Roy felt the rasp of a strand of barbed wire on his coat.

He gripped the reins tightly—to avoid losing his hold on them and being separated from his horse—and pushed forward a foot or two. He felt the wire in the darkness. The single strand was part of a fence, running across the trail they were following. Roy dimly remembered the direction from which the dog's barking had come, and he tugged the horse around and now walked ahead of the horse, guiding himself along the fence with one hand.

They stumbled along for several hundred yards, Roy breaking trail through the dense brush. The sleet was still lashing into his face with savage fury; and where the fence climbed the wall of the ravine and crossed a ridge of exposed land, the force of the gale was almost unbearable. Roy had to turn sideways, breathing in short gasps as the icy wind seemed to lift them at times from the ground.

He was gradually reaching a state of complete numbness and exhaustion. The dog's bark had not been heard since the first sound, and he could not be sure from what direction the sound actually came. Suddenly a small glow of light appeared in the night a few feet ahead.

Roy stumbled toward it; and the dog, somewhere beyond the light, began barking again. The light came from a glazed window of a dugout; and Roy lurched toward it and lay against the door. After a moment, he began hammering on the door and shouting. He heard the crash of an overturned chair, and a voice growled from within:

"Get away or I'll shoot through the door!"

Roy was too cold and exhausted to care whether the man shot. He kept hammering on the door, and shouting: "I'm freezing to death–let me in!"

Finally there was a sound of a bar sliding back. The door opened slowly, and Roy pushed into the opening, dropping the reins of his horse. A solidly built man stood back a few feet inside the room. He was pointing a rifle at Roy.

Roy reached up with his forearm and pushed his cap back from his forehead. The lower half of his face was covered by the bandana, which had frozen to his moustache.

The occupant of the dugout stared at him for a moment, then dropped the muzzle of the rifle.

"Hell, I know you! You're from Oklahoma!" Roy lunged toward a potbellied stove that glowed warmly in the rear of the dugout. The man grabbed his arm and swung him around.

"Be careful of that fire–or you'll kill yourself with frostbite!" he said, sharply. "Here–stand over here and get your clothes off. I'll fix some coffee."

Roy got his outer garments off, and the man helped him walk up and down the cabin floor to restore circulation.

Then he went out and tended to Roy's horse. When he came back, he was in a friendly mood.

"I recognized you from your eyes," he said. "You had some land next to me on Elm River, near Mangum."

He explained his wariness at Roy's arrival. He was a settler on the Matador land, holding eight sections.

"Everyone who has bought state land on the Matador has been run off or killed," he said. "I got these eight sections right in the middle of the ranch, and I aim to keep them. I figured you were one of the Matador hands trying to get me to come out so they could pot me—and nobody would ever know what happened. That's why I'm extra careful."

The settler prepared some hot food and more coffee.

"It looks like the stage got caught in the blizzard," he told Roy. "It was due here about sundown, and it's past midnight now. It's thirty below, and if the driver got caught out in this storm he probably froze to death."

While Roy was eating, however, the dog began barking again and a few minutes later they heard the skid of wheels on the frozen ground outside. The settler pushed the door open and the stage driver clumped in followed by a woman and a small child.

The driver, batting the snow from his gloves, explained that they had lost the trail and had wandered for hours in the blizzard before finding it again. The woman had wrapped a heavy blanket around herself and her child, and kept a lighted lantern under the blanket to keep them from freezing.

Their host made them as comfortable as possible for the rest of the night. When Roy awoke in the morning, cramped and sore, he went out to see how his horse had fared. The poor beast was standing dumbly in the small corral, partly protected by the rock ledge from the blast of the wind which still blew in a howling gale across the plains. He tried to feed the horse, but the animal made no effort to eat.

Roy was worried. By eleven o'clock the wind had subsided slightly, but there was a two-foot layer of snow on the ground. It would be rough going, but the stage driver decided to continue toward the Matador Ranch, a few miles to the southwest; and Roy saddled his weary horse and set out with the stage, intending to feed the horse at the Matador ranch house.

When they arrived, still fighting through the bitter "norther," the horse was too tired and frozen to eat the oats Roy got for him; so he pushed on, hoping to reach a small ranch near the lower rim of the Caprock and bed down there for the night. At nightfall he was still plodding along the trail, with no sign of human habitation. Just as the gray dusk began to close in, he saw a small dugout, and roused the owner. The man came to the door, but did not ask him in.

"The ranch is just ahead," he told Roy. "You better go on—they'll put you up for the night. I ain't got any room here."

The snow by this time had piled in deep drifts against the base of the Caprock, and the trail was invisible. The weary horse, forging through the storm by blind instinct, finally pulled up at a fence; and Roy saw a light ahead. He made his way up to the front of a small ranch house, and the owner—a rather friendly middle-aged man—came to the door.

"Get down off your horse and come in," he shouted cheerfully. The rancher pulled on a slicker, came out and took Roy's horse, leading it back to a stable in the rear. Roy went into the house and found the first semblance of a home he had seen since he left Oklahoma—a plain, but comfortable, ranch house, with a sixteen-year-old girl sitting at a checker board near the stove, where she had apparently been playing with her father.

The rancher came in and helped Roy take off his outer clothes.

"We ain't got much to eat," he said. "We've been snowed in here for a week—but you're welcome to what we have."

For two days Roy remained snowed in at the ranch, eating tough venison, blue biscuits, molasses and black coffee—and playing checkers with the rancher's daughter. The girl's appetite for checkers was insatiable—until Roy's desire to escape from checker playing was as strong as his wish to be on the trail again.

It was about two days' ride to Lubbock, high on the Caprock. Roy set out, his horse fresh once more after two days of warmth and food, and by nightfall reached the rim of the Salt River, which cuts a deep cleft into the southeastern edge of the Caprock. He descended along a narrow trail to the canyon floor, where one of the oldest stone houses in West Texas stood—the ranch house of "Captain Hank" Smith, a famous Indian fighter of frontier days. The grizzled old frontiersman's welcome was particularly hospitable when he found that his visitor was a nephew of Captain Bill Smith. "Hank" Smith had fought in the Indian wars with Captain Bill Smith of San Antonio, Roy's uncle.

The house, at the bottom of Blanco Canyon, was built of rocks, with walls thick enough to withstand almost any assault—a throwback to the days when Comanches and Apaches roamed the Caprock.

The lonely old recluse begged Roy to spend a few days with him, but Roy knew time was a vital element in getting to Lubbock. "Land rushes" did not last long, and he had already lost much time. He pushed on toward Lubbock early the next day, and arrived about nightfall. Lubbock was a small frontier settlement, one hundred and twenty miles from the nearest railroad and there was only one hotel in town, a two-story frame building with a half-dozen guest rooms. He managed to get a room, but when he went upstairs to his room, he found a stranger asleep in his bed, fully dressed, with his boots on—and wearing two Colt pistols!

Roy was too weary to argue. He managed to push his unexpected bed companion over to one side, crawled under the blanket and went to sleep. The next morning when he awoke, the stranger was gone.

Roy went downstairs and spoke to the hotel proprietor.

"I rented a room from you last night, and I found another fellow in my bed."

"Oh, him!" the hotel man laughed. "He's just a cattle rustler. They come in at night when it gets too cold and take any bed they can find. They always leave early—so the marshal won't find 'em here."

Roy made his way to the land office. There had been reports of rough work by some speculators, who wanted their agents to get all the land possible, and who even had strangers dragged out of the "chute"—a railed place where applicants for land lined up. In some cases men waited in line for days, without sleep, while friends brought food to them—or in some cases, changed places.

When he stepped into the land office, his heart sank. The railed "chute" was empty. Roy made a few inquiries of the land-office clerk and found the reason: The last of the Lubbock land had been disposed of the day before!

CHAPTER 6

"The damn rustlers have got our stock—and I'm going to get them back"

ROY CULLEN rode back over the rim of the Caprock and down across the rolling hills of the Matador Ranch where he had nearly died a week before, a disappointed but by no means discouraged young man. The eight sections of land he had hoped to take up on the Panhandle might have been a new stake for him—perhaps the beginning of a big ranch, and a home of his own. But he had failed by the slim margin of a single day.

Now as he rode back across the rough country where he had fought his way through the "blue norther," his tired horse threading down through the sloping gulches toward the Red River Valley, Roy's mind was busy with new plans.

He had often talked with his father about the possibility of further development of the 160-acre farm which Cicero Cullen had taken up on Elm River, before Roy came to Mangum. Roy decided that as soon as he returned to Mangum, he would spend some time looking over the possibilities of developing the farm.

The Cullen farm on Elm River was rich bottom land in places, and neighboring farms had grown excellent crops of cotton and corn. Roy's own homestead, three miles closer to Mangum, was hardly useful for anything. It was the last of the public land that was available in that part of the country, and Roy had filed on it because the hummocks of gypsum soil looked pretty. He had built a small dugout shack with a lean-to, and called the place "Gypsum Hill."

As soon as he cleared up the spring cotton buying at Mangum, Roy hired several farm hands and began to make plans to build up his father's farm. Cicero Cullen had a three-room farmhouse, one of the best in the area; and Roy bought four mules and three horses, and the most modern farm tools he could find in Mangum.

Several fields had been cleared and plowed, and he decided to cultivate these. There were about fifty acres of land that could be developed for late spring planting; and since Lillie was away in Europe, there was no reason for him to go south to Schulenberg until the fall buying season began.

So Roy labored through the hot months of early summer. His farm hands proved a bad investment: they did little work and he had to spend so much time watching them and telling them what to do that he decided to fire his help and do the work himself.

His first project was to plant a field with alfalfa, and the results were spectacular. The alfalfa grew rapidly, and in such quantities that Roy decided to go in for "scientific" farming. He knew that hogs were being raised profitably in the area, and gazing at his waist-high crop of alfalfa, he decided he would buy hogs, fatten them on the alfalfa—and perhaps add corn to the cycle. The crops of alfalfa and corn would furnish enough food to fatten the hogs, and the sale of the hogs would raise enough money to plant more alfalfa and corn, and thus he would be able to raise a larger number of hogs.

Roy began to figure his profits from this venture on the back of an envelope. He added up the returns from the first crops and the sale of the hogs, and then converted his earnings into more alfalfa and corn, and by the time he reached the bottom of the envelope he had pyramided the 160-acre farm into a prosperous farming business.

The only thing he had failed to record on the envelope was the weather. Oklahoma was subject to long and severe dry spells, and the results of such a dry spell were often disastrous to farmers.

Roy started with a small herd of Poland China hogs, black and sleek, and showing every evidence of fattening into good profits for the farm. He found it necessary to dig a well, because the water of the Elm River was brackish and salty. This was where Nature began to interfere with the alfalfa-corn-hog cycle.

A long dry spell set in early in the summer and Western Oklahoma became a dusty, waterless region. Roy's well began to dry up as the surface water receded, and the water from the Elm River seeped in. The Elm River water was salty, and the sleek black Poland China hogs began to turn a dirty brown. Instead of fattening up, they wasted away, until Roy finally decided he had better sell the hogs for what flesh was left on them.

One night rustlers invaded the Elm River farm and stole the mules and horses. Roy awakened the next morning to find his father's farm populated by a few dying hogs.

His dismay was quickly replaced by anger. He had lived in Western Oklahoma long enough to know that if a man did not look after his own property, nobody else would look after it for him. He went in and told his father: "Dad, the damn rustlers have got our stock—and I'm going to get them back!" He strapped on the Colt pistol he had bought for the trip to Lubbock, walked over to a neighboring farm, where he borrowed a horse, and started across the hills on the trail of the rustlers.

Rustling was a curious business in this part of Oklahoma. Most of it was done by men who knew the country thoroughly; and the stolen stock was usually driven at night, and held in small, fairly secluded valleys during the daylight hours. Roy was pretty sure he knew the direction the rustlers would take, and how they would travel. Mules usually will follow a mare, and among his horses was a fast mare that he had bought for his own use from a Kiowa Indian.

He figured the rustlers would take off with the mare, and the mules and other horses would follow. The natural route lay toward the west toward the North Fork of the Red River. There was about two miles of level land beyond the farm and then five miles of gypsum breaks where it would be difficult to follow a trail. Beyond that was a prairie-dog town known as White Flats, and another stretch of broken country, leading down to the North Fork.

Roy was seething with anger as he rode after his stolen stock; but he was also wary. He knew the rustlers were old hands at hiding in the hills, and if they spotted him on their trail, one of them might lay back and bring him down with a rifle shot. However, he wanted his mules and horses back, and he had no choice except to ride. There was only one place where the rustlers could cross the river, and he headed for that point.

He crossed the North Fork, and about two miles beyond, in a narrow valley, he saw his missing stock. The valley was surrounded by high cliffs; and Roy had a prickly feeling he might hear the crack of a rifle at any moment. However, he rode toward the grazing animals, and quickly herded them back toward the river. It was not until he had his stock safely across the river that he felt a sense of relief from the uneasy feeling that he was being watched from the hills.

He drove his stock back to his father's farm on the Elm River, and never saw the rustlers.

At the end of the summer, Roy decided that farming was a full-time job, and he did not have the time for it. He had put in a spring and summer of hard work, and had managed to produce a bumper crop of sorghum; but otherwise it was not too profitable a venture.

Meantime, the little town of Mangum was seething with political activity. An issue had arisen which literally split the county—and Roy, quite accidentally, found himself in the middle of the political controversy.

During the early days when Oklahoma and Indian Territory had been laid out by the Government, the Red River had been regarded as a natural boundary between Oklahoma and Texas. However, there were two Red Rivers—the North Fork and the South Fork, which split from the main Red River southeast of Mangum. Texas had always claimed the area between the North and South Forks as part of Texas; but when the Government surveys laid out the boundary between Texas and Oklahoma, the South Fork was specified as the dividing line.

When Greer County, which covered the area, was part of Texas, Mangum had been the county seat; and when the boundary was shifted, it continued to claim that distinction—a claim that was now disputed by the town of Altus, north of Mangum and above the North Fork, which wanted to form a separate county. The townspeople of the two towns developed a bitter feud over the question, and when Roy returned to Mangum to live, after his summer on the farm, he found Greer County had become divided, everyone taking one side or the other.

All the residents of Mangum—except those who had business interests in Altus—were on the Mangum side of the controversy. One of the exceptions was a restaurant owner named White, who also had property in Altus. He was a gruff, domineering man who was accustomed to having his views prevail in any discussion in which he offered an opinion.

Roy happened to be in a gathering of men in front of White's restaurant, listening to arguments on the county-splitting issue, when suddenly White thrust his head through the screen door.

"By God!" he roared. "Folks that own things in this country want Altus to be county seat of our county—and that's what it's going to be!"

Roy looked at White for a moment, wondering who he meant by "folks that own things." Then, on a sudden inspiration, he shoved the screen door against the restaurant proprietor's neck. White was caught like a mouse in a trap; and the harder he struggled to extricate himself, the harder Roy pushed.

"You stuck your nose in this," he said. "Now get it out."

White was trying to get it out, and Roy helped him by shoving the heel of his hand against White's nose. The restaurant man's face was outside the door and his hands inside, and all he could do was bellow each time Roy worked over his nose with the heel of his hand.

The men around Roy began to laugh—most of them being on the Mangum side of the dispute. Finally White got his knee against the door, and pulled his head through. He retired into the restaurant with red ears and a sore nose.

Then the night marshal, a burly Scotchman called "Mac," came up to Roy and told him he was under arrest.

"Everybody in town is for Mangum—except White!" Roy exclaimed. "You wanted someone to shut him up, and I did. Now you want to put me in jail!"

"Can't help it, Cully," the night marshal said. "I got to arrest you."

He grabbed Roy's arm, and Roy wrenched away. The next instant the two were out in the square, slugging toe to toe. Roy was smaller and thinner, but much faster than the heavy-set law officer.

"Drop your guns, Mac!" someone shouted, and the marshal pulled back and unstrapped his guns. Roy waited until the man had shed his weapons, then the fight was resumed. It was quickly evident that Roy, although smaller than the bulky lawman, had an advantage in his speed. He stepped in and jabbed, and then slipped out of the marshal's reach time and again, until the guardian of the law was puffing like a winded horse. Finally, the night marshal stopped, picked up his guns and walked back to his office on the square.

Roy rode back to the farm on Elm River, thinking the account was closed; but when he returned to Mangum the day marshal—also called "Mac"—met him and said, quite stiffly:

"Mr. Cullen, the Mayor wants to see you."

Mayor McMillan—the third "Mac"—was also justice of the peace. The formality of the marshal's tone disturbed Roy; everybody in Mangum called him "Cully."

"What does he want me for?" he asked the marshal.

The man shrugged. "It's on a serious matter—assaulting an officer."

Roy hurried to the Mayor's office, a small frame shack

which also housed the court—since the Mayor was also justice of the peace.

"What's up, Mac?" he asked.

Mayor McMillan wagged his head solemnly.

"I've got to fine you, Cully, for resisting an arrest and fighting an officer."

"Hell, Mac!" Roy exploded. "Everybody in town agreed with what I did—when I got White's head stuck in the door. You're supposed to represent the town, aren't you?"

The Mayor—now acting as justice of the peace—again shook his head.

"Maybe you did us a favor, but under the law I've got to fine you."

"How much?"

"Nine dollars and twenty-five cents."

Roy stared steadily at the Mayor for a minute. He was barely twenty, but he knew that he was liked and respected in Mangum; and to be fined for taking a position the whole town agreed with seemed outrageous. He reached in his pocket and slowly pulled out nine silver dollars and a quarter. Then he pointed his finger at Mayor McMillan.

"I'm going out and fight you, Mac. You and the two marshals will never be elected in this town again!"

Without waiting for the election—which was several weeks away—Roy began stumping the square, moving from bank to stores to saloons, making speeches denouncing the "three Macs" at every restaurant or store where he could collect people to listen. Soon a crowd was following him, loudly cheering his words; and however decisive the effect of his speeches may have been, the three officials were defeated at the next election.

Roy's accidental introduction to politics filled him with

a new interest in public affairs. He had no desire to run for office; but the taste of public reaction to his speeches aroused in him a Warwickian urge, and at the next county election he plunged into a hot political campaign in behalf of a young Pennsylvania lawyer, who had come out to the Territory to make his fortune and was running for County Attorney. Roy had met the young man in Mangum, and liked him.

The young man from the East was running for an office regarded as a sensitive post in the affairs of the county, since the county attorney had the right to initiate investigations into land claims, and was an arbiter of most of the legal activities of the county.

Roy approached the young attorney.

"I'd like to help you in the election," he said. "If you don't mind."

The Pennsylvanian was delighted to accept Roy's offer. The latter's efforts in the campaign for city offices, which resulted in the defeat of the "three Macs," had enhanced his position in county political circles. Roy promptly began to plan the campaign of the young lawyer, acting in the capacity of political counselor as well as stumping the county in behalf of his candidate.

For several weeks Roy Cullen spent much of his time making rousing political speeches for his man as he toured the county on business. The situation looked good, up to election eve. Everyone assured Roy his candidate would win. But Oklahoma was a hard political school, with few rules and no scruples in vote-getting campaigns.

Roy left his protégé on the day before election, flushed with anticipation of victory; and with a few final words of advice.

"Move around a lot—shake hands with everybody, and let everybody see you," he advised. "Better not do any drinking—there are a lot of folks against whiskey in this county."

Everybody saw the young candidate, but not exactly in the condition Roy had expected. The Pennsylvania lawyer was making his final rounds of gathering places, delivering a few last appeals for votes, when one of his henchmen suggested he go up to a room in the hotel and meet some important citizens. One of the citizens had a bottle, and offered the young lawyer a drink. He took it; and a few minutes later he began to feel groggy. The drink had been doped.

The rest of the whiskey was poured over the young lawyer's shirt, and he was led out into the street where he curled up in front of a saloon and went to sleep—in full view of the electorate. The night marshal found him, sprawled against the wall, and hauled him to jail, where the young man spent election day sobering up.

In spite of this set-back to his candidate, Roy lost no prestige in the election. His championing of the cause of Mangum in the county-seat fight had made him popular; and although his espousal of the cause of the young Pennsylvania lawyer did not result in a political triumph, it increased the respect of the local citizens for Roy himself.

As a young man hardly of voting age, he was also gaining a solid reputation as a serious-minded young business man. Cotton men knew him as a fair trader; and since cotton trading was a rough business, with various devices and tricks for getting the best of a bargain, Roy had to learn to take care of his end of a trade and do it in an honest and straightforward way.

He made friends quickly; and it was perhaps this—and his complete faith in himself as well as in his fellow-men—that had earned him a place in the business world of Western Oklahoma.

Lillie had returned with her father and mother from Europe, and Roy planned an early visit to South Texas for the fall buying season. He visited his mother in San Antonio; and then went on to Schulenberg, where he found Lillie delighted to see him. He remained in South Texas as long as he could, and then returned to Oklahoma.

Western Oklahoma offered little comfort in those days for a young man in love. It was a hard, bleak country; and the rough-and-ready night life in the prairie towns offered little for Roy Cullen. He often spent his evenings with his father on the Elm Creek farm, riding across the rugged country in the evening and listening to the wail of coyotes, sending their long-drawn cry of loneliness across the flatlands at dusk. Roy developed a friendly feeling toward the untamed creatures, whose perennial loneliness seemed to echo that in his own heart, as he dreamed of his blue-eyed sweetheart in far-off Schulenberg.

In the spring of 1903, when Roy was in Mangum, he received a letter from his sister, Daisy Knight, who had moved from Schulenberg back to San Antonio. She gave him the news of the family, and then wrote that Lillie Cranz was planning to visit the family of a banker named Gross, in San Antonio. Roy immediately decided to visit his mother; and on April 18, 1903, he packed his bag and left for the South, arriving at his mother's home in San Antonio two days later.

One evening he gave a "Tally-Ho" party, hiring one of the high-backed wagons which were popular in those days; and as he sat beside Lillie on the high seat next to the driver, he asked Lillie to set a date for their wedding. Lillie thought they should be married right after Christmas, and this was agreed. Roy was now nearing his twenty-second birthday; and he had become well established in the cotton business as a buyer, both in Oklahoma and South Texas. He was sure he would be able to support a family.

The following day he decided to leave for Houston to renew his contract with Clarkson; and Lillie left with him, riding on the train as far as Schulenberg, although she had intended to stay longer with the Gross family. They had decided not to make an announcement of their wedding plans until Roy had an opportunity to speak to Lillie's parents.

The following July Roy returned from Oklahoma to Schulenberg for the beginning of the cotton-buying season, and lost no time in telling Gustave Cranz that he and Lillie planned to be married. He went directly to the Cranz home and asked Lillie to tell her father he wanted to speak to him.

Roy waited on the veranda for the older man to come out. He was quite excited, and so, he discovered, was Gustave Cranz. He stumbled slightly as he came out on the steps, and Roy noted this.

"Mr. Cranz," he said, without preliminaries, "I want to marry Lillie."

The merchant looked at Roy for a few seconds. He was a gentle, kindly man, with a wealth of wisdom in his deep blue eyes.

"What can you offer Lillie in the way of a living, Roy?" he asked. "Can you support a wife?"

Roy nodded firmly. He said he planned to return to Western Oklahoma, and as soon as conditions were right, he was going to set himself up in business as an independent cotton buyer. The older man nodded. He suggested that he might help Roy into a banking firm in Texas, but Roy shook his head.

"I want Lillie to know I am supporting her," he said.

It was decided the wedding would take place in the Cranz home in Schulenberg on December 29, 1903; and as soon as Roy finished his cotton buying in the South, he hurried back to Mangum. Just before Christmas he returned to San Antonio by way of Schulenberg, spending Christmas Eve at the Cranz home. Then he continued to San Antonio on the midnight train, and spent the next three days with his mother. On December 28 he returned, with his mother and Daisy, to Schulenberg.

The wedding was at noon the following day. Only members of the Cullen and Cranz families were invited to the wedding. It was a simple and beautiful ceremony, in the spacious Cranz home. Lillie, her blue eyes shining, wore a snowy white crepe-de-chine wedding dress; and Roy, his straight, slim figure more stiffly erect than ever with the realization of a new and greater responsibility, stood beside her while the Rev. T. J. Windham intoned the marriage vows . . . "Do you, Hugh Roy, take Lillie . . ."

They left that afternoon for San Antonio, and there was an opera party that night at the old San Antonio Opera House, where a traveling musical company was playing a popular musical comedy of that day, *Princess Chick,* featuring a song called "The Tale of the Kangaroo."

The next day Roy, filled with great hopes and determination, set out with his bride for Oklahoma—the raw, untamed frontier Territory where he planned to make his home and his fortune.

MANGUM
MAN

CHAPTER 7

"I don't ever expect to work for anyone but myself again"

THE LONG, dusty ride from Dallas to Chickasha exposed the utterly drab and dreary prospect of the Western Oklahoma plains. The train arrived about noon in Chickasha, where it was necessary to change trains for the final one-hundred-mile trip down to Mangum. It was New Year's Day of 1904, and the wind blew great clouds of sand across the plains, obscuring the buildings of the town in a yellow haze.

Roy helped Lillie down from the coach; and they decided to have New Year's dinner at the Geronimo Restaurant, one of the better eating places in Western Oklahoma. Then they boarded the train for the final journey across the plains to Mangum.

Roy and his young bride stepped out on the dusty little station platform at Mangum. The town was a mile off the railroad, having been built during the stagecoach days; and they climbed into a station coach furnished by the hotel to transport passengers into Mangum. Lillie looked out across the flat country toward the little cluster of gray buildings she would call "home."

The rooms at the hotel—recently built of native rock—were small and clean, but they were not luxurious. Roy realized that life might not be too pleasant for Lillie, in the hotel. A few weeks after their arrival in Mangum, he made arrangements with the Reverend Davidson, a Presbyterian minister, and his wife to rent two rooms at their home.

The night they moved in Roy brought home two thick steaks from the butcher, for Lillie to broil. He settled himself comfortably in a chair in the parlor-bedroom, waiting for Lillie to call him to dinner. He waited about a half hour . . . and she didn't call. Finally, he arose and went into the kitchen.

The steaks were lying untouched on the kitchen table. Lillie was standing in front of the table, plainly puzzled.

"Honey, whatever is the matter?" He walked over and put his arm around her shoulders. She looked up, and smiled ruefully.

"I don't know how to broil a steak . . . Do you?"

Roy laughed.

"I sure do." He quickly arranged a grill over the wood stove, and in a few minutes the steaks were sizzling.

Lillie learned quickly; it was the last time Roy ever had to broil a steak.

Roy took Lillie out to Gypsum Hill shortly after they arrived in Mangum, and they spent a night in the shack. Under the land laws of the Territory, homesteaders were required to live on their land at least two days in each calendar year, as well as to make certain improvements. Roy and Lillie returned to town after the first night, but when they came back to spend the second night, the shack was gone. A sudden "twister" had blown up during the day and completely demolished it.

That fall Roy took Lillie back to Schulenberg, where she

spent the winter with her family—and there young Roy Gustave Cullen was born.

When the baby was three months old, they brought him to Oklahoma. It was a long, dreary ride across Texas, and the baby became violently ill with "summer complaint" on the trip across the plains of Oklahoma. Roy and Lillie watched anxiously as the train crept slowly toward Mangum.

The worried couple took young Roy to the hotel at Mangum; and as soon as he seemed to be well again, they drove down to the homestead. The new house, which Roy had built while Lillie was away in Schulenberg, looked fresh and clean. The first night in their new home, however, a rainstorm blew up, lashing the Elm River Valley and drenching the new house. In a short while water began to drip through cracks in the roof.

An umbrella was rigged hastily over the baby's crib, and Roy stretched a tarpaulin over their bed. The next day he brought several rolls of tar paper from Mangum, and made the roof water-tight.

One day, when he rode in from Mangum, he said to Lillie:

"Honey, I'm going to quit working for Clarkson."

"Quit your job, Roy?" Lillie's blue eyes widened as she looked up at him.

Roy nodded. His face was already beginning to show deep lines which outdoor life, and the need of fighting for his place in the world, had gradually engraved upon his young features. His mouth was set in the expression Lillie knew so well.

"I'm going in business for myself. I don't ever expect to work for anyone but myself again."

When the cotton-buying season closed, Roy took Lillie and young Roy back to Schulenberg. Roy went on to Houston to see W. B. Clarkson, his employer.

"I'd like to resign, Mr. Clarkson," he told him. Clarkson was surprised.

"You've been doing very well, Roy. Aren't you happy in your present work?"

"Yes . . . but I'm a married man now. I've got to get started in business for myself."

Clarkson was plainly astonished. He pointed out that a married man had increased obligations, and required a steady income to meet them. He offered a substantial raise in salary, but Roy shook his head.

"I appreciate all you've done for me, Mr. Clarkson. But if I keep on working for you now, I'll always be working for somebody. And that means my family will always depend on somebody else for a living. I want them to depend on me."

Clarkson asked Roy if he had considered the problem of financing his business. The young man shook his head.

"I'll get money . . . somehow. I know the business pretty well, and I think I can make a success of it. If I do—I want it to be my success, not somebody else's."

The little family—increased to four with the birth of Lillie Cranz, their second child—returned to Oklahoma. Roy went to Chickasha where he called on a banker who had carried his accounts when he worked for Clarkson. His name was Henry Johnson, and later he became associated with the Kleberg cattle empire at the King Ranch in South Texas and became a breeder of blooded horses. Roy explained to Johnson his decision to leave Clarkson, and to go into the cotton-buying business himself.

"I need credit," he said, simply. Johnson looked at the young buyer with appraising eyes, drumming his fingers on his desk.

"How much do you need?" he asked.

"Fifty thousand dollars."

Johnson continued to drum his fingers. Then he said:

"All right, Roy—you can have that."

"How much margin do you want?" Roy asked.

"You won't have to put up any margin, Roy. Your business for Clarkson has been good . . . and I've watched you. When the season opens this fall, you can draw up to fifty thousand dollars."

As the fall seasoned opened, Roy began buying from the men he had traded with during past years. Within two months his credit had gone up to a quarter of a million dollars.

Cotton buying in those days was a migratory profession. Cotton buyers moved across the country with the cotton-picking seasons; and after buying what they could of one crop, they would move on to the next location as the harvesting progressed.

Roy moved with this circuit, traveling south into Texas and as far west as Seguin. The buyers purchased the cotton and arranged shipment to the compresses, where it was put through the first stages of processing. Roy learned that steamers, bringing cargoes into Texas ports during July and August, had no regular freight for return voyages; and as a special inducement to shippers, they offered low rates for cargoes shipped at this time. Roy began to confine his purchases during this period to places along the Southern Pacific Railroad, where he could get immediate shipment. At times he would work all night with freight crews, loading the cotton, so that he could have it rushed to the compresses for preparation for shipment.

In Oklahoma his operations were mainly along the Rock Island and Frisco Railroads. He would be on the road for days at a time during the heavy buying season; and this worried him, because it left Lillie home with the two children. Many times he worked all night to complete a deal, and then caught an early morning train to get home.

Roy sooned moved his family to Chickasha, where he and Lillie established their first real home. He was driving himself with unrelenting energy to build up his independent business as a cotton buyer. It was an intensely competitive business, and he was competing with eastern buyers and the new and growing firm of Anderson, Clayton and Company, of Oklahoma City. It was here that he first met William L. Clayton, a rising young cotton man of Oklahoma City, who later built Anderson, Clayton, now of Houston, into the largest cotton-buying firm in the world.

Anadarko, a large town west of Chickasha, was then a junction point for all telephone lines to Western Oklahoma, and therefore a key point in the cotton business, because it was here that all telephone lines to points to the west were controlled.

Roy gave the telephone company each day a list of about twenty-five names of cotton merchants and ginners throughout the Western Oklahoma area. At three o'clock, when the cotton exchanges closed, he began to place calls to these merchants and ginners, tying up all the trunk lines to the East, North and South. The other cotton firms were unable to get through to their various offices until Roy had gotten the first chance to buy the cotton.

Late in 1905 Roy joined with other cotton men in the area, forming the Oklahoma Cotton Exchange; and by the end of the year he was known as one of the most active cotton buyers in Western Oklahoma. He had a wide circle of friends, and had established himself as a fair and straightforward dealer.

There was a particularly tough cotton merchant in Mangum, who was popularly known as "the Bull." He was a heavily built man, with an aggressive manner, who drank a great deal of whiskey and said little. He knew all the tricks of the cotton-trading business, and usually managed to get from fifty cents to a dollar a bale the better on every trade with a buyer.

Roy Cullen needed three hundred bales of high-grade white-staple cotton to fill out an order, and he agreed to buy this from "the Bull." Then he went out to the cotton yards, about a half mile from Mangum, to "class" the cotton. The buyer and seller walked along the rows of bales, standing on end. The other man slashed open each bale with a sharp knife, and pulled out a handful of cotton. Cullen examined each sample, and classed it.

He noticed that "the Bull," as he called out the grade, classed each sample a grade higher than Roy did. If Roy classed it as "middling" cotton, the other man would call out "strict middling"—a grade higher. Roy said nothing; but he wrote down the tag numbers as "the Bull" called them out.

At the end of the row the man laid down the knife and asked Cullen to give him the classes so he could enter them in his tally-book. Roy reached for the knife and said:

"Let's class this cotton again—and this time we're going to do it the right way!"

The other man stared at him a few seconds. Then, without a word, he walked back along the row, and Roy repeated the classing, pulling out the samples. When they had finished, they drove into the bank at Mangum, "the Bull" still saying nothing.

As soon as the bank clerk had added the figures, and Roy had made out the check—according to his figures—the man turned and said:

"Will you have a drink with me?"

Roy nodded. "Sure!"

They walked over to the Palace Bar. "The Bull" turned to Roy:

"Straight?"

"Straight."

He poured the drinks, and they tossed them off. The man did not say another word until they turned to leave. Then he asked:

"Cullen, will you buy any more cotton from me?"

Roy looked at him steadily, and "the Bull" continued:

"You can buy all the cotton you want from me, Mr. Cullen—and you'll get it right. You've got plenty of guts, and I like you."

CHAPTER 8

"I'd as soon trust Roy Cullen as I would my banks"

THE YEAR 1907 was fateful for Oklahoma and the nation. Oklahoma and Indian Territory became a state in that year; and panic swept the country, breaking the markets from San Francisco to New York.

The shift from territorial status to statehood inadvertently plunged Roy Cullen into politics again—and it was his first entry into a major political field. Immediately after Oklahoma was voted to statehood by Congress, various political factions began to emerge in a roaring fight for the Governorship.

Roy Cullen was an independent voter, who supported the man, not the party. Nearly everyone in Oklahoma was a Democrat; and the only political contests were in the primary elections, with Democrats vying for the various nominations. However, Roy had little active interest in the gubernatorial race, except the desire to see honest and capable men in office. Then—as seemed to be customary in his political adventures—he became embroiled in a political controversy.

The affair was quite accidental, and except for a small

amount of pistol-waving, had no dangerous consequences; but it thrust Roy Cullen into the middle of the state political battle.

The two principal candidates for the Democratic nomination for Governor—which was equivalent to election—were Lee Cruze, a prominent Oklahoma City lawyer, and a land promoter named Haskell. On general principles, Roy favored Cruze. But he had little use for Cruze's campaign manager, named Morman Pruitt. Cruze seemed to be a straightforward, conscientious and experienced attorney; but Roy regarded Pruitt as a typical politician.

Roy happened to be in the lobby of the Lee Huckins Hotel in Oklahoma City one evening, reading a paper. He had come to Oklahoma City to ship some cotton, at a time when the political campaign was seething, with nearly everyone in Oklahoma taking sides for Cruze or Haskell.

Morman Pruitt and a crowd of his political henchmen swarmed into the hotel and gathered in the corner of the lobby near Roy's chair. They were noisily forecasting Cruze's triumph at the polls, when an unobtrusive stranger walked up to the group and said quietly:

"Would any of you gentlemen like to make a wager?"

"On who?" one of the Cruze men asked.

"On Mr. Haskell."

Pruitt's crowd was silent for a moment, as they inspected the mild-mannered stranger. Then one asked: "How much do you want to bet?"

The man pulled out a roll of bills. Roy had glanced up to follow the exchange, and the roll looked good for several thousand dollars.

"Any part or all of it," he said, still not raising his voice.

One of the group suddenly confronted the stranger and

began cursing him. Suddenly the mild-mannered man found himself in the center of the crowd. Roy listened to the barrage of curses and taunts for a while; then he arose and walked over to the group. Nobody paid any attention to him at first.

"Why don't you cover the mans' bet—or let him go?" Roy asked.

Pruitt and his men turned, as if by common impulse, and stared at the new interruption. Then Pruitt pushed through the crowd toward Roy.

"Who the hell are you?"

Roy looked at the man.

"I'm an American citizen who believes in fair play," he said. "And you're a bunch of damned cowards trying to bully this man—when you won't cover his bet!"

Pruitt reached under his coat and started to drag out a gun—which was a common feature of men's wearing apparel in those days—when one of his companions grabbed his hand.

"You want to sink Cruze?" he said sharply.

The mild-mannered stranger had departed during this new altercation, as quietly as he had come; and when Roy saw that the subject of his interference had left, he turned and walked back to his chair. After he sat down and began reading his paper again, he could see that the Cruze faction had gone into a huddle, and several of the group were directing glances at him. He knew a few of the men casually, and he was quite certain they knew him also, because he was well known in Western Oklahoma.

After several minutes in a huddle, the Cruze men left the lobby, and the next morning Pruitt met Roy Cullen in the lobby and apologized for what happened the evening before. Roy accepted his apology, but that did not end it. The man who offered the wager apparently had gone directly to Haskell and reported the incident. The paper that supported Haskell blazoned the affair on its front page the next day.

The incident became a campaign issue. Haskell's supporters charged Cruze and Pruitt with hiring thugs in their efforts to smear his opponent; and they loudly praised Roy Cullen for his "courageous stand—as an American who believes in fair play!" Haskell won the nomination, which assured him the election.

He wrote Roy, stating that he attributed the margin of victory to the public sympathy aroused by the incident in the Huckins Hotel. He added that anything Roy Cullen wanted, within political reason, would be his for the asking.

Cullen wrote back a brief reply:

"All I want you to do is be a good governor."

Meanwhile, the gloomy clouds of national depression were climbing ominously over the horizon. The smaller banks in Western Oklahoma began to run out of cash . . . and this brought home to Roy Cullen the first impact of an economic panic.

He had been a boy, in the process of quitting school, when the panic of 1893 struck the country. He had felt its effect only indirectly, in the pinch of family finances. But now it became a tangible thing, an enemy to be reckoned with; and with Roy's characteristic directness, he tackled the problem without much beating about the bush.

He knew the banks that had backed his independent cotton-buying venture, through extension of credit to him, were badly pressed for cash. Their money had been made available to him for buying cotton, based on their absolute assurance that he would repay the money as soon as the cotton was sold. At that time he had a special arrangement with several banks, under which he held bills of lading and receipts for cotton delivered, until it was actually received at the compresses and paid for. In this way, he held the collateral on money advanced by the banks, and when the deal was completed he would turn the money over to the banks to pay off their advances.

When the bottom dropped out of the market during the panic of 1907, it was necessary for Roy to sell the cotton quickly in order to return the money to the banks. But there were no buyers . . . and for the first time he felt the pressure of a falling market against extension of credit. Roy went to the banks.

"I'll get your cash," he told them.

Within a few days he arranged for quick disposal of all the cotton he held. He sold cotton to an English firm, T. W. Stewart, at Galveston, and the French firm of Algeyer and Company at Houston, for half cash and half exchange credit—which he could not use at the time. He turned the cash over to the banks.

It was a costly operation. Roy had to accept New York exchange credit, but the New York banks were as badly pressed as the Oklahoma banks, and the exchanges were not immediately honored.

Roy meanwhile had stopped shipment on all the cotton he could reach, and had it brought back to the compresses. Again he lost, his normal profit being wiped out; but he saved the collateral and was able to refund it to the banks.

He learned in a hard school the rigors of financial panic. And he also found time to measure the effects of his own standard of honesty against the engulfing tide of economic disaster. A quarter of a century later, when the depression of the early 1930's swept over the country, Roy Cullen was able to draw from his personal history a principle of rigid adherence to the common rules of fair economic practice—and it was this insight that turned him against the so-called "economic reforms" of the Roosevelt New Deal.

He had lost from one to three dollars a bale when he liquidated his cotton holdings; but he enabled the banks that had trusted and supported him to remain liquid. And the "payoff" on this came shortly afterward.

A Dallas cotton firm, Harrall and King, moved into Cullen territory during the period of financial stress; and knowing the banks were hard pressed for money, they went to Colonel Boone D. Hite, who owned several banks in Western Oklahoma, and suggested a special arrangement.

"We know your cash is short—as all banks are," they said. "We'd like to work out a deal with you under which we could handle our deals through your banks, and reduce the amount of cash you would need to handle them."

Colonel Hite shook his head.

"Sorry," he said. "Roy Cullen uses all the money we have available."

The Dallas cotton buyers said they would turn over all collateral papers, such as bills of lading and receipts, for money advanced by the bank.

"We understand Roy Cullen keeps the collateral until he ships the cotton," one of the men said.

Colonel Hite nodded. "Yes—that's a fact," he said.

"We'll let you hold the receipts, so you'll be in possession of the collateral at all times," the man from Dallas said.

The banker laughed.

"When we got hard pressed for cash," he said, "Cullen sold his cotton at a loss—to get us the cash. He's the sort of fellow we like to do business with, and I reckon we'll keep on doing business with him. I'd just as soon trust Roy with the collateral as I would my banks."

But Roy was getting worried. He was doing business, all

right; but at the end of the year, when he totalled up his figures, there wasn't much left. He knew he was doing as much business as any other cotton firm in Western Oklahoma. Yet he was not making money.

One day Colonel Hite met him on the street, and said:

"Roy, I see you're making some pretty good money now."

Cullen shook his head.

"Hell, no," he said. "I'm losing money."

"Your accounts don't show it," the banker said.

"Then the accounts are wrong," Roy replied. "Let's go look at your books."

They checked at the bank, and after going over the figures, Roy straightened up.

"There's a check for $33,000 missing," he said.

They prowled through the desk drawer, where he knew the bank teller tossed the checks he turned in. In back of the drawer, stacked with a pile of old envelopes and pieces of paper, was a check for $33,000 signed by "H. R. Cullen."

Colonel Hite laughed. This was the "margin of profit" Roy was supposed to have in his business.

Early in 1905, Roy moved his little family to Anadarko, Oklahoma. However, Anadarko was not much different from Chickasha and Mangum, as far as doing cotton business was concerned. There was plenty of business, but little return in the way of net profits. Roy found himself handling hundreds of thousands of dollars' worth of cotton in Western Oklahoma, and shipping to all parts of the world. But at the end of the season, when he reckoned up his earnings, there was hardly enough to support his family—which had now increased to five with the arrival of Agnes Louise, who was born in Anadarko in 1908.

"I work like hell," Roy told Colonel Hite, "but the banks get all the money."

He began to check with other cotton buyers, including those representing large firms, and found the story was much the same with them. The price of cotton, driven down by the market break of 1907, had not risen enough to make much margin between the buying and selling prices. Roy had become a successful trader, and he knew he held his own—but it wasn't enough.

He began to reckon up his assets. He had virtually unlimited credit with the bankers of Anadarko, Chickasha and Mangum. Since the day when Henry Johnson had agreed to extend Roy's credit "up to fifty thousand dollars," he had never had to worry about money to handle his cotton business. At times his credit piled up to several hundred thousand dollars, and he knew his reputation in this respect was something men work a lifetime to acquire.

It would require a great deal of sheer nerve to toss away that credit—which was pure gold in the business world. But Roy had made a similar decision several years before, when he gave up his job with Clarkson and launched himself—a young man of twenty-two, just married and with the responsibilities of a family—into a career as an independent cotton buyer.

He went home to the house at Anadarko one night, determined to think out the problem . . . and reach a decision. He had obtained several maps of the United States, and he spread these out on the floor. He studied the maps a long time . . .

Along the eastern half, across the Mississippi River, there were several large ports. The raw materials and goods produced in the Ohio River Valley, and around the Great Lakes, flowed down toward New Orleans; and east of that, beyond the Appalachian Mountains, they flowed down to the

Atlantic Coast—to New York, Philadelphia, Boston and Baltimore.

But west of the Mississippi the situation was different. Here, in the vast basin formed by the Missouri and the Mississippi, there was no dividing line. From the great lumber regions of the North, the cattle ranges and corn and wheat lands of Nebraska, Kansas and Iowa . . . the vast cattle and cotton country of Oklahoma and Texas . . . here it was all a single mighty bowl, scooped out and pouring its wealth of meat and grain, wool and hides, minerals, lumber and oil —all of it down across Texas to the city of Houston!

Here was the greatest area of productivity on the American continent—perhaps the greatest in the world; its products all pouring down across the map. And at the bottom of the map was Houston!

The next day he looked at Lillie. He smiled, but his face, already cast in rugged lines, was firm and his jaw was set.

Lillie smiled a bit uncertainly. She had come to recognize that glint in Roy Cullen's gray eyes.

"Honey," he said, "I think we're going to move to Houston."

CHAPTER 9

"Jesse Jones is a powerful man— but I'm a citizen of Houston!"

HOUSTON had been the capital of Texas seventy years before Roy Cullen moved there—but, because of the oratorical enthusiasm of Roy Cullen's illustrious grandfather, Ezekiel Cullen, it had ceased to be the capital in the year 1841. In a speech before the lawmakers of Texas, he had hurled every epithet he could muster—and his arsenal was prolific—at the damp, swampy, malarial *bayou* country that surrounded the city that later became Texas' greatest metropolis.

"That abominable place—that wretched mudhole—that

graveyard of men—the City of Houston!" he called it, shouting his maledictions from the floor of the Third Texas Congress; and his eloquence was so persuasive that the Government was moved to Austin—where it remained.

Ezekiel Cullen had been the first politician of importance in the Cullen family. Descended from a line of Scottish and English forebears who came to Virginia in 1670 and became large landholders there, Ezekiel Cullen had the blood of pioneering forefathers. The Cullens were the direct lineage of John Wimberly, about whom Louise Cullen had told Roy during his boyhood days in San Antonio.

John Wimberly, a "gentleman of Lancashire, England," had established the family in North America; and his son had moved to Windsor, North Carolina, in 1710; and after the American Revolution, the family—now joined with the Scottish Cullens—had moved to Georgia.

It was here, in the luxurious plantation home of Frederick Cullen, that Ezekiel was born; and it was with the hardy instinct of his pioneer ancestors that he decided to migrate to the seething Mexican province of Texas in 1835, when the first flames of Revolution were being fanned by Colonel Sam Houston, Stephen Austin and Mirabeau Lamar.

Young Cullen was possessed with the same deep sense of public spirit that later propelled his grandson into Oklahoma politics—and ultimately into Texas and national politics. He wanted to bring his old friend and fellow-Georgian, Lamar, back to Texas to unseat Sam Houston, and take over the political leadership of the new Republic.

He had hung out his shingle—"E. W. Cullen, Esq."—in San Augustine, the provisional capital of Texas, while the Revolution was in progress; and from here he wrote Lamar in Columbus, Georgia, in 1837:

> You are a brother Georgian, and much more talented and experienced than myself; hence I do not consider myself competent to give advice. But what I say is with the best of motives, and I hope you will take it in good part. Don't be absent from Texas at present . . . Watch closely the interests of the people at large. Don't be led or duped by monopolies and speculators . . . The election of President is close at hand, and you have it in your power to be what you please.

Ezekiel Cullen's subtlety and finesse in the art of "king-making" became a legend in Texas; and it is cited here because the arrival of his grandson at the scene of Ezekiel's political triumphs some three score and ten years later seemed to have ignited a startlingly similar sense of political and public interest on the part of Roy Cullen.

When Mirabeau Lamar, with Ezekiel's encouragement and prompting, was elected as the second President of the Republic of Texas in 1837—succeeding Sam Houston, the "hero of San Jacinto"—Ezekiel was also elected to the House of Representatives. He promptly launched a bitter attack on General Houston's namesake city, which was then the seat of the peripatetic government of Texas.

In the years following the Texas Revolution, Texans were even more uninhibited—geographically speaking—than they are today: the western boundary was not even defined, and Lamar claimed all the land as far as Santa Fe; and there were even a few who wished to extend the boundary to the Pacific Ocean. Ezekiel Cullen argued that so vast a domain should have a centrally located capital, and not a city situated—as Houston was—almost on the eastern border.

In addition to its unfortunate geographical location, Ezekiel pointed out that Houston was surrounded by swamplands and plagued with mosquitoes and yellow fever. The waters along the bayous were unhealthy; the death rate from disease bred by bad water and filth was extremely high. In a resounding speech in the House of Representatives, in 1839, he said:

"It would be better to legislate in tents—in a high, healthy section of this country—than to inhale this poisonous atmosphere; to drink polluted water; to be subjected to deprivation and want of comfort incident to life in Houston."

As a spokesman for Lamar's party, he advocated moving the Government to a pleasant place in the hills along the Colorado River of Texas—where President Lamar had once shot a buffalo. As a result of Ezekiel Cullen's eloquence, that is where the Government went—to Austin, named after Stephen Austin, the "Father of Texas."

And so—three-quarters of a century later—Ezekiel Cullen's grandson decided to move to "that abominable place—that wretched mudhole—that graveyard of men—the City of Houston!"

It might seem foolhardy for a young man, hardly out of his twenties, with a steady business and a growing family, to pick up his family and his belongings and migrate into a new city—which he did not even like as a place in which to live. It took a species of courage, and faith in himself—and in the city of his choosing.

But there was a streak of stubborn courage in old Ezekiel Cullen's grandson—the same kind of courage that had led Roy's grandfather to give up his Georgia home and head into the untamed lands of the Southwest "where a man could have all he could hold." The same flinty determination that Louise Cullen had seen in the eyes of her son, when he decided to quit school in San Antonio and go to work, was in Roy Cullen's eyes as he headed south for Houston.

The sprawling city by the bayous, in the census of 1910, had a population of 78,000 souls. It had become, in the decade between Roy Cullen's departure for Oklahoma and his return to South Texas, the center of a new and exciting gift of nature—oil! On January 10, 1901, the great "Spindletop" had poured its black geyser of liquid wealth into the sky near Beaumont—the first big production discovered in Texas. Three years later the "Moonshine" well on the newly developed Humble field brought oil within fifty miles of Houston.

Roy's decision to move to Houston was not a hasty one. He had thought the matter over carefully, weighing the advantages and disadvantages—because if he moved to Houston, he intended to make it his home for the rest of his life.

He had visited the city by the bayous many times in the course of his business with Clarkson; and he hated the dank, dreary climate, the drizzling rain and the swarming mosquitoes from the swampy lowlands around the city.

But he had noted one overriding fact: Houston had just completed the dredging of a ship channel which would bring ocean-going vessels and foreign trade directly into the city. He believed the port of Houston, if properly expanded and developed, would become the natural gateway to one of the world's richest areas—the Mississippi and Missouri River basins, covering a third of a continent. Thus Houston would inevitably become one of the world's major cities.

He knew, also, that his growing family would be better off, even in the rainy climate of Houston, than on the barren plains of Western Oklahoma. Lillie would be closer to her family in Schulenberg; and his mother, still living in San Antonio, would be able to visit them. His father had died in San Antonio in 1911, the same year Roy decided to move to Houston, so there were no real ties holding him to Oklahoma.

It was characteristic of Roy Cullen's growing sense of mature responsibility that he moved into Houston not as a refugee from the barren plains of Oklahoma, but with the eager enthusiasm of an emigrant to a new country and with every intention of becoming an active and useful citizen. His first act was to write to more than a hundred large port cities throughout the world—most of which he knew in a business way from his years of exporting cotton—and request information and data on their port facilities. He wanted to know how man-made harbors were made—and how successful they were. What were the breakwater and dredging problems? What transportation factors helped or hindered a growing port?

He received enough material within a few weeks to fill one corner of his tiny office.

Houston had almost finished dredging the Ship Channel from Galveston Bay—a natural harbor on the Gulf of Mexico—fifty miles inland to the heart of the land-locked city. The information Cullen gleaned from replies to his letters indicated that most of the great ports of the world also were similarly man-made.

Liverpool, England, had a moving dock—Prince Albert Wharf—which rose and fell to conform with the tides. The port of Hamburg, Germany, was a huge frog-pond until they dug a ship's channel through the harbor. New York—the largest shipping gateway in the world—would have been a shallow bay if they had not dug Ambrose Channel through the Narrows. Shanghai, Hamburg, Liverpool, Wilmington Harbor near Los Angeles—all were built and dug by human enterprise.

He knew, from these reports, and from other data he collected, that Houston would never be bothered by settling sand—the bugbear of river ports—as New Orleans had been bothered. There would be "dead water" at the head of the Ship Channel, cut through the bayous, with no floodwaters to fill it up with sediment. The breakwater at Galveston was built so that the tide perpetually scooped out the sand from the ships' entrance, furnishing a natural clearance of the outer channel. The first section of the Ship Channel had been completed in 1905, to bring ships as far as Harrisburg.

Armed with these facts, Roy Cullen was confident that there was a future for him in Houston. He did not like the climate—the drizzling rain and cold, damp winters. But twenty-five feet of water brought to docks in the center of Houston meant future commerce and industry; and it meant the kind of growing city Roy Cullen wanted to grow with.

The Cullens arrived in Houston early in 1911. Roy had a small amount of capital, built up in the years he had been in business in Oklahoma. He rented a house on Hadley Avenue, a mile south of the bayou, from a Houston attorney named Hugh Montgomery, who lived next door, on the right. On the left lived R. C. Holmes, who later became president of The Texas Company.

Roy lost no time getting his feet solidly planted on Houston soil. He had decided to invest in real estate. After making a survey of the land adjacent to the Ship Channel, he bought a tract on the Channel across from cotton wharves owned by Weld and Neville. His land had about 1400 feet frontage on the Channel, varying from 130 feet to 565 feet in depth. It had been owned by the Kessler Estate in Schulenberg; Lillie's grandfather was a Kessler, and Roy bought it from her father, Gustave Cranz, for seven thousand dollars.

Houston needed two things—a non-political Harbor Board and a City Engineer. Roy had learned this from studying the reports of Chambers of Commerce and the Boards of Trade in the foreign port cities to which he had sent his requests for information. Roy felt it his duty to present the results of his researches to the city, so he went to the editor of the Houston *Post*.

He explained that he wanted to place an advertisement in the paper concerning the land he owned along the waterfront of the Ship Channel. He extolled the future of Houston in such glowing terms that the editor became convinced that Roy Cullen would become one of the civic leaders of Houston. He published Roy's statement.

Shortly afterward the name "H. R. Cullen" greeted the citizens of Houston for the first time in a headline over a statement advocating a bond issue for the financing and construction of municipal wharves to handle incoming shipping.

"Houston's Ship Channel is more important than Houston, with all her improvements," the statement said. "For if Houston were entirely destroyed by some catastrophe, this present generation would take advantage of our inland waterway and build a greater city in its place."

He flung a final challenge to the voters: "Shall we be content to stand still like the average city, or shall we continue to progress and be among the leading cities of our country?"

The city electorate voted for the $3,000,000 bond issue, three to one.

Roy plunged into the affairs of Houston with increasing fervor. He had stacked the pamphlets and data from other port cities of the world—which he received in reply to his letters—in one corner of his small office, and pored over as many of the reports as he could. He soon became one of the best informed men in Houston on port developments; and among other things, he developed a friendship with a tall, brusque Texan named Jim Cheek, who occupied an office in the same building.

Cheek was a big landowner in Houston, and he had some property along the Ship Channel near Manchester, a few miles below Houston. He agreed to deed it to the city, if the city would agree to build wharves and harbor facilities provided for by the bond issue. The final segment of the Ship Channel had been opened, with its 1300-foot Turning Basin at the upper end, and put into official service by President Woodrow Wilson, pressing a button at his desk in the White House in Washington, D. C., on November 10, 1914.

The real-estate business was not so thriving as Roy had hoped; but he dug into it with energy and determination. He had spent more than twelve years learning the cotton business, and now he found himself in an entirely new field—with a growing family in a new town!

One of his first prospects for the land along the Ship Channel was a friend of his neighbor, Mr. Holmes, who introduced him to Roy. His name was R. E. Brooks, and he was a former judge and president of the Producers' Oil Company. Roy made an appointment with Judge Brooks to look over the land, and rented a boat for the inspection trip.

For more than an hour—with Roy at the oars—they cruised up and down the Channel. There was not much port activity, and Judge Brooks showed little enthusiasm as a buyer. The banks of the Channel were caving in at some points, and he assured Roy that this "ditch" would never become a thriving port of entry. The "inland waterway" would be little more than a haven for water moccasins and mosquitoes.

Even after they completed the tour, Judge Brooks continued to express his disillusionment as to the future of the port of Houston. Roy listened to him until they pulled up at the curb at the Texas Building, where the judge's office was located. Then Roy turned to his prospective customer and shook his finger at him.

"You've been knocking that property ever since I showed it to you," he said. "I know why you are doing it—and let me tell you something right now. As far as you are concerned, the price I quoted to you is the price of the land, and it will never be one penny less!"

Judge Brooks stared at the young real-estate salesman in some surprise. Then he climbed out of the car and started across the sidewalk toward his office. After a few steps, he turned and came back.

"All right, Roy," he said. "Bring the maps up to my office, and I'll pick out the piece of land I want."

The real-estate business was not exactly booming in Houston in those days. The city was small, and the streets were often impassable during the rainy periods. Greenish water covered the ditches along the sides of the roads—since the city itself was only fifty feet above the bayou; and few of the downtown streets were paved.

However, Roy persisted with determination and confidence that the city would grow—and if it did, his real-estate business would have to grow with it.

Meanwhile, Roy's family was growing. Young Roy had become a sturdy, blond-haired boy, already showing an interest in science. By the time he was twelve years old he had become a charter member of the Houston Radio Club, and was dabbling in such things as transmitting sets and crystal receivers. The two girls—Lillie and Agnes—were in school; and Roy decided to move his family into a larger home.

They acquired a two-story house on the corner of Alabama Avenue and Austin Street, about two miles from the heart of the city, and moved into their new home in 1915. Roy's mother became a frequent visitor to the new home. She had mortgaged her home in San Antonio, to pay Lucien Beck's way through medical school, and had lost the home before Roy had enough income to pay off the mortgage. She still had an income, however; and traveled a great deal, visiting her various children and relatives from Mexico City to

Florida: Daisy in Florida, where she and Frank Knight had moved; or Roy's oldest brother, Lucien, who was living in Monterrey, Mexico; or Louise, who was then in New York. Roy's mother was now in her seventies, but she was still a lovely woman, and her cheerful friendliness warmed the new home of the Cullens whenever she visited them.

On each visit, Roy's mother would bring presents for the children—a bright Mexican blanket, or strange desert plants; and even canary birds. On one visit she brought a box of Malaga grape roots from Florida, where she had been visiting members of the Beck family. She spent most of her latter days in the Cullen home in Houston until she died, early in 1920, in San Antonio at the home of her son, Dick Cullen.

The development of the Ship Channel meanwhile had struck a political shoal which drew Roy Cullen unexpectedly into conflict with Houston's biggest real-estate operator, Jesse Jones.

After Jim Cheek had made his offer of land for building wharves, the Portland Cement Company of Texas chimed in with a promise to build a big cement plant in the area, if the municipal wharves and facilities, authorized by the bond issue, were built on the Cheek land. However, during the two years that followed the opening of the Ship Channel, nothing happened.

In April, 1917, two and a half years after the bonds had been voted, the Harbor Board, of which Jesse Jones was chairman, addressed a letter to the City Council asking that the deal with Jim Cheek and the Portland Cement Company be repudiated. The alternative suggested was to build docks further into the heart of the city.

The Houston *Chronicle,* owned and published by Marcellus E. Foster, and later taken over by Jesse Jones, began berating the City Council for not heeding the suggestion of the Harbor Board. Foster wrote an editorial giving ten reasons supporting the Harbor Board position.

Roy Cullen read the editorial, and then he stormed into the office of Mayor Ben Campbell, who had been leading the fight for the city, charging the Harbor Board with "sidestepping their moral and legal obligations."

Roy brandished the newspaper before the Mayor, but Campbell threw up his hands. "My term of office is ending, Roy," he said. "I'm getting out of politics. I've given all the facts—why keep brawling about it?"

Roy pointed out that the reputation of his administration and the city of Houston was at stake: an agreement had been made with the cement company, and with Jim Cheek; and he pointed out further that the docks built in the area where the land had been given the city would expand Houston's development, rather than confine it to the center of the city.

The Mayor shook his head.

"If you won't answer it—let me answer it for you," Cullen said.

Mayor Campbell shrugged. "Go ahead, if you want to, Roy."

Roy went back to his office, and pecked out on his typewriter a letter to the editor of the Houston *Post*. Then he returned to the Mayor's office.

"I'll pay for a full-page ad to print this," he said, "if you'll put a footnote on the ad, saying you approve of what I've said."

Campbell read the letter, and said: "All right, Roy—go to it!"

Cullen took the letter to the *Post*—and also to the *Chronicle*. The latter at first refused to accept the letter without getting the approval of Marcellus Foster, who was in New York. Finally the advertising manager took the letter as a paid advertisement—and was subsequently fired for his mistake. The *Post* printed the letter the following morning, and Roy Cullen found himself in the middle of the biggest political fight he had thus far experienced.

The campaign to pick a mayor to succeed Ben Campbell was reaching its highest pitch. J. J. Pastoriza, who supported the Manchester wharf-site faction, was running against Judge Ben Davidson, backed by the *Chronicle* and Jesse Jones.

Cullen lost no time throwing his support to Pastoriza. The local betting odds were quoted by Judge Davidson's adherents the day before election at three-to-one in favor of the Judge's election; and when Cullen heard these odds on the Houston Cotton Exchange, he stamped into the headquarters of Judge Davidson, confronted two of the Judge's backers —Ed Campbell and Murray Jones—and offered to bet a thousand dollars at the prevailing odds on Pastoriza's election.

Political ballyhoo was one thing—but a cash bet was another. Jones and Campbell hedged; and after some dickering, they agreed to bet seven hundred dollars on Judge Davidson to Cullen's one thousand dollars. Cullen asked them to jot it down in a written memorandum.

This was about 3 P.M. on Election Day. Roy knew the labor vote would come in late in the day, so Pastoriza's campaign manager phoned all the polling places, giving them information on the bet and announced that the odds were "ten-to-seven for Pastoriza." The story swept the town—and Pastoriza won the election by a few hundred votes.

In the same election, the Harbor Board issue was put up to a referendum of the voters; and they approved the city's original agreement for the Manchester wharf by a vote of two to one. This marked Roy Cullen's first victory over Jesse Jones.

COON CREEK
SCHOOL

CHAPTER 10

"Gentlemen, I'm a cotton man, not an oil man!"

HOUSTON was a lusty, brawling city in the years just before Word War I, the pride of the Southwest and the capital of King Oil; and Roy Cullen was determined to grow with the city. But political prestige did not necessarily bring a concomitant of economic advantages: After the first stormy years in Houston he found that he had done little to improve his finances. He had scored a triumph over the redoubtable Jesse Jones in the Harbor Board fight, but he was still struggling for a foothold as one of Houston's young business men.

The sale of land to Judge Brooks had brought in some money, and there were a few other good deals that had made a profit. But real-estate operations—as practiced by successful land owners and operators—required a kind of trading that ran counter to Roy Cullen's personal ambitions. He was a skillful trader, but as he had once said, referring to the admonitions of his mother: "I never tried to out-trade anyone in my life, and I never let anyone out-trade me if I could help it."

He had finally put his cash assets into a stock company,

called the Texas-Oklahoma Wharf Company; and since he also had a seat on the Houston Cotton Exchange, he decided to return to the cotton business, using the new company as an exporting firm.

He placed advertisements in Texas and Oklahoma newspapers, announcing that he would now handle cotton exports; and the response he received was immediate and stimulating. People all over the Southwest began shipping cotton to him.

His credit with bankers and cotton men in Oklahoma and South Texas was still good, although he had been away from the business for seven years. His old friends now began to ship cotton to him—four and five hundred bales in a shipment—without any collateral except Roy Cullen's personal reputation.

A firm friendship had grown between Jim Cheek and the young man from Oklahoma; and the older man knew Roy was having a tough time making his real-estate and cotton business pay. The three Cullen children were in school; and the problems of a growing family were increasing.

Jim Cheek had made money in several subdivisions of the city, and had turned his attention toward oil operations. One day he and Roy were chatting on their way up to their offices, and Cheek suddenly turned and said: "Roy, I've got a proposition for you. Can you come into my office for a minute?"

Cheek was a big, hearty man with an open face and an open-hearted manner. He liked Roy from the time they met; and he had appreciated Roy's battle to force the city to keep its agreement on the Ship Channel wharf site, which Cheek had given to the city on its promise to build municipal wharves. He also had a healthy respect for young Cullen's ability to deal with men.

He explained his interest in the oil business: it was new to him, but it was also new to most of the men in Houston who were making money in oil ventures. New wells were coming in at the Humble field and Goose Creek; and Cheek had turned his eye toward Coryell County, where there was a lot of land that had not been leased by any oil producers.

The custom was for the landowner to lease the land for oil prospecting at a nominal sum—usually a few cents an acre—with a percentage of oil royalties if oil were found. Since unleased land obviously was virgin land—as far as oil was concerned—it was a gamble for both sides, but the oil prospector took the financial risk.

"I don't know anything about oil, Jim," Roy told his friend. "And if you're looking for money—I haven't got it."

Cheek shook his head.

"I want you to try to get leases for me in Coryell County—the new Ranger field has just been opened there."

"I've never read an oil lease in my life," Cullen said. "Why don't you hire a lease man? You can get a good one—for a hundred and fifty a month and expenses."

"No, I want you to come in with me, Roy," Cheek replied. "I'll give you a drawing account of five hundred a month, plus expenses—and one-fourth of all the business we do."

Cullen shrugged. It was good business—and he was not doing too well in real estate and cotton. There was one condition. He had never worked for anyone since he left Clarkson.

"I think you're crazy—but I'll go in with you, Jim," he said. "There is just one thing I want understood. I'm working with you in this business, but not as an employee. You advance the cash for my expenses, and you get three-quarters of whatever the leases bring in. I'll take the other quarter."

Cheek agreed. A few days later Roy set out for Coryell County. Jim Cheek had told Roy to contact a man at Flat, Texas, a village in Coryell County. A meeting was arranged at the Coon Creek School, where farmers from all over the county gathered to hear about new oil prospects. Roy Cullen had never made a formal public speech before—except for his abortive electioneering in Mangum—but he had spent several days, before embarking on this new venture, reading up on oil geology at the Houston Public Library.

He stood for several seconds before the farmers and their wives, growing more embarrassed each moment. Finally, he said:

"Gentlemen, I'm not an oil man—I'm a cotton man. But I'm going into the oil business—and if you'll give me leases on your land, I'll do everything possible to get the oil rights developed."

His candor apparently was convincing. The next day he signed forty-three leases—"for one dollar and other valuable considerations"—and returned to Houston. Jim Cheek was enthusiastic. He had a map of Western Texas marked out over the great open plains west of the Pecos River—Pecos, Sutton and Val Verde Counties, and Crockett County east of the Pecos.

"There's oil in Eastland," he said. "Let's try and get leases south of there."

The oil fever was sweeping across Western Texas, and most of the big ranchers were getting from ten cents to twenty-five cents an acre for oil leases, giving the leaseholders the right to drill for oil. Each of these agreements provided for a percentage of royalties to be paid to the landowner, in case of an oil discovery.

Roy Cullen headed for Western Texas, starting from Del Rio, in the Rio Grande Valley west of San Antonio. After several days' scouting, he reported to Cheek that land was not being leased for "one dollar and other valuable considerations" out in Western Texas; most of the ranchers wanted real cash for the leases.

One evening, sitting in the hotel in Del Rio, he watched a tall man in a checked suit, who seemed to know everyone in the hotel. He followed him into the dining room, and walked over to his table.

"My name is Roy Cullen–" he began, and the big man shoved his hand across the table, and said heartily:

"Glad to know you, Cullen–my name's John Blackmon. Sit down."

Roy sat down. They had dinner together: and the big man explained that he was a cattle and goat rancher near Rock Springs, northeast of Del Rio in Edwards County; and he owned about 60,000 acres of land. After listening to Roy's story of his search for oil lease land, he invited him to come up to his ranch.

"This is lambing season–I'll be busy for two or three days. If you can wait that long, I'll go with you and talk to some of the other folks up there."

Roy traveled with Blackmon to Rock Springs, and helped with the lambing; and then he and Blackmon set out together. At Rock Springs they met a congressman from El Paso, Claude Hudspeth; and through him they met Judge Davidson of Crockett County. There was a good deal of suspicion of oil leases in the Pecos River country; and Roy found it necessary to convince the ranchers that he was leasing for development–not speculation.

Judge Davidson sent him to the county clerk of Crockett County–a man named Noland–and he was able to lease approximately 400,000 acres of land, sitting in the hotel lobby entertaining Judge Davidson, while Noland corralled the leases. Each lease was for "one dollar and other valuable considerations"—the "considerations" being Roy's option to drill for oil, or release the leases.

It was near Langtry, the almost legendary site of the "court" of Judge Roy Bean, that Roy first met the redoubtable Babb family—"Old Man" Babb and two of his three sons. Wallace Pratt, chief geologist for the Humble Oil Company and one of the world's authorities on oil lands, had come out to join Roy at Ozona, under a joint arrangement between Roy Cullen and the Humble Company, to look over an area of about 60,000 acres of land of the Babb Ranch, on which Roy had a nominal lease.

The Babb Ranch sprawled over the rugged country west of the Pecos River, where the southwest corner of Crockett County joins Terrell County. Old Man Babb had settled on a part of the country known as "the Langtry section," named after Roy Bean's town. William Dodd, Babb's "right hand man," later told Roy that in the earlier days when Old Man Babb walked into Roy Bean's saloon in Langtry, where he held court, the famed "Judge" of "law west of the Pecos" would slip out the back door.

Ranchers in the area had a simple and effective method of handling rustlers. They would allot a percentage of cattle each year to the biggest rustlers, and thus avoid the necessity of having Cattle Association men and their own riders shot up.

Roy Cullen and Wallace Pratt headed west from Ozona toward this formidable country, crossed the Pecos River and rode up to the Babb ranch house. There were four United States Deputy Marshals staked out around the house, armed with Winchesters. One of the Federal men explained that there had been a "shooting across the River" and they had come to collect one of the sons.

"I've got business with Mr. Babb," Roy said, and he and

Wallace Pratt walked toward the door. As they approached the ranch house, the door opened and John Babb stepped out.

He looked at Roy Cullen, and Roy called out:

"I'm Roy Cullen—I want to talk about the oil leases on your ranch." He pointed to Wallace Pratt, who was standing a little way behind. "This is Mr. Pratt—he's a geologist."

John Babb motioned them inside.

"Come on in and eat . . . we're just settin' down." He looked at the U.S. Marshals. "Why don't you boys come in and eat with us?"

The lawmen declined, explaining they had already had dinner. Roy and Wallace Pratt went into the ranch house. Sitting at the table was Old Man Babb, a huge, glowering man in his late fifties. Roy explained the purpose of his visit, and John Babb listened attentively. Wallace Pratt, he said, wanted to have the land explored by geologists for the Humble Company.

"That's fine," he said, cordially. "Let us know if we can help you."

After Roy and Wallace Pratt had returned to Houston, leaving a geologist to make the survey, he received word from the latter that Old Man Babb had voiced threats against Roy, threatening to shoot him if he returned to that part of the country. Roy had some legal matters to attend to at Del Rio, south of the Babb Ranch on the Rio Grande River, and when he arrived there he found his lawyer was disturbed over the reports of threats by Old Man Babb.

"The Babb boys are in town," he said. "Old Man Babb is dissatisfied with the leases you got on his land. He thinks you got the best of him, and I'd advise you to get out of town to avoid trouble."

"My geologist wrote me about that," Roy said. "The Babb

boys seemed all right to me . . . I sent John Babb a couple of hunting dogs, and I don't think he'd make trouble. Anyway, I came here to attend to my business, and I'm going to finish it before I leave."

The lawyer left for lunch, and Roy agreed to return at two o'clock. He was also disturbed about the reports of the Babbs. He had sent a pair of bloodhounds to John Babb, after his visit to the ranch, and he wondered at this sudden hostility. Besides, he could not see that there was anything wrong with the leases that could not be adjusted.

At two o'clock he returned to the lawyer's office. A wide-shouldered pleasant-looking man was sitting in the waiting room. The lawyer came out as Roy entered and looked startled. He glanced at the young man, and then said:

"Mr. Cullen—this is Mr. Boy Babb."

Boy Babb had not been at the ranch the day Roy was there with the U.S. Marshals. He greeted the man, extending his hand. Boy Babb shook hands and smiled cordially.

"Glad to see you, Mr. Cullen. Those bloodhounds you sent John are wonderful dogs to catch lobo wolves and panthers." He hesitated, then said: "John is in town—he'd be mighty glad to see you."

John Babb and his younger brother were down at a photographer's shop, and Boy Babb offered to wait for Roy to finish his business and take him there. Roy walked down the street with Boy Babb to the little shop, not knowing what to expect. Babb was friendly, but the clan had a reputation for quick triggers, and Roy had carefully slipped a Colt forty-five into one pocket of his brief case.

As he entered the room where the Babb brothers were sitting, he realized that he had forgotten which pocket held his pistol; and when he laid his brief case on a table, he slammed it so he could locate the gun. Then he planned to reach into the brief case, ready to pull the gun out and start shooting if any hostile move were made.

Nothing happened. John Babb came over and shook hands warmly. Roy pulled out the lease instead of the gun with his free hand, and said:

"I understand you aren't satisfied with the lease, Mr. Babb. You can have it back if you want it."

John shook his head, and looked a bit embarrassed.

"The old man had been drinking a little," he said. "Maybe he talked too much. We made those leases with you in good faith—and we're sticking to them."

John thanked him again for the dogs, and Roy left. Later he found the rumors of threats to kill him had been stirred up by others who wanted the lease.

Meanwhile, Roy had been building up a large and varied assortment of oil leases, ranging from the Edwards Plateau, east of the Pecos, along the river through Val Verde, Crockett and Pecos Counties. Several wildcat wells were drilled on his leases, but all were dry holes.

Ira Yates, who owned a big ranch in Pecos County—less than a mile from one of the Cullen leases—begged Roy to lease his land. Roy had set up headquarters for a while in San Angelo, and Yates also had a home there.

Yates finally offered Cullen a lease on all his land—at fifteen cents an acre—but geological reports had been negative, and the offer was turned down. It was a costly mistake on Roy Cullen's part. Ten years later the great "Yates field" was brought in—one of the most productive in the history of Texas oil discoveries.

Roy Cullen had explored much of West Texas, and leased thousands of acres of land—but he had not brought in an oil well. At one time he had under lease more than a million acres of land on what was known as the "Edwards Plateau," each lease being for "one dollar and other valuable considerations." The "other considerations" were Roy's promise to try to develop the oil rights by drilling wells.

A representative of a large Eastern oil company asked Roy to meet him in Dallas to discuss the transfer of his leases on the Edwards Plateau for one million dollars, which would have financed Roy's drilling operations for a considerable period of time.

However, the offer was turned down, after the oil company man refused to give specific assurance that a development plan would be carried out.

"I promised the ranchers that wells would be drilled on their land within a reasonable time, or the leases would be relinquished," Roy said. "I mean to keep my word. If you take over the leases, I have no assurance that you will drill the wells—and I can't return the leases."

By this time Roy Cullen had become a full-fledged wildcatter. He had traveled across the western plains and plateaus of Texas, working on the small reserves of capital he had from his Houston real-estate operations, and money he borrowed from Houston banks. A few drilling operations were carried on by outside groups, under royalty arrangements.

The results of three years of hard and unrewarding effort left Roy exactly where he started when he headed west to lease land for Jim Cheek—with one important exception. He had found nothing in the way of producing wells; but he had learned a lot about wildcatting for oil; and his lack of success had not dampened his hopes.

He had learned the curiously undefinable thing which he called "creekology"—the wildcatter's natural sense of the values of surface geology. And while none of the wells drilled on his leases had struck oil, he had found out among other things that the "structural traps," in which oil collects far below the ground level of the earth, are far more difficult to find than the "salt domes" of Eastern Texas.

The structural traps are the result of folding or displacement of layers of rock, where extreme pressure or the release of pressure has caused a layer to break or slip in such a way that a fault is created; particles of oil moved along in slow underground seepage will collect in these traps and form pools. These structures are common in West Texas; whereas the salt-dome formations are found in South Texas.

And so, after three years of unremitting search for the "black gold" in the rocky plateaus of West Texas, Roy Cullen returned to Houston, prepared to tackle the salt domes.

CHAPTER 11

"The trouble with this business is everybody expects to find oil"

SALT DOMES are huge beds of salt gypsum that lie at varying depths below the surface of the earth, formed from the evaporation of waters of the sea millions of years ago; and they are harbingers of oil. They thrust up formations of porous rock or sand into which bits of plant and animal life, distilled into oil after aeons of underground pressure, filter into pools or traps formed by faults in the earth structure. These pools and traps are great natural deposits of oil.

A few miles southwest of Houston was a place called Pierce Junction. Fifty-two dry wells had been drilled in the area. Roy had many occasions to study the field—and the location of wells drilled there. It was known that the Pierce Junction field was over a salt dome; but the location of oil pools might be at the crest of a salt dome, where porous rock has been pushed up; or it might be on the flanks, where shifts in the earth structure may have created gaps or faults. Or there might be nothing but salt water sand!

One good "gas well" that had been drilled on the flank of the dome at Pierce Junction interested Roy Cullen. One day he took a piece of white cloth to the gas well and tried holding it over a small valve outlet. He found it showed no color, which would have indicated oil. But Roy was not satisfied. He continued the experiment every day for two weeks, and one day the cloth began to show a yellow color. This intensified on successive days until it was a deep yellow.

After studying the amber-colored rags, Roy hot-footed over to the offices of L. P. Garrett, the Gulf Oil Corporation's vice-president in Houston. He spread a map on Garrett's desk.

"Let me have a lease on this land," he said, pointing to an area along the flank, "and I'll drill you a well."

"On the Howe land?" Garrett looked at Cullen in some surprise. "It's too far off the dome, Roy. You won't do any good there."

"Give me the lease anyway," Roy said. "If the well is no good, you won't lose anything."

Garrett agreed, and Roy left with a lease.

He brought together about a dozen men—Judge Brooks, Captain Jim Baker, Will and Joe Rice, H. M. Garwood, Sam Streetman, Abe Levy, J. M. Link, J. E. Duff, and others. They formed a company called the Pierce Junction Oil Company, elected Judge Brooks president, and took over Cullen's lease from the Gulf Company. Forty acres—or two-thirds—went to the company; and Judge Brooks and Roy kept twenty acres in a separate partnership. The group raised $40,000 to finance the drilling.

Forming an oil company may be kept a secret, as long as the associates feel like it—but locating and drilling a well is seldom a secret. One of the best-known "wildcatters" in Texas—"Trapshooter" Reilly—had followed Roy Cullen out to Pierce Junction one day and saw him check on the coloration of cloth from the gas well on the Gulf Company site. Reilly asked Roy what he planned to do, and Roy told him about the Pierce Junction Company. He also told Reilly that all the interests were taken up.

Reilly immediately gathered a few associates and leased land adjoining the Cullen lease—and the race was on!

A contract to drill the well was given to Judge Brooks' son, Emory Brooks; but the drilling rig was not immediately available, and it was several weeks before the equipment was rigged on the locaiton. Meanwhile "Trapshooter" Reilly had brought his driller, Wynne Crosby, into the field and Crosby's crew began drilling.

Reilly struck oil; and Roy was now sure his well would come in. A few days after the Reilly well "blew in," Roy was called to the field. Emory Brooks showed him a "core," or sample, of oil sand and after looking at the core, they ordered the crew to set the casing, or pipe, for a test.

The Pierce Junction well came in with a blast of pressure, blowing off the "Christmas tree"—the arrangement of valves placed over the top of the pipe to cap and control the flow—and ran wild. It was on a Sunday, and around the field, on the off-wind side, were those who had put money into the Pierce Junction Oil Company, and their wives.

Roy and Lillie brought the children out, and they were there—in Sunday dress. Lillie, sensing that this was to be "an occasion," had dressed little Roy in a white suit, with a white Russian blouse and a blue collar. When the spray of oil and sand shot into the air, spreading a huge, murky cloud over the field, she tugged young Roy and the girls quickly to the far edge of the field, but the little boy ran excitedly toward a "mud pit." The wind whipped the spray in all directions, and young Roy's white blouse soon looked like a grease-monkey's shirt.

The well was soon brought under control, and produced about twenty-five hundred barrels a day and flowed about two years. The company hired Emory Brooks to drill three more wells. All three were dry holes, and the company released the property back to Howe.

Roy and his associates moved over to Damon's Mound—another salt-dome formation—fifty miles southwest of Pierce Junction, and began to drill in this area.

This was the most heartbreaking of all his early ventures. For three years they moved the derrick from location to location on Damon's Mound.

At the end of three dreary years on Damon's Mound, Roy abandoned operations. In the meantime, the Pierce Junction well had stopped flowing.

Roy still had a spark of faith, in a secret corner of his mind, in the Pierce Junction field. He was sure the oil was there—and the drying up of his discovery well, coupled with the three dry holes young Emory Brooks had drilled, did not dampen his faith.

Three years after the Howe land was released, he decided to go back to Pierce Junction and try another well on the Howe lease—and this time he brought in a small trickle of oil—about sixty barrels a day. He decided to drill deeper, and struck a pool almost as big as the first one he had drilled at Pierce Junction.

"The trouble with this business," he told his partners, "is that everybody expects to find oil on the surface. If it was up near the top, it wouldn't be any trick to find it—and it wouldn't be worth much. You got to drill deep for oil."

Roy's family had now increased to seven—two more children, Margaret and Wilhelmina, having arrived during the years he was at Pierce Junction and Damon's Mound. Young Roy was preparing to enter college. He had showed a great aptitude for scientific subjects, and it was decided that he should go to Rensselaer Polytechnic Institute, near Troy, New York.

A workshop had been rigged up over the garage, and young Roy had installed various electrical gadgets with which he constantly experimented. He read of the experiments of Thomas Edison and Marconi, and particularly of Nicholas Tesla, the great Italian physicist who had anticipated many of the world's great discoveries in the field of electricity.

One day Roy went up to the workshop to watch his son, hard at work with complicated circuits, home-made batteries and strange creations of copper. He watched the boy for several minutes, and finally young Roy reached into a maze of wiring with his bare hands and "drew" the crackling electricity from the wires.

Roy was startled.

"Aren't you afraid you'll get a shock, Sonny?" he asked.

The boy looked up, smiling.

"No, Dad—I read about it in Tesla's book, and he's never wrong about anything."

Roy Cullen nodded. He had no such faith in Tesla, but he had faith in other things that were not unlike his son's faith in the great scientist. He began to recognize in his son a trend that was not unlike his own firm belief in himself—except that young Roy's mind was turned toward science, and the deep reservoirs of knowledge that lay before him.

By the fall of 1923 young Roy was sent off to Rensselaer, and there was a noticeable gap in the closely knit family circle. However, the new arrivals in the family were taking up much of the attention of the household, and as they grew up from babyhood the house was full of the laughter of children once more.

Roy was away from home much of the time; but the times

of his return were occasions for great celebration. In the evenings when he drove in from Damon's Mound Lillie would wait for him in the closed porch, or veranda, in the rear of the big house, and Roy would clump up the stairs, sometimes soaked and muddy from his boots to his collar.

"Help me get my boots off, Lillie," he would say, "and I'll go upstairs and get a shave and a bath—and tomorrow's another day."

She knew on these occasions that the well was dry, but the children never knew it. During the evening Roy would sit with the two youngsters, and tell "continuing stories"—each night a new "episode" to the stories. Later in the evening he would sometimes quietly talk over the affairs at the field with young Roy . . . but otherwise the members of the family knew little of the struggle and the heartbreaking disappointments that had been going on since that exciting afternoon at Pierce Junction.

Lillie worried at times about Roy's health. She knew he was working at a terrific pace, slogging through the mud all day . . . directing the rigging of the derricks, and watching through long nights as the crews kept the drills biting deeper into the ground.

During these lean years when Roy was away much of the time, the burden of keeping the family together fell upon Lillie. The two older girls were in high school, and young Roy was in Rensselaer during the school year. The babies—Margaret and Wilhelmina—would wait each night for another episode in the continued stories; and when Roy was unable to get home, Lillie would take them upstairs alone.

During the summer months, when young Roy was home from school, he would sit with the two youngsters during the evening, brewing hot chocolate and telling stories, while Lillie watched over her brood, quietly and calmly.

Years later, young Roy said: "Mother's the best engineer I've ever known. If I could run an oil rig as smoothly as she ran that house, I'd be the best in the business."

In the evenings when the familiar sound of the Cullen car announced Roy's arrival, Lillie would always be at the door of the rear veranda, waiting for him as he plodded across the pathway from the garage, smiling cheerfully and waving his hand to her and the two young children.

"I'm glad you could get home tonight, Roy," she would say. "You know how Baby is waiting for the rest of that story."

Roy would laugh, and gather the two youngsters in his arms. His stories in the evening were always improvised; and both Margaret and Wilhelmina would sit wide-eyed while he unfolded each tale.

Sometimes, when they sat together on the veranda and Roy stretched out his legs, slowly pulling off his mud-soaked boots, Lillie would look at him with the deep tenderness he knew so well in her blue eyes, and would say:

"I'll be so glad when you can be home every night, Roy. All the other children on the block have their fathers home at night, and our children want you at home, too."

Roy would nod and smile, the lines of his face deepening.

"We got to keep going a while longer, honey . . . I want the children taken care of. Just let me get upstairs and get these clothes off, and get a shave, Lillie—and tomorrow'll be another day."

Tomorrow was always "another day"! From one well to another—some fair, a few good, but most of them dry—Roy Cullen pushed on from field to field. In 1927, he moved into Blue Ridge.

By this time Roy Cullen was beginning to be known as a "wildcatter" with uncanny "luck." He seemed to have a knack of striking oil where the big companies had failed. His wells at Pierce Junction and Blue Ridge had been on land which geologists had surveyed and found negative—or which the bigger companies had abandoned.

One Saturday afternoon, when Roy was in his Houston office, Big Jim West phoned him and asked him to drop over to his office.

When Roy came in, West—a bluff, square-jawed man who was known as a successful cattleman and lumber operator—asked him to sit down.

"Roy," he said, "I've made a success in the lumber business and in the cattle business. But so far I haven't done very good in oil. I'd like to make a success of that, too."

"I hope you do, Jim," Roy said.

"I've got three million dollars lying around—that I'm not using. And I've got the West Production Company—which don't amount to much. I'll put the three millions in my oil company, and give you one-fourth interest—if you'll go in with me. You'll be president—and have complete charge of the company."

Roy thought this over for a moment.

"I'll think it over," he finally said. "I'll give you my answer later."

The following Tuesday, when Roy had not called West, the big cattleman called him.

"Look here, Roy—I made a proposition to you last Saturday, and since then I haven't heard a damn thing from you. I offered to give you almost a million dollars, and you haven't even taken the trouble to reply. What's your answer, Roy?"

"I'm not interested," Roy said.

There was a moment of silence at the other end of the phone. Then West said:

"Not interested! My God—what do you want?"

"I'll tell you what I'll do, Jim," Roy said. "I'll go in the oil business with you—fifty-fifty. For every dollar you put in, I'll put in a dollar. But only on condition that I have full charge—no interference."

West hesitated again; then he said:

"Roy, I didn't know you had that kind of money."

"I'll put up five thousand dollars," Roy said, "and you put up five thousand. We'll each have a half-interest in the company."

West was dumbfounded.

"I offered you three million dollars, Cullen—and you'd get a quarter of that. You'll turn that down and put up five thousand of your own money?"

"That's right," Roy said. "And I'll be 50 per cent owner. I won't be working for you."

West agreed. They met and flipped a coin to see which name would be first in the partnership name. Roy won, and it was "Cullen & West."

Shortly after the firm was formed, they incorporated the South Texas Petroleum Company. Roy bought two big Union Tool drilling rigs and moved the equipment to the east side of Blue Ridge.

Jim West objected to the location.

"I've drilled wells on that side of Blue Ridge," he said. "Jim Abercrombie has drilled there; so has the Texas Company, and Humble. There isn't any oil there—and you'll be throwing the money away."

Roy Cullen looked at his partner.

"I'm supposed to be in charge—isn't that it, Jim?"

"Sure you are," West said. "But—"

"Then that's where we drill," Roy said. The rig was on what was known as the Bassett Blakely tract on Blue Ridge; and on the first hole bored, they struck oil. They bored four more wells on the same land, and all four brought in oil! The South Texas Petroleum Company was a going concern.

CHAPTER 12

"Sixty million dollars is a lot of money—but I'm not interested"

THE LEGEND of "Cullen luck" began to range up and down the oil fields, from Blue Ridge down the coast to Matagorda and Calhoun County. He seemed to have a knack of finding oil in "abandoned fields," which did not make the geologists too happy, since their judgment was placed in a precarious position by this man who found oil where they said there was no oil. It was also financially distressing to the larger oil companies. Many of them had to buy back their own fields at increased prices.

The oil geologists were baffled by the uncanny prescience of this wildcatter, who kept finding oil in supposedly worked-out fields. Other wildcatters, who had followed the oil trail from one end of Texas to the other, sought some reasonable explanation for Roy Cullen's "nose for oil."

Actually, it was neither luck nor uncanny skill. It was closer to being ordinary "horse sense." During the dozen years Roy had spent in the oil fields—from the time he set forth in quest of oil leases for Jim Cheek, until he struck the golden gusher at Blue Ridge—he had studied oil geology with the same persistent thoroughness that he had employed as a boy, when he spread maps on the walls of his room to study the history of the world . . . and later in Anadarko, when he laid the maps on the floor and decided that Houston, Texas was to be his future home because it was a natural port.

He had pored over books on oil geology. He had followed the course of rock formations for miles over the rugged terrain west of the Pecos River, until he knew the face of the land with an intimacy of long acquaintance.

He used the new instruments that had been developed by oil geology—the early "torsion balance" which measured minute difference in the gravitational pull of the earth at different places, thus detecting differences in underground structure; and was the first oil man in Texas to realize the possibilities of the "gravity meter," which gave a clear picture of the varying density of sub-surface rock at various levels.

Later he began to employ the "seismograph," an instrument developed to measure the intensity of earthquakes, or tremors in the earth's crust. The original ponderous seismographs, built on great blocks of cement to register earthquakes thousands of miles distant, were reduced to small, sensitive instruments which could be mounted in a small truck and hauled across country, taking measurements of tremors that travel through the underground structures of the earth. The speed of these tremors, and the rapidity with which they are reflected back—like sound waves measured by the sensitive instruments of an ocean liner to determine the depth of the ocean floor—became a picture, in the mind of the geologist, of the kind of rock formations he would find if he drilled far below the surface.

Roy used these instruments—as did all oil prospectors of

his day; but he added another ingredient. That was the general "shaping up" in his mind of all the facts and impressions he had gleaned from his "creekology," and geological and geophysical studies.

Oil prospectors had begun to employ "geochemical" methods, studying surface samples of soil and rock, and testing them for traces of oil. Even where the pools of oil were buried thousands of feet under the surface, chemists had found that minute particles of oil tended to migrate upwards to the surface, sometimes creating a "halo," or ring of traces of oil. Later, when the electromagnetic surveys used by Professor Schlumberger of France to detect coal—by passing an electrical current into the ground to detect the presence of the more highly resistant coal formations—became known, Roy Cullen began to adapt these methods to oil hunting.

"Cullen luck" was actually the application of common sense to all these things he observed or learned—both from physical inspection of the ground, and from geological and geophysical reports. In his early days of exploring West Texas for oil lands, Roy Cullen had studied great bench-land formations, and topographical sweeps of land running for hundreds of miles across the surface earth structure of Texas. He had observed where shoulders of rock, thrust out of the soil a hundred miles inland, would have a basic similarity with formations and ledges nearer the coast, five hundred to a thousand feet lower down.

He applied his knowledge of the earth's surface to problems of drilling—and it was this knowledge that enabled him to conquer the bugaboo of Texas oil drillers for a quarter of a century: the so-called "heaving shale," known to geologists as "Jackson shale."

Shortly after the South Texas Petroleum Company got under way—following the strike on East Blue Ridge—Roy

Cullen turned his attention to the Humble fields, once a booming cluster of oil wells, and now nearly played out. West was disgusted when Roy announced his intention of drilling again on the Humble land.

"They've drilled so many wells out there that there isn't room to put down another hole," he said. "even if there was any oil left—which there isn't."

Roy pointed to a place on the map.

"I think there's room for one more—over here on the southeast side."

West wanted to know when he was going to inspect it.

"I've already decided where to drill," Roy said. "All I need is a lease."

"You're going to lease it without even looking at it?" West demanded. "Are you crazy, Roy?"

"It has been intensively drilled and we have geophysical reports on the entire area," Roy said. "Looking at it won't add anything to that. It won't mean anything."

"Well, it will to me," Big Jim roared. "I'm going out there!"

"Go ahead, Jim," his partner said. "I'd go with you, but I'll be too busy getting ready to drill it."

West inspected the field, and returned protesting more loudly than ever. The field was honeycombed with dried-up wells.

"You'll have to tear down old derricks to find a place to drill a hole," he told Roy. "You'll have to fill in the slush pits. The field is like a piece of Swiss cheese right now!"

When they began to drill, they found many of the wells in the area had gone into water. Roy had already figured out why this was so. About three thousand feet down there was a layer of blue mud, known to drillers as gumbo; and below that about five feet of salt water sand; and then below that another layer of thin gumbo.

When the drillers reached the layer of thick blue gumbo, they would set their "casings"—an outer pipe which is lowered into the hole to shut off the flow of water. When the drill bit into the salt water sand below the thick gumbo, they got water.

Roy decided to set the casings down in the thin gumbo, dropping them past the layer of salt water sand, thus cutting off the water.

This was exactly what was done; and the first well came in with "pipeline" oil—that is, oil that was so pure it could be moved directly into a pipeline without treatment.

However, Roy had already decided to drill deeper. For years drillers had battled in vain to get below the treacherous "heaving shale"—a softer, shifting layer of shale that crumbled and closed in on the wells. Roy had studied reports on previous drillings at the Humble field, and anticipated this. He knew they would strike the Jackson shale about three thousand feet down.

It had been customary to "set screens" at the level where the drill first struck oil sand. The "screens" are sections of iron pipe with holes punched in the casing, set in the oil sand, so the oil can seep through from the sand. Where there was "heaving shale," the crumbling rock would sift in and clamp down on the pipe, "freezing" it; and the well and pipe would have to be abandoned.

When the driller had the "screens" about four hundred feet from the bottom of the hole, the shale began to press in, threatening to freeze the pipe. The pumps had almost choked down.

Roy ordered the driller, Dalton Brown, to "thin up"—

which meant pumping water instead of mud until it washed and cleared the screen of mud shale. This was not a normal procedure, but Brown—after a startled glance at Roy—complied with the order.

In a few minutes the pumps began to work more freely.

"Use only water and no mud," Roy ordered. "Work the pipe up and down, and try to punch it through the bridge."

The driller manipulated the heavy pipe like a pile driver, lifting it and driving it against the bridge. Under the heavy blows, the bridge of shale gave way, and the pipe slipped down into the oil sands. The "screens" were set.

It was midnight. Roy had been directing the setting of the screen for hours, and now he told Brown, the driller, that he would lie down on the ground and get some rest.

At 4 A.M. Brown aroused him.

"Wake up, Mr. Cullen! I think she's coming in!"

Roy arose, stretched and yawned, and then walked over to the well. Oil and gas was blowing up through the hole so violently that a four-inch "flow line," which connected the well to a 1600-barrel storage tank, was bucking like a wild snake in the darkness.

Roy ran to the storage tank, scaled the ladder, and climbed out on the top of the tank and sat astride the flow line until Brown could call out the rest of the crew and tie it down.

The next day the well was under control, pouring out five thousand barrels a day. Roy Cullen's feat made oil history—for the first time demonstrating that the dread "heaving shale" could be conquered.

Another drilling company, the Texas Company, which owned land adjacent to the area where the Cullen well had been brought in on the Humble field, drilled what is known as an "offset" well opposite the Cullen well on their land. They agreed to space additional wells the same distance apart on each side of the dividing line—in order to distribute equally the flow of oil. Four Cullen wells were drilled, all bringing in oil. The other outfit was unable to pierce the Jackson shale, and brought in dry holes. Finally, on the fifth well, the superintendent of the crew came to Roy.

"Mr. Cullen, will you help us?" he asked.

"Sure," Roy said; "if you'll do what I say and pay no attention to your field manager."

The driller followed the same procedure that Roy had worked out for his first well, and a gusher came in, pouring out seven thousand barrels a day. A short while later, the superintendent came over to the Cullen rig.

"Mr. Cullen—you were kind enough to help me drill that well. I want to show you something."

He led him over to the well. The two organizations had a "gentleman's agreement" to control the flow of wells on both sides of the line by a half-inch "choke," permitting only a half-inch flow from the well.

"It's a half-inch choke, all right—on this side," the superintendent said, pointing to the flow pipe. "But it's flowing through a four-inch choke on the other side."

Roy laughed.

"Tell 'em to keep it up," he said. "In a little while you'll be drawing water out of that well, and I'll still be getting oil!"

Roy Cullen was awarded a degree of Doctor of Science by the University of Pittsburgh for the "originality of thought, daring and vision in the development of methods of drilling deep wells" which enabled him to drill the Humble field wells through the "heaving shale" that had defied oil-well experts for three decades.

With the Humble wells now bringing in oil, Roy shifted the focus of interest of the South Texas Petroleum Company back to Blue Ridge. One Sunday morning a Houston lawyer,

John Price, who had a royalty interest in the Blue Ridge field, drove out to the Cullen well to see how it was progressing. A "norther" had blown up during the night, and a freezing wind whipped across the oil field. The boiler had been fired up, and on the south side—partly protected from the wind—Roy Cullen was lying on several sacks, with his overcoat over him.

"What's the matter?" Price asked. "Is he sleeping off Saturday night's binge?"

The fireman looked down at the sleeping figure.

"He's been handling four fields—day and night, Mr. Price. He's been jumping from one field to another, working with the drillers, until I guess he's forgotten what a bed feels like. He works for four or five days without taking off his clothes."

Shortly after the Blue Ridge and Humble fields were brought in, Roy Cullen went to New York—and a group of Wall Street investment men approached him with a proposal to set up a corporation and sell shares to the investing public.

"We are interested in your oil properties," the spokesman for the group said to Roy. "We want to make you a proposition."

"What do you know about my properties?" Roy asked.

"We know all about them. We know enough to make you a proposition."

"Maybe you know more than I do," Cullen said. "But let's hear it."

The proposal was to form a corporation, in which Roy Cullen would be president and would agree to run it for at least ten years. Bonds would be issued up to $60,000,000 to be sold by the company, of which half would be turned over to Cullen and West as profit. The remainder would be placed in the treasury as capital of the corporation to run the business.

"Sixty million dollars is a lot of money," Roy said. "But I'm not interested."

The investment bankers asked him why.

"I'd be afraid to spend any of the money," he said. "If the company didn't turn out to be a success, I wouldn't have any right to the fifteen million—I'd have to use my portion to pay back the bondholders."

By 1930 Roy Cullen had not only established himself as one of the most successful oil prospectors in Texas, but he had passed beyond the stage of the so-called wildcatter. He had built up huge oil reserves for Cullen & West, and had become an established oil operator. Most of the fabulous oil discoveries in Texas—such as the great East Texas field, discovered by "Dad" Joiner in an area where no one but the farmers who owned the land thought there was oil—were made by wildcatters, but few lived to enjoy personally the full fruits of their discoveries.

Roy Cullen was one of the notable exceptions. He had made his greatest developments in oil fields that had already been explored, and in some that seemed to have been worked out. There was still ahead of him the most spectacular discovery of his career, and one of the most fabulous in the history of oil in Texas—the finding of the Tom O'Connor oil field; but as the 1920's drew to a close, he had moved into the class of sound and solid oil production, and no longer depended upon discovery wells.

He had tapped the fields at Blue Ridge, Humble and Pierce Junction—all supposedly "worn-out" oil fields—for millions of barrels of oil, which were pouring into the big refineries in a steady stream. And he had made fortunes for those who had put money into his ventures . . . ventures in which Roy Cullen always put up the major money and took the major share of the risk.

Jim West's five-thousand-dollar "ante" in the firm of Cullen & West had already paid him back several millions; and Roy's own fortune was large enough that he could have retired with a comfortable income for life.

The long, hard years in Oklahoma and in West Texas were things of the past. The bitter fight to establish himself in Houston—after he had cast aside the years he had spent building up a cotton business in Oklahoma—was now only a hazy memory. He had had the raw courage and persistence to stake his whole future on his judgment . . . and he had won. The going had been rough at times.

But the long, hard years were beginning to pay off. Young Roy, who came home from Rensselaer to Rice, and left school a few weeks short of graduation, was now with his father's company, and rapidly becoming an "oil man."

Margaret and Wilhelmina were in grade school, and Agnes was engaged to marry young Roy's roommate at Rensselaer, Ike Arnold. Only Lillie Cranz had left home. She had gone to Los Angeles with "Aunt Louise"—Roy Cullen's half-sister, Louise Beck—to visit Aunt Louise's daughter, Margaret; and there she had met a young Italian actor, Paul Portanova, and married him.

Young Roy had an experimental and inventive turn of mind that might carry him far in the field of technology and research.

It was about a year before the Blue Ridge well was discovered that he had come to his father and announced that he had decided to leave school.

"I want to go to work, Dad. I don't want to wait for my diploma. I've seen a lot of men with diplomas and degrees—and that's not what I want."

Roy Cullen looked at his son gravely. He remembered another scene, strikingly similar, many years ago, when he had stood before his mother in the garden of their San Antonio home and said: "Mother, I'm quitting school."

He was fairly sure he knew what had prompted young Roy's decision. He knew Roy had met a girl at Rice, and that he planned to get married; and he knew the same deep pride that had prompted his own decision nearly forty years before was now prompting the decision of his son.

He laid his hand on his son's shoulder, and his face crinkled in a smile.

"Sonny, you do what you believe is right in your own mind—and I'll back you up."

The bond between the two, which had always been deep, had grown with the years of hard work and struggling—even while the boy was away at school and Roy was out in the oil fields. Many years before, when young Roy was a small boy, his father had found him playing with matches. He took the boy into his study.

"Sonny, your mother told you not to play with matches, didn't she?"

The boy nodded.

"And you've disobeyed her, haven't you?"

Young Roy nodded again.

"Well, I'm not going to punish you, Sonny—even if you were bad. I won't whip you. But the next time you disobey your mother, I'm going to take off my coat and you'll have to whip me."

A strong, enduring affection had bound the members of the Cullen family closely together, during the days of adversity as well as success. It was a family that shared happiness and love as other families shared food. Roy Cullen looked at his son—tall and straight, with his mother's deep blue eyes.

"Have you decided what you want to do, Sonny?" he finally asked. "We're got plenty of jobs you can handle in South Texas Petroleum."

Young Roy shook his head.

"I've got to work for somebody else, Dad. I'll know that whatever I'm doing is on my own—not with your help. It's the only way I'll ever know what I really can do."

His father nodded. A few days later he saw Wallace Pratt, of the Humble Company, and Pratt quickly agreed to take young Roy into their research department. He was sent to Breckenridge, Texas, where Humble was drilling; and he went to work in the research department, converting oil gas into alcohol and other by-products.

For nearly a year he remained with the Humble Company, working on technical projects, and learning much about the science of oil research. But he was not happy, and Roy realized that. One day he met Wallace Pratt in Houston, and Pratt said to him:

"Roy, your son isn't satisfied up at Breckenridge."

Roy Cullen looked at his friend.

"What's the matter with Sonny?" he asked.

"Your boy thinks faster than most people, Roy . . . and it's hurting him more than it's helping where he is. He needs to be among men who are out doing things. These fellows are buried in scientific thinking up there."

Roy nodded. A few days later he called his son on the telephone.

"What's the matter, Sonny?" he asked. "You in love?"

Young Roy laughed. However, he agreed to accept his father's offer to come back to Houston and work for Cullen & West. This brought a deep satisfaction to Roy Cullen. He had watched his son grow in experience and stature with real pride; and he knew from early indications that Roy Gustave would develop into a first-class oil man. He had quickly understood Pratt's remark: young Roy would be "buried" if he remained in the research laboratory at Breckenridge.

Shortly after young Roy returned to Houston, he married his schoolgirl sweetheart, Katherine Thompson, whom he had known at Rice Institute. Roy and Lillie suddenly realized that their family was indeed "growing up." It seemed only a few short years ago that they had bundled up their belongings at Anadarko, and headed south with the three children to Houston.

A little more than a year after young Roy's marriage to Katherine Thompson, the first grandchild had arrived in the Cullen family—Roy Henry.

"It would be nice to settle down and just live with the children," Lillie told Roy; and his rugged face softened again in a gentle smile; but he shook his head.

"We can't settle down yet, Lillie . . . not until all the children are taken care of. You've brought up a fine family, honey. Sonny is doing well, and he's going to be a great oil man. When Agnes and Ike are married, and their children come along, we'll have a bigger family. But right now there's still a lot of work to do. You remember at Pierce Junction, some of the people that came in with us wanted to salt away what they had and quit. A few of 'em did, and now they wish they hadn't."

Lillie nodded, and took his big, rough hand in hers.

"We've had a good life, Roy . . . even if it was a bit hard at times. I hope nothing ever happens to spoil it."

He nodded.

"Yes, it has been good . . . We've got a good family, and that's the best any man can ask in life. The country is in a pretty bad mess, but the folks that have faith in themselves and in other people will pull it through. We saw it in 1907, and again in 1917 when the cotton market broke, and in

1921. The country will come through, but it will take a lot of faith—and a lot of work. God gave us a good country, Lillie, but he didn't guarantee anything, and it's pretty much up to us what we do with it . . ."

A few days later he got a telephone call from L. P. Garrett, of the Gulf Company—the man who leased the Howe tract at Pierce Junction. He said:

"Can I come over to your office, Roy . . . I've got a good proposition for you."

CHAPTER 13

"I'm not going to find any more oil fields for you to give away!"

Garrett walked into Roy Cullen's office. Roy nodded as he sat down, and began chewing on a cigar. It was almost ten years since he had talked Garrett into leasing the Howe land at Pierce Junction, and Garrett had tried to talk him out of it.

"Roy," Garrett said, "I want you to drill an oil well for us."

Roy continued to chew his cigar; then he slowly shook his head. He was almost fifty years old—solidly built, with a shock of black hair barely showing streaks of gray. His face was moulded in deep lines, and his expression had a way of settling into an expressionless mask when he was studying another man, or thinking out a problem.

Finally he said:

"I've never contracted to dig a well, Mr. Garrett."

"We'll pay you a good price," Garrett said.

"Where is the well?"

"On Lockwood's land in Fort Bend County, near Thompson."

Roy Cullen nodded. "I know the place."

It was known as Rabb's Ridge, and three wells had been drilled there—all dry holes. Roy also knew Hiland Lockwood, a Houston real-estate man who had dabbled in oil. Lockwood was a fairly close friend.

"Why do you want me to drill it?" he finally asked.

Garrett explained that Lockwood had made that provision. He owned three thousand acres on Rabb's Ridge, and he had agreed to lease half the land to Gulf—if Roy Cullen drilled the well.

"I'll tell you what I'll do," Roy said. "I'll match acres and dollars with you, and I'll drill on a fifty-fifty basis. The Gulf Company can put up its acreage, and I'll get 1,500 acres of Lockwood's land. We'll split the cost of drilling. Then each of us will own half interest in any oil produced."

Garrett agreed. Cullen telephoned Lockwood at the Rice Hotel. He told Lockwood of his arrangement with the Gulf Company, and asked if he would lease half of his tract.

"Sure," Lockwood said.

"It's a deal," Roy said.

Cullen had examined the maps before he talked to Lockwood. He knew the tract, and was familiar with the geological reports, and previous drillings.

Cullen chose the east half, where no wells had been drilled. He had already surveyed the general contours of the country, and found that the Brazos, winding east of the Thompson field, had apparently been shoved into that course by the rising land—which indicated the probable presence of a "salt dome" far below the ridge.

Cullen's first survey was based on his "creekology"—a study of the courses of the rivers and creeks winding around hard formations of the land on Rabb's Ridge. This would reveal the action of pressures of rock deep in the earth.

He knew the Gulf geologists and survey engineers had

gone over the area. But he was also pretty sure they had not made a physical survey. The swamplands were too rotten, and there were too many rattlesnakes and copperheads to encourage that kind of survey.

After Roy had selected the site, Garrett told him the Gulf geologists had picked another site for drilling, about a mile and a half south of the ridge.

When these objections were made known by Garrett, Roy Cullen's face set grimly.

"Didn't we agree that I was to decide the location?" he said.

Garrett nodded. "But our engineers have all the geological data," he told him. "They think you should drill further south."

"To hell with what they think!" Roy snapped. "I've studied the ground myself, and I've got the gravity meter reports. They bear out the 'creekology' of the place. I'm going to drill on top of the ridge."

The drilling itself was a back-breaking job. A corduroy road had to be built across the slough to the side of the ridge to carry machinery, derrick rigging and pipe to the well site. The first heavy loads sank into quicksand, and tractors finally had to be used to drag rig and pipes up to the location.

Cullen and his crew worked night and day, getting up the rig and finally drilling the well. It was several weeks after the job was started that the drill bit through a layer of Miocene sand and the core of oil sand was brought up.

It was on this night that Roy got the telephone call at his home, and drove fifty miles to Rabb's Ridge. The following night, after he had leased the additional land from Hiland Lockwood, Roy returned to the drilling area.

For several hours the pressure underground had been increasing almost visibly. The derrick, standing gaunt and bare against the early morning light, was trembling so violently it seemed suddenly to have become alive. And around the derrick platform, where the mud hose and the pipes lay in coils, the ground itself seemed to be "alive."

The superintendent of the Gulf Company and his assistant were standing near the rig; and suddenly as the derrick began to heave convulsively, they sprinted toward the outer rim of the cleared field. The crew at the rig, seeing the two men leave, ran after them.

At that instant the well blew in. The "Christmas tree" of valves capping the well pipe jerked violently under the impact, as the underground torrent rushed upward with a pressure that seemed about to tear the derrick, rig and all, from the ground. Roy Cullen, standing on the derrick floor, saw that the rig had been abandoned. There were no men at the valve to close it down and control the rush of the erupting oil.

He jumped on the flow lines from the derrick floor, and the oil pressure was so great coming from four-inch lines that as it hit the pumps it rebounded, and literally covered him with oil. The pipes were shaking violently as he made his way across the few intervening feet until he reached the valve control wheel. Then it required several seconds before he could apply enough pressure to turn the wheel.

Once he turned and shouted, but the sound of escaping air and the racket of the vibrating derrick drowned out his words. Finally a "roughneck"—one of the derrick workers—started across the clearing, plunging like a green ghost through the shower of oil. He jumped up beside Cullen, and together they were able to twist the valve shut.

Late that day Roy returned to Houston, tired and grimy with oil and muck. Blue Ridge had made him a millionaire; but Rabb's Ridge had catapulted him toward the "wildcatter's dream"—a hundred-million-dollar oil field!

On that day, Roy Cullen might have retired—and he would have become one of the world's richest men. Cullen & West had a half-interest in a field that would produce oil for more than a hundred years. Yet Roy not only did not stop working; he didn't even slow down.

A year after the discovery well came in at Rabb's Ridge, Roy got a telephone call from his production chief, Lynn Meador. The original Thompson well—known as Sharpe and Lockwood No. 1—had "blown out." That meant it had gone out of control. He hurried to the field and found Meador at the well. It was an awesome sight. The gassy hurricane was blowing up through the mouth of the well with a deafening roar. A mile-long coil of black pipe had shot out of the well and was hurled across the live-oak trees around the rig, writhing and twisting like a gigantic black python. It lay across the limbs of trees and around nearby derricks, in a hideous tangle of oil-blackened steel.

The sand was shooting up through the ground with a force that had sheared off sections of the steel-plate flooring of the well rig, as if they were cardboard. Great rocks had been belched up through the ten-inch casing with such terrific speed that they had expanded when they struck the air and could not be dropped back through a twelve-inch casing!

After looking over the wreckage, Roy shook his head. The Rabb's Ridge discovery well "ran wild" for several months until it "blew itself out." Other wells had been drilled in the area and were still producing—and Sharpe and Lockwood No. 1 had paid for itself a hundred times over.

It was not long after this that a second well in the Thompson field—known as "A. P. George No. 3"—blew out. This was far more serious than the discovery well's finale, because it was pure oil and gas, and a spark might ignite it into a flaming inferno. Meador was at the well when he heard one of the crew on the derrick shout, and then he saw the man scramble down the ladder.

"It's coming up!" he shouted to Meador.

The next instant the black casing pipe shot into the sky, and the oil and sand followed in a black geyser. In a matter of seconds the entire field was drenched with the spray of oil, sand and rock, while the ground shuddered under the gathering force of the underground blast.

In a few minutes the oil and gas was roaring through the mouth of the well in a constant stream. Roy Cullen arrived at the field a short time later, and immediately pulled on his boots and headed across to the shattered skeleton of the derrick. It was necessary to cap the well immediately, since the combination of oil and gas might catch fire any second and explode.

Roy took charge of the capping operation. It was decided to suspend an open valve over the pipe, stretched on guy ropes, and try to lower it over the pipe. Roy stood on the derrick floor, his face and clothes black with oil, while the oil spray enveloped the rigging and derrick like a cloud. A single spark would have detonated the explosive mist of gas and oil, and killed everyone near the derrick . . .

Finally, after hours of effort, the open valve was dropped on top of the casing. The collar of the valve was made of die-metal, hard enough to cut its own threads into the well casing; and once it was lowered over the head of the pipe, it was quickly screwed into place.

It required several hours to bring the well under control. Roy remained at the derrick until the oil was again flowing in a regulated stream, and then drove back to Houston.

The Rabb's Ridge area continued to be highly productive, with well after well brought in until the once-abandoned Thompson field was a liquid gold mine. One day the Humble Company approached Jim West with an offer to buy out Cullen & West's interest for twenty million dollars. West wanted to accept the offer, but Roy scoffed at it.

"The stuff in that field is worth a hundred million dollars," he said. "Maybe two hundred million."

This was more than a clash of opinion as to the productivity of an oil well. It was a conflict of fundamental viewpoints. Roy had fought through the muck and mud, crawling over the rocks in search of oil; and when it came in, he felt as if it were part of his own life blood pouring out of the rocky crust of Rabb's Ridge. To Jim West it was "just another oil well"—and Humble's offer of twenty million dollars was a business proposition that would enable Roy and himself to pull out with enormous profits, and no further risk.

The argument became bitter. Roy explained his reasons for wanting to refuse the offer: The Thompson field was now proved . . . and it was as yet untapped. The wells they had drilled would produce oil for more than a hundred years.

Jim West was adamant. He said that with two wells "blowing out" the field might begin to dry up. And the Humble Company's offer would enable them to pull out with a clear profit and no further risk that the field would fail.

Roy laughed.

"Jim—that field is worth at least a hundred million dollars! Do you think I want to sell it for twenty million?"

West still wanted to sell, and finally Roy agreed.

"All right, Jim—we'll sell. It's your company as much as mine, and if you want to sell, we'll sell. But after this deal is closed, we're through as partners. I'm not going to find any more oil fields for you to give away!"

The partnership of Cullen and West was terminated after the sale of the Thompson field to Humble. The field continued to produce—as Roy had said it would.

The dissolving of the Cullen and West partnership left Roy Cullen once again a lone operator—and that was the way he liked to operate. He had already carved out a fabulous record in the history of Texas oil development; and two years later, on the sandy humps of land along the Gulf Coast southeast of San Antonio, he was to write the most fabulous chapter of all—the discovery of the great Tom O'Connor field, which became the real "wildcatter's dream."

CHAPTER 14

"I'm not and never have been a candidate for anything"

FAITH," ROY CULLEN SAID, "is the greatest thing in the world! Faith in your fellow-man . . . and in yourself. It is greater than love, because if you have faith—in yourself, in your friends and neighbors . . . then you've also got love."

It was a homely philosophy, and not too complicated; yet it told in many ways the story of Roy Cullen's life. Many years after he became the most successful wildcatter in Texas, he met the Reverend Billy Graham, the evangelist, and he asked Roy—who had given millions to Methodist, Episcopal, Baptist, Catholic and non-sectarian hospitals—why he had not become a regular member of any church. Cullen took the evangelist out on the lawn in front of his home, and pointed to the sky.

"See that star up there? It's probably a million light years away from us. And over there is another star—maybe a million light years away from the first one. My church is up there somewhere . . . and I haven't been able to locate the exact place where it is."

Roy Cullen's philosophy had been built on a hard core of

self-reliance, which he had learned in the lean years of his early life in Oklahoma, and in the oil fields. He had been deeply pleased to find these same qualities in his son. He knew they were necessary for whatever a man had to do in life; they were tested qualities, and they were the source of a man's individual strength.

His own sense of self-reliance and determination was based primarily on his belief in individual dignity and self-respect. His mother's words—"never give an insult, and never take one"—were ingrained in his nature. And although there might seem to be a conflict between this rugged self-reliance and determination, and the sympathy and natural generosity which his mother had also instilled in him, there was no conflict in Roy's mind. Both facets were part of an orderly pattern of thinking . . . "I never tried to out-trade a man in my life, and I never let a man out-trade me if I could help it," he told Jim West; and this was his creed.

It was perhaps this seemingly conflicting combination of driving determination and generosity toward other people that prevented Roy Cullen, who was as good a fighter as the next man, from becoming ruthless. And it was natural that he should turn his attention—as fortune heaped its wealth upon him—to the economic distress that was engulfing the country.

As hard times descended upon Texas, and upon his own community, he began to think of ways in which he might help to alleviate the troubles of other people.

One of these efforts began to take shape in his mind shortly after the discovery well came in at Rabb's Ridge. The big house on Alabama and Austin had been the Cullen home for almost the span of a generation. The older girls and Roy Gustave hardly remembered Oklahoma; and the two younger girls had never known any other home. But the family was growing up, and the older children were moving out into the world.

One day Roy said to Lillie: "It looks as if we won't have the older children with us much longer, honey."

"Roy and Agnes will be here," she said. Lillie Cranz had gone to Los Angeles to live, after she had married Paul Portanova; but the others had homes in Houston.

"What I mean is—we're in the middle of a depression now, and a lot of people are out of work, and this would be a good time to help some of them. You remember that 'big white house' we used to talk about, Lillie—that I dreamed of when I was a boy out in San Antonio?"

Lillie nodded.

"Well, I think maybe now is the time to build it."

"With the children moving away—you think we need a bigger house, Roy?" Lillie laughed, and kissed her big husband. "I know what you mean, honey—and I think so, too."

"We'd have a big home, so all the children and their children would be able to have parties . . . and Margaret and Wilhelmina are growing up."

So it was decided to build a new home. Roy acquired four acres in the new "River Oaks" district, where some of Houston's most beautiful mansions were springing up; but after going over the plans with their architect, John Staub, he shook his head.

"Let's make it bigger, Lillie," he said. "We always wanted a big garden—with the kind of flowers and trees we like."

Two more acres were added, and the "big white house" began to take shape. Roy issued one positive order to his contractors:

"I want you to pay the highest wages paid anywhere for this kind of work."

This was not merely to be a new house; it was in a small

measure a civic enterprise, to help people who were out of work in the dark days of depression. Even the garden became a project. Roy had a deep passion for flowers; and when he was out on the rocky plains of West Texas, tramping over ledges and gullies looking for outcroppings of rock, he often clambered down cliffs to look at some particularly dazzling bit of color on the petals of a tiny flower.

"I never was much of a hand for picking flowers," he explained. "I just liked to watch 'em grow."

He was able to "watch 'em grow" to his heart's content as the big garden took shape at River Oaks. Roy sent a horticultural expert roaming through South Carolina, Alabama and Louisiana to find azalias, camellias and rare shrubs. His flower-hunting zeal almost provoked a crisis with Louisiana. State officials at Baton Rouge, alarmed by the Cullen raids on Louisiana's flowers, threatened an embargo, but the people of the state let out a howl of protest. The Cullen garden was furnishing needed stimulus to the flower growers, who also were hit by the depression, and they wanted no interference with his buying.

Meanwhile, the nation was moving into an ominous cycle of unemployment and low markets. Roy watched the developments with increasing worry—not because of any immediate effect it would have upon his own fortunes, but because he was afraid of the consequences to the national economy.

In the election of 1928 Roy had thrown his personal political preference to Herbert Hoover, abandoning his lifelong faith in the Democrats. While he had no personal political ambitions, he had never lost his active interest in the political affairs of his city, or the state or nation. Seventy-five years before, Ezekiel Cullen had left Texas to follow the political banner of General Zachary Taylor; and while Roy had no intention of leaving Texas, he began to look with concern upon the national scene.

Roy had made frequent trips to New York and other cities of the East; and he had become increasingly concerned over the trend in national political developments leading up to the elections of 1932.

Depression and social unrest had stacked the cards against President Hoover. Cullen had not lost faith in Hoover, however, nor in the principles for which his party had stood . . . and in the political pastures of Texas a Republican was a strange maverick, needing courage and determination to maintain his political views.

But he knew the country was in desperate straits, and the people were looking anxiously for a Moses to lead them out of the economic wilderness. When Franklin Delano Roosevelt was nominated by the Democrats in the summer of 1932, and began to make ringing speeches across the land, it looked as if a new Bryan had arrived on the political horizon.

Roy had supported Herbert Hoover in 1928; and he still believed Hoover's policies would restore the nation's crumbling economic life, applying rigorously the hard principles of governmental budget balancing. But a new school of economic thought was gathering force. Roy was a firm advocate of the age-old creed of "enlightened self-interest." The new political and economic school was like a chameleon; he was not sure of its colors. At one time it held unswervingly to individual liberty; and then it seemed to advocate more governmental controls . . . a socialized democracy!

It became increasingly evident, however, that the people were looking for a "new prophet"—and the new prophet had emerged in the person of Franklin Delano Roosevelt.

Roy read with interest the Democratic campaign pledges

to "remove the Government from all fields of private enterprise except where necessary to develop public works and natural resources in the public interest."

Roosevelt, as the head of the party, pledged a "covenant with the people, to be faithfully kept by the party entrusted with power." He spoke of "rigid governmental economy" by a "stern and unremitting administration policy of living within our means."

This all sounded like good horse sense to Roy Cullen. If Governor Roosevelt planned to carry out these policies, then he felt that it would be better to elect him than to return President Hoover to office—with a hostile and obstructing Congress.

He decided to take a trip to the East and see for himself what kind of fellow this new Roosevelt actually was. He wanted to join Agnes and Ike Arnold, who were visiting in Buffalo, where the Arnold family lived; and at a reception given by Mrs. Arnold, he had an opportunity to talk with many New Yorkers.

He met a New York State official who knew Roosevelt and he asked him what he thought of the Governor.

"There's no particular harm in him," the man said. "He's like all the Roosevelts—he has a big mouth."

In New York Roy Cullen continued to press his inquiries. He knew a number of New York financial men, with whom he had been dealing in his various oil transactions; and wherever he found men willing to talk about the Governor, he listened. Many of the men with whom he talked wondered what reason this tall, rugged-looking Texan might have for his persistent efforts to find out things about Franklin Roosevelt. But when Roy Cullen returned to Texas, he had a firm and decided impression of the man who was to lead the Democrats to victory in the elections of November, 1932.

"Everybody says Governor Roosevelt is big-mouthed but harmless," he told his friends back in Houston. "I don't believe he's harmless—I think he's dangerous. Governor Roosevelt can hurt this country if he's elected—and I'm going to fight him."

Roy had not been in a political fight of any consequence since he fought Jesse Jones on the Houston Harbor Board issue twenty years before. But he decided this was too critical an hour in American history for anyone to remain on the sidelines.

Republicans were never very strong in Texas; and there was little or no organization. So Roy turned to his own resources once more, as he had in the Harbor Board fight. He went to the Houston *Post* with a letter urging Texans to support President Hoover, and warning them against placing the country's future in the hands of the glib-tongued Governor of New York.

His pleading fell on deaf ears. Texas—like the rest of the nation—was crying for any kind of change, and Roosevelt and the "New Deal" was swept into office in the elections of November, 1932.

There was an early reversal of many of the campaign pledges: the plunge into Government borrowing and spending, which the President had inveighed against in his election speeches; the swift change from the policy of keeping the Government out of business, which had been his campaign slogan, to increasing bureaucratic involvements in industry which Roy Cullen described as "creeping socialism."

"This country became strong by keeping two basic principles," Cullen said. "The first is our system of free enterprise, without the Government interfering with the rights of the states or the rights of the people; and the second is building a tariff wall that can protect us from cheap foreign markets. The New Deal is abandoning the two things that have made us strong."

By the end of Roosevelt's first term as President, Roy Cullen was convinced that the danger of socialism was not merely an academic play on words—it was real and imminent. He opened a broadside of telegrams on members of Congress, and began to follow closely the actions of every congressman and senator. When Senator Alben Barkley led the fight to revise the Supreme Court through legislation by Congress—the celebrated "Supreme Court packing" issue—Roy Cullen bought a page advertisement in the Louisville *Courier-Journal,* Senator Barkley's home-state newspaper, bitterly attacking the Senator.

He warned the women of Kentucky, to whom the letter was addressed, that the election of Senator Barkley would help President Roosevelt and the New Deal carry out a plan which would result in ". . . the end of free speech, the direct control of the farmer and laborer, and result in a dictatorship for our country." He pointed out that primary elections in Pennsylvania, Iowa, Virginia, Missouri and Texas had already repudiated the New Deal.

"Citizens of Kentucky!" he wrote. "Will you not join with these states in helping to retain the freedom of your country by voting against Barkley?"

Barkley was elected; but Roy Cullen turned immediately toward an attack on the "court-packing" bill. A veritable flood of telegrams and letters poured over the wires and through the mails from Texas, directed at congressmen and senators, warning them of the danger of abrogating their rights to the pressure from the executive side of the Government.

When the "court-packing" bill was defeated, in its original form, which would have empowered the President to revise the Supreme Court at will, Cullen wired congratulations to those who had defeated the bill, charging that "the 196 congressmen who voted for the bill admitted by their vote that they lack the necessary ability to carry on the functions delegated to them by our Constitution"; and he suggested that "all of these 196 congressmen should resign."

The message did not produce any wholesale resignations in Congress, but it did impress upon quite a few members of Congress that the craggy Texas oilman, who had been quietly inquiring around New York and Washington about the caliber of the President—when he was still Governor of New York—was a new political force in Texas.

Several Texas Democratic leaders began to view Roy Cullen's activities with new respect. John H. Kirby, an unreconstructed Texas Democrat of the old school, wired Cullen from New York:

> The vigor with which you are attacking national conditions is heartening to all of us old-fashioned Americans, who believe in the Constitution and the Government created for us by wise and patriotic forefathers. The voice of a private citizen, however wise and capable he may be, has not the power of achievement behind him. I suggest that you permit us to send you to Congress.

Cullen thanked him, but said that he had no thought of running for any office. "I can do more good helping other candidates—doing what I can to see that the good men get into office and the bad ones are kept out, than I could ever do in public office myself," he told friends. "I am not and never have been a candidate for anything."

CHAPTER 15

"There's a mile-deep pool of oil down there"

AFTER ROY CULLEN broke with Jim West, he decided to go "on his own," bringing into his company the members of his family and perhaps a few close personal friends, like Harry Holmes, his attorney. The first thing he needed was a name.

One day he was fishing with Harry Holmes on the Brazos River, near Freeport, where the river empties into the Gulf of Mexico. They drifted past a small scattering of tumbledown shacks on the bank, a few miles above Freeport, and Holmes remarked:

"That's all there is left of old Quintana."

The place had been a flourishing port on the Brazos when Houston was only an inland village. Roy looked at the dilapidated remnants of the town, and suddenly said: "Quintana. . . . You know, Harry, I like that name. The old place hasn't anywhere to go, so maybe it won't mind if we borrow the name. . . ."

The next day Quintana Petroleum Company's charter papers were drawn up, with Harry Holmes as general counsel, Ike Arnold as chief engineer, Roy Gustave Cullen as vice-president, and Roy Cullen as president.

The big house on River Oaks also was coming along; and in 1933 it was finished. With Roy Gustave, Lillie Cranz and Agnes married and living in other homes, the "old folks" settled down with the two younger girls, Margaret and Wilhelmina, in their spacious new home.

It was a "dream castle" come true . . . a huge white mansion, built of Texas stone, with a broad portico and white columns facing upon a huge courtyard. On the east end was a reflection pool, that reflected the sky and the trees; and on the west end was a small colony of garages, garden toolhouses and servants' quarters. Inside the door was a big T-shape rotunda, ascending to the second story; and the walls and floors of the entrance foyer were plated with black-and-white marble brought from Italy.

Imposing as the house looked from the outside, it was warm and comfortable inside. Lillie's home-making touch could be seen everywhere—in the light colors of the "living room," the comfortable stuffed chairs, the warm colors of the paneled dining room and the music room, finished with a delicate saffron of English harewood. The bedrooms upstairs were well furnished, in varying colors, with the same warmth pervading each of them that had been achieved in the downstairs area. And in the basement was a huge game room. All round the house were wide lawns, and the garden of azalias and camellias.

In the years that followed friends flowed in and out of the house in a constant stream, and Roy's genial smile and Lillie's calm, graceful hospitality warmed the hearts of many a visitor to Houston. The "big white house" was a reality . . . with that rarest of qualities, the almost visible warmth of love and affection which had flowed through the Cullen family for three generations.

The new home soon became a gathering place for the Cullen clan—including a new generation of grandchildren. Both Roy Gustave and Agnes now had families of their own.

Roy Cullen had passed the half-century mark in his life, and he might have looked back with pride and satisfaction on all that he had achieved . . . From the time he had quit school at the age of twelve, and assumed a responsibility for his own life—and later that of his family—he had worked unceasingly and unswervingly to provide for those he loved and for whom he felt responsible.

He had made some difficult decisions in discharging that responsibility. When he quit Clarkson a few months after he married Lillie Cranz, he had made a decision that might have staggered many an older and more experienced man . . . the decision to take a young wife, used to the luxury and comforts of a wealthy merchant's home, into the wildest country in the Southwest, among the rough, brawling inhabitants of a small frontier town.

That responsibility had been carried out, as had been the responsibility for moving his family back to Houston, leaving the home and business he had established in Oklahoma. None of these tasks had been easy, and it had required a kind of courage that is not often found to carry them out . . . And now, with the pinnacle reached—with every goal attained—it should have been simple for Roy Cullen to retire quietly from the battle.

But whatever it was that drove him into Oklahoma, and into Houston . . . was still driving him now. He had become known as the "King of the Wildcatters" after he brought in the Thompson field; but the name never really fitted him until he moved out into the rolling cattle lands that rise from the Gulf of Mexico toward the plateaus of West Texas. And it was out there, on the monotonous miles of dusty range land known as the "O'Connor Ranch," that Roy Cullen struck the most fabulous of all wildcat oil fields.

Tom O'Connor's forebears had come to Texas exactly one hundred years before Roy Cullen turned his eyes toward these great empty spaces of land, dotted with cattle and mesquite.

In 1830 two enterprising Irishmen, James Power and James Hewitson, had secured from the Mexican Government the right to bring settlers into the land between the Nueces and the Guadalupe Rivers.

Cabeza de Vaca had explored the land a century before; and the Frenchman, La Salle, had penetrated west from the Mississippi as far as what is now the city of Victoria. For the most part, however, it had been inhabited by savage Karankawa Indians, reputed to be cannibals. Land records of 1832 show that three members of the O'Connor family—James, Thomas and Charles—came with about two hundred Irish immigrants to settle on the Power and Hewitson grant. The original Tom O'Connor Ranch was a square league on Saus Creek, in what is now Refugio County, filed on September 28, 1834 by "José Jesus Verdaurri," apparently the Mexican magistrate. An extra league was added because O'Connor had married a Mexican.

Hardly had the O'Connors settled on their land when the Texas Revolution broke out. The year Ezekiel Cullen came to Texas, the O'Connors were fighting with the "Refugio Volunteers" against the Mexican Army; and an O'Connor signed the Texas "Declaration of Independence" at Washington on the Brazos on March 2, 1836.

It was natural that Tom O'Connor, descended from the first "cattle kings" of Texas, should have one main idea about oil: and that was to keep out trespassers and interlopers who wanted to invade his domain with chuffing boilers and tall derricks, spreading like strange land-ships against the flat, cloudless skyline.

Roy Cullen always worked on the principle that there was more than one way to skin a cat; and instead of approaching Tom O'Connor directly—and getting rebuffed, as others had—he telephoned him for an appointment. O'Connor was polite, but not encouraging: he would be glad to meet Mr. Cullen at his ranch office in Victoria.

Roy drove with Harry Holmes to Victoria. It was a thriving little town, with a main street and a row of two-story buildings. When Roy and his lawyer got out of their car in front of the building where Tom O'Connor's offices were located, the rancher was standing at the window, watching them. He turned to one of his men and said:

"These fellers may be kidnapers—keep an eye on 'em!"

This was in 1932; and the precaution may have been prompted by the kidnaping scare that spread through the country in the wake of the Lindbergh kidnaping. However, neither Roy Cullen nor Harry Holmes gave O'Connor's aides any cause for alarm.

After a lengthy discussion, during which Roy carefully explained why they wanted to lease the land for oil surveys—and what they intended to do—O'Connor said he would "let them know."

This was indefinite; and after several weeks, during which Roy received no word from the rancher, it became more indefinite. Roy Cullen was never one to wait for events to shape themselves; he decided to take further action. He knew other oil men had cast covetous eyes on the O'Connor Ranch, and it was only a matter of time until someone cracked the rancher's resistance.

Roy knew that one of his oil field acquaintances, Chad Nelms, who had drilled a neighboring well on one of the leases at Blue Ridge, was a friend of Tom O'Connor. So he went to Nelms. He asked him to go to Victoria and find out why O'Connor had not replied to their first request for a lease.

Nelms drove to Victoria, and told O'Connor he had come there representing Roy Cullen.

"Cullen?" O'Connor thought a moment. "Oh, sure—he was here with the lawyer feller. I said I'd write him a letter—but you know how I hate to write letters. Is he all right?"

"I wouldn't be here if he wasn't, Tom," Nelms said. The cattleman nodded.

"All right—I'll give him the lease. I'll have my lawyer, Mr. Vandenberg, draw it up. But look here, Chad—you tell this feller, Cullen, that if they change one damn word, or dot an 'i' or cross a 't'—they can tear up the paper."

Nelms reported the results of his meeting, and Roy and Harry Holmes drove down to Victoria again. The lawyer, Vandenberg, had prepared the lease; and Roy signed it exactly as it was written. He paid a dollar an acre for the right to survey the ranch, and the right to select two 7,500-acre blocs for drilling. Nelms was given an overriding royalty amounting to about 2 percent, and the deal was closed.

The first hole drilled on the O'Connor land brought salt water at 4,450 feet. Roy sent young Roy out to the O'Connor workings to direct operations for reworking the first hole. When the drill had gone down another four hundred feet, the "cores" indicated they were close to the oil sand.

Meanwhile, Humble Oil had become interested in the

O'Connor operations. Wallace Pratt, who had been with Roy in the days when he had visited the Babb stronghold in the Pecos River country, and was still chief geologist for Humble, had tried to make a gravity-meter survey of the O'Connor land, but the rancher had refused permission. When Pratt learned that Cullen had leased 15,000 acres on the O'Connor property, and already had a survey, he went to the Quintana office.

Roy told him of his drilling commitments, which included at least two wells. Then he showed Pratt the survey maps.

"If Humble wants to come in, you can have half interest," he told Pratt. "Dollar for dollar—we'll split the cost."

Pratt stared at the rugged face of his old friend, and suddenly turned without a word and started for the door and opened it. He was halfway out of the office when he turned again. Roy stared at him with level eyes. Pratt shrugged and walked out. Ten minutes later the telephone rang in Roy's office. It was Wallace Pratt.

"All right, Roy," he said. "We'll take half."

Humble had already drilled a well on adjacent land, owned by another of the O'Connor clan—D. M. O'Connor; and now they were deeply interested in the progress of the Quintana drillings. Roy was confident they would strike a vast oil reserve.

On the day the drillers expected to test the oil sand, all of Quintana was on hand—Roy, Holmes, Ike Arnold, young Roy directing the drilling operations from the slushy derrick platform; and with them were Chad Nelms and O'Connor himself. It was a tense afternoon. Roy examined the samples as the drill went down.

"There's a mile-deep pool of oil down there," he told O'Connor. "This will be one of the biggest oil fields ever discovered."

Chad Nelms called Roy aside. He explained that he had not made a stake yet in the oil business, and he needed some sure money.

"If you think a good well is sure to come in, I'll sell you back part of my royalty," he said.

Cullen looked at the young man.

"I'll give you twenty-five thousand for an eighth of your share, Chad—but I think you're making a hell of a mistake!"

Young Nelms considered this.

"You got about forty minutes to think about it," Roy said. "And you'd better think hard."

"I've thought hard," Nelms said. "If you'll pay me twenty-five thousand for an eighth of my share, it's a deal. I want to sell—for better or for worse."

They shook hands; and twenty minutes later the well came in with a rush of pure pipe-line oil. Roy Cullen's prophecy had held true; and the first of the great O'Connor wells was in production.

On the way back to Houston, Cullen rode in the Nelms car. Nelms tried to conceal his disappointment, and finally Roy laughed, and put his arm across the younger man's shoulder.

"You feel pretty bad about that deal, don't you, Chad?"

Nelms grinned rather ruefully.

"Not too bad," he said.

Roy slapped him on the back. "Forget about it, Chad—call it off! Just figure nothing was said about it."

Nelms slowly shook his head.

"Mr. Cullen, you've risked your judgment on almost every well you've drilled. I risked mine—and I was wrong, that's all. If the drill had gone into salt water sand, you'd have paid me twenty-five thousand dollars just the same. It's a big well —and it's your royalty."

Roy put his big arm around young Nelms' shoulder.

"I'd rather call it off," he said. "But you've shown fine character, Chad—and that's more important than all the oil wells in Texas."

How close Chad Nelms came to winning a bet was revealed in subsequent exploratory drilling. The place where Roy Cullen had drilled the "O'Connor A-1," as the discovery well was called, was on the brink of the oil pool, and a few yards further and it would have been a dry hole.

However, Roy Cullen's uncanny sense of where to dig for oil had held true once more; and within a short time the great O'Connor Ranch became known as "the billion-dollar oll field." Wells were drilled back toward the center of the producing area, until the flat prairies that once had been dotted with longhorn cattle now bristled with a cluster of derricks that soon began to look like a forest.

It was the "wildcatter's dream" that Roy Cullen and every other oil prospector in Texas had hunted from one end of Texas to the other. Hundreds of wells were drilled, and with the output "choked off" by valves—which is the way scientific oil production controls the flow and prevents draining off the top of the oil pool and losing the force of underground pressure—the wells would continue to pour out oil for a hundred years.

Roy Cullen's name had become famous in the oil fields after he struck oil at Blue Ridge and Babb's Ridge; but now it was a legend.

He could have retired on his laurels—not only as "King of the Wildcatters," but as one of the world's richest men—but the word "retire" apparently was not in the Cullen vocabulary. He went to Tom O'Connor and asked him if he would lease an adjoining block of land. O'Connor, who had doubled his wealth almost overnight, readily agreed. Roy kept on acquiring leases until he had eleven separate tracts on the O'Connor field.

As rich as the first O'Connor field was, it was only a fraction of the oil produced in later developments. And through it all the fable of "Cullen luck" continued to grow. On one tract, Roy measured off five miles from the border that joined the new lease with his old field, and at a point just inside a fence which cut across the range, and said:

"We'll drill here."

The well came in, and he worked back along the five-mile strip, bringing in gusher after gusher. A hundred yards beyond his first well, another oil company drilled, and got a dry hole.

CHAPTER 16

"I've got to help them learn the things they have to know"

QUINTANA PETROLEUM had set up offices in the Sterling Building—the same building that had housed Cullen & West. Young Roy and Ike Arnold by now were solid cornerstones in the establishment, Roy as vice-president in charge of field operations and Arnold as chief engineer. The firm now had operations stretching from Houston beyond San Antonio, and new explorations were going on farther west, on the rocky lands Roy Cullen had traveled over when he was hunting oil leases for Jim Cheek.

Lillie had often asked Roy to retire, or at least to leave the bulk of the burden of managing the company to the younger members of the family.

"It's pretty dangerous in those oil fields, Roy," she said to him. "Every time I hear of somebody getting hurt—I think you may be the next one."

Roy smiled gently, but again shook his head.

"Nobody can stand still, Lillie," he said. "You've got to move forward or go back. Sonny is coming along fine—I've got him in charge of all our field operations now, and he's learned the business from the bottom up. One of these days maybe we can sit back and rest . . . and I'll look at you and think: 'What a fine lot of children you've brought into this world, Lillie, and raised to be good men and women!' But right now they've got a few more things to learn, and I've got to help them learn the things they have to know—so they can carry on the way they should."

The Cullen family had grown up in two layers—first Roy Gustave, Lillie Cranz, and Agnes Louise; and then the two younger girls, Margaret and Wilhelmina. By the middle 1930's young Roy also had a growing family, with three children—Roy Henry, Cornelia Agnes, and Harry Holmes Cullen. Agnes and Ike Arnold had been married in 1931; and Lillie Cranz, the oldest daughter, was now Mrs. Paul Portanova, living in Los Angeles. Margaret had entered Kinkaid School in Houston; and Wilhelmina was still in grade school.

Young Roy had not only developed a thoroughly competent knowledge of the technical side of oil production; he also had invented several pieces of oil-well equipment, including a pump for light gravity oil—one of the bugbears of oil production. He had worked out a method of combining the valves of a "Christmas tree" into a single cast-iron block which would control pressure up to 20,000 pounds per square inch.

Roy was proud of his only son. He had followed young Roy's interest in scientific work with keen attention, and had watched him work his way up through the oil business, from a field "roughneck," or derrick hand, to chief of field operations.

Young Roy absorbed responsibilities as rapidly as they were offered. He directed the drilling of the second well—the "O'Connor A-2"—on the Tom O'Connor field; and the following year, in 1935, when his father was away on a trip through Europe with Lillie and the two younger girls, he assumed active charge of the Quintana field operations.

By 1936, the Tom O'Connor field was going full blast, its great cluster of derricks pouring out thousands of barrels of oil daily into the vast flood of Texas' oil production, and the company began to extend its interest into Western and Southwestern Texas.

Young Roy went down to the southern tip of the state to supervise emergency drilling operations at a field near Edinburg, where the drilling pipe had "frozen" in the well. The derrick and rig used for the drilling was not Quintana equipment; it had been rented from another drilling company for the operation, and was built on a wooden base, with an iron pipe clamped to the derrick legs for bracing.

"Be careful about that rig, Sonny," his father had told him before he left. "It's not as solid as our rigs."

The young man nodded. "I'll be careful, Dad—and I'll be back in a few days."

It was in May, and young Roy drove alone in his car to Edinburg—a trip of more than four hundred miles. When he arrived at the field, the drill crew was trying to work the pipe loose by lifting and turning the pipe.

The well was then down to about seven thousand feet, and the pipe—more than a mile and a quarter in length—was being stretched like an elastic hose in an effort to dislodge it from the walls of the well, where it was frozen fast.

Young Roy immediately went on the derrick, where the driller, Chester Kraft, was trying to free the pipe. The derrick was trembling under the tremendous pressure of the machine which was drawing the pipe from the top, stretching it several feet every time the pressure was exerted. Each time Kraft pulled the lever, lifting the upper end of the pipe, a pressure gauge indicated the extent of power applied, and young Roy checked this carefully.

The "junk pusher" of the drilling crew was a young man named Johnny Warren. His job was to provide the pipes and other equipment needed for drilling, and he was usually a privileged man in the oil field drilling crews. He kept in touch with the head office, as a sort of unofficial liaison man between office and field crew.

Johnny Warren had been called to the telephone by the Houston office, shortly after young Roy arrived at the field, and when he returned to the well he said to young Roy:

"Your dad says you are to come down off that derrick, Roy. He says it's an old rig and he doesn't want you to take any chances."

At each successive pull of the lifting device, the pipe seemed to have stretched a few inches further, indicating the lower end might be slipping from the frozen grip of the well walls. Actually, the derrick floor was sinking into the mud under the terrific pressure.

Young Roy shouted "Okay! I'm coming down!" above the clanking din of the well machinery. He checked the pressure indicator again, and then turned to Kraft:

"I think she's coming loose, Cheety. Pull her wide open."

Kraft pulled the throttle open, and the derrick seemed to vibrate from top to bottom, trembling under the tremendous power being exerted to draw the pipe free.

There was a sudden shudder, and one of the bracings on the legs of the derrick snapped loose. Young Roy shouted:

"Look out, Cheety—she's coming down!"

The driller turned to jump and at that instant the big derrick began to crumple and collapse. A length of hose, torn from its connection, snapped around and flung Kraft clear off the derrick.

The tangle of twisted steel and wood crashed down upon young Roy. Several of the drilling crew, who had dashed for safety at the first sign that the derrick was coming down, ran back and found him pinned under the wreckage. A piece of the bracing pipe, which had snapped off as the derrick collapsed, apparently had struck him on the head. He was unconscious when he was pulled from the wooden platform.

He was rushed to a hospital at Edinburg, and a phone call was immediately placed to Houston. Roy Cullen, with Lillie beside him, started out within the hour on the four hundred-mile trip to Edinburg, driving his own car.

By the time he arrived in Edinburg, the doctors in attendance had decided young Roy's leg would have to be amputated; it had been crushed by a falling beam and the operation was necessary if his life was to be saved. The surgery was performed, and young Roy seemed to rally.

Two days later, his father put a call through to his office in Houston.

"The operation on Sonny's leg was successful," he told Ike Arnold. "It looks now as if he'll pull through."

Two hours later another message came from the hospital. Young Roy had died, without fully regaining consciousness.

The tragic death left a deep imprint of sadness at the Cullen home on River Oaks Boulevard. Margaret and Wilhelmina were at home during the summer; but in the fall when they left for school, Roy and Lillie were alone in the big mansion with its white-and-black marble foyer, its spacious halls and wide lawns.

To all who knew them, the terrible tragedy of their only son's death seemed all the more tragic because it had been so unnecessary. Young Roy had chosen to go into the field when he could have remained in the office, holding down an easier job in his father's vast domain. But he had the same mould of character that his father possessed; he had refused to remain inactive or avoid the responsibilities of life for which his native ability fitted him.

Roy Cullen's deep pride in his son's character had a full measure of vindication in the manner in which he died; and yet no amount of pride could absorb the shock and hurt caused by the loss. His rugged face became a mask of his emotions; and he seemed to many of his friends to have withdrawn into a hard shell of reserve. Only Lillie understood the deep pain which the passing of his only son had brought to him . . . a pain which she shared with the gentle kindness which had been the bond between them for half a lifetime.

It was several months after the tragedy at Edinburg that a tall, graying man wearing rimless spectacles, with the gentle, earnest countenance of a scholar, came into Roy Cullen's private office at Quintana. With him was John T. Scott, chairman of the First National Bank of Houston. Scott had telephoned Roy that he wanted to see him on "an important matter."

He introduced the man—Dr. E. E. Oberholzer, formerly head of Houston's public school system and the founder of Houston's only public "institution of higher learning." It had been known as Houston Junior College until two years before, when Dr. Oberholzer had succeeded in having it raised to the status of a "University."

"Brother Cullen," Scott said, looking at Roy over the tops of his glasses, "I want you to meet a man who needs some help."

Roy Cullen grinned at the banker. Scott always called him

"Brother Cullen." Then he looked at the man who "needed help" for several seconds. Roy was then deeply engrossed in the coming Presidential election, in which Governor Alf M. Landon of Kansas was running against President Roosevelt; and he had little time for any activity outside of the business of Quintana and the national elections.

He had already written to Governor Landon, assuring him that he could expect the support of Texas Republicans equal to that given Herbert Hoover in 1928; and Governor Landon had replied expressing "deep appreciation for the many kind things you have said," adding: "I hope you will keep in touch with me and give me your suggestions on the campaign in Texas and elsewhere."

Even in the midst of his personal grief, Roy Cullen had taken time to wire Landon shortly after he was nominated:

> All worthy Americans feel that you represent something bigger than a political party and that you will stand for and work for freedom and justice and . . . will help to save for these United States the form of government known to our forefathers.

In the midst of this preoccupation, he took the time to listen to John Scott's plea in behalf of Dr. Oberholzer. The Houston educator was planning a campaign to raise money to enlarge the embryo University of Houston until it would have full university stature and be accredited with the Association of Southern Colleges and Universities.

Dr. Oberholzer spent only a few minutes with Cullen at this time; but he left with the oil man's promise that he would listen to Dr. Oberholzer at greater length after the election campaign.

"I'm putting in most of my time trying to beat Roosevelt," he said, chewing impatiently on his cigar.

"We've got to have a campus and some buildings," Dr.

Oberholzer said. "Mr. Scott said you were a nice fellow to know—and we need the help of some businessmen to get them."

"I'll have to think it over," Cullen said. "Come back some time later, and we'll talk about it."

On the way out of the office, Dr. Oberholzer asked Scott what he thought Cullen might contribute to the fund.

"Probably twenty-five thousand," the banker said. "Maybe more."

It was several weeks later that Dr. Oberholzer came back. This time he was accompanied by Dr. W. W. Kemmerer, Assistant President of the new University. Governor Landon had lost the election by the most lop-sided vote in the history of the Republican party; and Roy Cullen now had lots of time to talk on this occasion.

He fished a cigar from his desk drawer, bit off the end, lighted it and leaned back in his chair.

"Tell me about this University," he said. "Will it provide education for all the young folks—kids whose fathers have to work for a living? I don't know much about colleges—I quit when I was in the fifth grade and went to work. My son, Roy—" he paused, as he always did when the name of his son was mentioned. "Roy quit Rice just before he was ready to graduate, and went to work—so he never got a degree."

Dr. Oberholzer's eyes lightened up.

"That's exactly what we are planning, Mr. Cullen. The main thing we want to do is provide educational opportunity for young people who don't have the money to go off to college—the sons and daughters of working people. And we want to offer an opportunity for working people themselves, who can attend classes in the evening and get vocational and technical training, as well as study academic and cultural subjects."

Roy nodded.

"That's the kind of college I'd like to help," he said.

Dr. Kemmerer produced preliminary plans for the first building—to cost about $150,000. He explained that they were preparing a brochure outlining the plans for the University.

"I'd like to have you look at it when it's ready," he said.

"I'd like to see it," Cullen said.

That was the extent of the second meeting. But Dr. Oberholzer and Dr. Kemmerer went to work on the brochure, and before it was ready for final printing they sent an advance copy to Cullen.

After giving the brochure a chance to sink in, Dr. Oberholzer made his third trip to see Roy Cullen. This time Scott came back with him. During the interval between his second and third visits, a good deal had been done to further the campaign: Two grants of land had been obtained from Julius Settegast and Ben Taub providing one hundred ten acres of land upon which to build the University.

However, the campaign for funds had been progressing rather slowly. Scott broached the matter they had come to discuss.

"Brother Cullen, we need somebody to serve as general chairman of our finance committee to raise funds for the new University—and we think you're just the man for the job."

Roy listened while they explained the progress made thus far.

"It's just a nominal job," Scott said. "Not much work to it."

Cullen agreed; but he soon found that the "nominal job" entailed more personal attention than his oil wells.

He called up his friends and associates, and enlisted their aid. And meanwhile in his mind there was the germ of an idea: More than a half-century before, a western railroad builder, Senator Leland Stanford of California, had lost a son; and he had said: "The children of California shall be my children!" The result had been Stanford University, one of the great educational institutions of the country.

Roy Cullen had investigated the background of the University of Houston. Years ago a group of educators in Houston had formed Houston Junior College, mainly for the purpose of providing educational opportunities for students who could not afford to leave Houston for their college work—and who were not eligible to enter Rice University, then the only other institution of higher learning in Houston.

A degree at Rice had not been enough to prevent young Roy Cullen from quitting school to go to work. He had gone into the oil fields to work—when he might have stayed in college . . . And his father began to think that the most fitting thing he could do as a tribute to the memory of his only son was to help provide education for young men and women who had no choice, who could not afford to leave Houston to go to college.

Houston Junior College had been the University of Houston for nearly three years; but it still had no home, and classes were held in temporary buildings erected on the grounds of San Jacinto High School.

Roy Cullen decided that a permanent home for this University was something worth working for. With characteristic energy, he plunged into the task of organizing the fund-raising campaign. But before the campaign was fairly under way, he had already settled the future of the new University. It was going to have a home—if he had to build it himself!

The deeds to the lands given by Settegast and Taub required that buildings be started by January 1, 1938; but Roy called up Julius Settegast and Ben Taub and assured them the building would be started. At a dinner given for the two hundred members of the fund-raising committee, Colonel Joseph W. Evans, an old friend from his early days in the cotton business, was toastmaster.

He introduced Roy, as chairman; and then Lillie Cullen, who was with him at the dinner. And then he announced that Roy and Lillie Cullen had donated the entire sum needed for the first University of Houston building.

The announcement of the gift—the largest endowment to education in Houston since William Marsh Rice had endowed Rice Institute nearly a half-century before—brought tumultuous applause; and then Colonel Evans added that the building would be in the nature of a memorial.

"It will be the Roy Gustave Cullen Memorial Building," he said.

Roy Cullen arose, his eyes wet and his voice choked with emotion, and handed Colonel Evans a check for $260,000.

"There is only one condition to this contribution," he said. "The University of Houston must always be a college for working men and women and their sons and daughters. If it were to be another rich man's college, I wouldn't be interested."

ROY GUSTAV CULLEN
MEMORIAL

CHAPTER 17

"There can be no compromise with a threat to our freedom"

THE GIFT of more than a quarter of a million dollars to the University of Houston—large as it was—had far more far-reaching and beneficial effects than the size of the donation itself. It kindled a spark in Roy Cullen's mind. He had given little thought to educational institutions since he quit school at the age of twelve—except to make out checks covering the expenses of his children's schooling. But now he became acutely aware of the philosophy of his grandfather, Ezekiel Cullen, who had declared to the Third Congress of Texas, six years before its admission to the Union:

"Intelligence is the only true aristocracy in a Government like ours; and the improved and educated mind has and will ever triumph over the ignorant and uneducated mind."

He listened to Dr. Oberholzer, at a meeting of campaign workers for the University Fund, declare with calm and reasoned persuasion:

"There are thirty thousand young people here who would like to return to school. The University will afford them new hope. Its doors will be closed to none. It is a community service college. Those without a high-school diploma will be welcomed as well as those with a diploma . . ."

This was grist for Roy Cullen's emotional mill. He turned his energy and decision—which had carried him through oil and cotton businesses, and in politics—toward the accomplishment of something that he now felt was as truly necessary to the greatness of Houston as the Ship Channel had been a quarter of a century before.

Roy Cullen had the knack of driving a logical point into the track-bed of his own experiences, the way a railroad spike is driven into a tie. He remembered a few years before when he had rammed his drilling bit through the "heaving shale" at the Humble field, and the University of Pittsburgh had awarded him a degree for this conquest of one of the most troublesome obstacles in oil-well drilling. Roy had talked at that time with Dr. John G. Bowman, the president of the University. Later Dr. Bowman had visited the Cullen home in Houston. Roy had learned from him how the University of Pittsburgh was built by the donations of the people of that city, who raised more than twelve million dollars to build it.

"Are the people of Houston going to admit that the people of Pittsburgh are more civic-minded, more patriotic, with more love of education, music and art than the people of Houston?" he asked.

He answered the question himself.

He knew that many of the men who had made fortunes in oil in Texas had started as poor boys—just as he had. These men intended to use their fortunes for the betterment of Houston and the state of Texas . . . and he could see no reason why they should not begin their "betterment" while they were still living.

"Suppose William Marsh Rice, the founder of Rice Institute, or George Hermann, who gave Hermann Hospital and Hermann Park to Houston, could look back from the world beyond and could live their lives over," he said. "Do you suppose they would wait until the end to do their great work of giving? Or would they start giving a little sooner—so they could see the sunshine and light of their own creations?"

This philosophy of philanthropy was new; yet it sank deeply into the hearts of many men in Houston, who had amassed fortunes—and who intended some day to leave part of their estate to welfare institutions. With Roy Cullen sounding the tocsin, money began to pour into the coffers of the new University.

The next goal set by the committee raising funds for the University was a million dollars—and Roy "opened the pot" by increasing his original gift from $260,000 to $345,000. He brought into his fund-raising team names that were later to be famous in Houston and Texas: Neal Pickett and Judge Roy Hofheinz, both of whom became mayor of Houston; Oveta Culp Hobby, wife of the former Governor of Texas—who became the founder of the Women's Army Corps during World War II and later national Secretary for Education and Public Welfare in the administration of President Eisenhower.

The campaign was a roaring success. While it was going on, ground was broken for the Roy Gustave Cullen Memorial Building to house the College of Liberal Arts of the new University. Roy held an umbrella over Lillie's head during a driving rain, while she lifted the first spadeful of earth for the new building.

Roy stood in the blue gumbo mud oozing over his shoes—as it had many times when he was slogging through muddy oil fields—and shoveled as the rain poured down, dripping from his shaggy black hair.

That year the first class was graduated from the University—one hundred and seventy-four students, completing a full year's curriculum of work for an accredited bachelor's degree. Roy, proud and beaming, was the baccalaureate speaker . . . And by this time his mind was filled with a memory that had long been dormant: the memory of things his mother had told him, back in the San Antonio days, about Grandfather Ezekiel Cullen, who became the "Founder of the Texas School System."

Ezekiel Cullen had become chairman of the Committee on Education of the Congress of Texas back in the first days of the Republic of Texas; and he had formulated the policy which President Lamar expressed in his inaugural speech: "It is admitted by all that the cultivated mind is the guardian of democracy; and while guided and controlled by virtue, the noblest attribute of man. It is the only dictator free men acknowledge, and the only security free men desire . . ."

Ezekiel Cullen had written in his first report to the Congress on January 4, 1839:

> Your Committee views it as one of the first and paramount duties of the Congress to provide a system of general education . . . and we should lay the foundation while it is in our power, making suitable appropriation of the public domain . . . to establish primary schools and colleges. Nothing is so essential to free government as the general diffusion of knowledge and intelligence of every kind. It is the foundation of civil liberty, and constitutes our national strength and glory.

A hundred years later, almost to the day, the first Cullen building was dedicated on the campus of the new University of Houston; and within the year plans were started for the huge central building of the new campus—the Ezekiel Cullen

Memorial Building, to cost more than five million dollars, and the outright gift of the Cullen Foundation.

Meanwhile, the Cullen oil domain, under the banner of Quintana Petroleum, was extending its borders and bringing in new sources of oil wealth—a great part of which was being immediately siphoned off into the educational project upon which Roy Cullen had embarked.

In 1940, Chad Nelms, who had arranged the original meeting between Roy Cullen and Tom O'Connor, went to Fort Worth to talk with the owners of the big Washburn Ranch, west of San Antonio. There had been a good deal of oil prospecting on the vast, rolling lands which comprised this ranch—one of the largest in Texas. One of the foremost geological survey companies in Texas, the De Golyer firm of Dallas, had surveyed the area, and reported there was no indication of oil.

Then Roy sent Nelms to Fort Worth to talk with John Pearson, one of the owners of the Washburn Ranch.

"I represent H. R. Cullen of Houston," Nelms announced.

"Never heard of him," Pearson said.

Nelms was startled. He pointed out that Roy Cullen was one of the biggest independent oil operators in the country.

"Good for him," Pearson said. "I still don't know him—but I'll tell you what I'll do. I'll call Randolph Bryan in Houston. If he says you and Cullen are okay, we may make a deal."

He phoned Bryan.

"A man in my office says he's Chad Nelms, and he represents H. R. Cullen of Houston. Do you know them?"

"Is he a bald fellow, with a little moustache?"

"That's the man," said Pearson.

"Let him have anything he or Mr. Cullen wants," Bryan

said. The result was a lease on 30,000 acres of land, which later was increased to more than 100,000 acres on the Washburn Ranch in La Salle County, which was to become one of Quintana's most important oil fields.

After the deal was closed for the Washburn lease, the location for the first drilling was made, based on logs and maps showing forty-six test holes which the Sun Oil Company had drilled on the property. A short time later Roy Cullen attended a cocktail party and dinner at the Rice Hotel, at which a number of prominent Texas oil men were present.

The oil men began to talk about the new Cullen lease on the Washburn Ranch, and Lee Blaffer, of the Humble Company—which had been Roy's partner on many oil deals—laughed at Cullen.

"That's the graveyard of Texas," he said. "You're a hundred miles from oil down there—everybody has prospected it and given it up."

Cullen looked at Blaffer a minute, then he said:

"Lee, I'll bet fifty thousand dollars I'll get a producing oil well on the first well I drill on that land."

William C. Potter, Chairman of the Board of the Guarantee Trust Company of New York, was in the group.

"I'm Cullen's banker," he said, "and the fifty thousand dollars is up. Do any of you boys want to cover?"

Jim Abercrombie, one of the wealthiest oil men in Texas, had his hand in his pocket, but he pulled it out empty. Nobody covered the bet; and shortly afterwards the first well on the Washburn field drilled by Quintana brought in oil—and the next three were dry holes!

Roy sent a seismograph crew to "shoot" the property, and a fault was discovered to the south of the earlier drillings. He decided to sink a well in this area, where he felt the oil pools might lie. The first well at the new location came in with oil, and thirty more wells were drilled in the same area, all producing oil.

Roy Cullen had now emerged as one of the leading independent producers in Texas, and was spreading his network of producing wells throughout the state and into neighboring Colorado and Wyoming.

His drillers had worked over most of the old fields in the neighborhood of Houston—Pierce Junction, Blue Ridge, Damon's Mound, the Humble field, and Thompson. Now Quintana, fully organized, was developing new major oil fields.

There were many reasons offered by men wise in the ways of the oil business to account for the phenomenal success of Roy Cullen and Quintana. He had always adhered to two basic principles: "Flank the old domes—and drill deeper!"

Drilling deeper was almost a religion with him. In the 1940's, Joe Redding, one of Quintana's drilling contractors, telephoned Cullen one day from a small store near a drilling rig, explaining that they had gone down about as far as he thought advisable.

Then he held the receiver to his ear and listened. After about five minutes, he said, "Okay, Mr. Cullen," and hung up. Then he turned to Lynn Meador, who had been standing beside him:

"When they say the last rites over Mr. Cullen, and get ready to lower him into the ground, I'll bet he'll look over the side of the casket and say, 'Better dig a little deeper, boys!' "

Roy Cullen's faith in "flanking the old domes" and "drilling deeper" had brought in Pierce Junction and Blue Ridge and Humble after they had been worked out by other drillers; and it was the same persistent courage to "drill deeper" that drove through the "heaving shale" at the Humble field and brought in wells where all other drillers had abandoned the field.

As his years rounded the half-century point—which he reached in 1931—Roy Cullen's philosophy of "drilling deeper" had begun to communicate itself to his political and cultural life. The rugged axiom that he had learned early in life—"don't try to out-trade anyone, and don't let anyone out-trade you"—had mellowed into a mature sense of public responsibility during the years he had struggled for a foothold in Houston.

And now, in his baccalaureate address to the first full graduating class of the University of Houston, he was able to put his philosophy into words.

> . . . Use carefully and accurately the senses God gave you, and you can make them of great value in your life work . . . I sometimes believe that we underestimate our capacity for endurance. Most men and women give up after one try; whereas, by all the rules of the game, they are entitled to a hundred trials . . . If you will learn, when adversity floors you, to start climbing again, there is no height on the ladder of success beyond your reach.

And at the close of his speech he said:

> There is as much honor in being a successful farmer or mechanic as there is in being a successful lawyer, or doctor, or financier, or statesman . . . The station of life does not make the man; on the contrary, it is the man who must make the station . . .

The wealth that had poured up out of the ground had become a sacred trust to Roy Cullen. In a speech at San Antonio in March, 1941, at the annual Oil Men's Jubilee, one of his old friends who had gone to school with Roy and the Beck boys in San Antonio—John Boyle—turned to Roy Cullen, his eyes brimming with tears, and said:

"You have become one of the greatest men in Texas . . .

Roy Cullen!" And then, turning to the other oil men: "Mr. Cullen has discovered more oil fields and contributed more to the material growth of this state than any other citizen within its borders. Many others in this land of great wealth and natural resources have accumulated wealth; but few have recognized—as Roy Cullen has—that this wealth is a trust, to be administered for the well-being of our fellow-men."

Roy Cullen's interest in his fellow-man was not confined to the boundaries of Texas, however. His voice had already been heard—among bankers and politicians—during the decade since he had first opposed the election of Roosevelt in 1932; and now as the fires of war were kindled on the world's horizons, the old fears that he had felt before the Roosevelt election began to stir again in his mind.

His youngest daughter, Wilhelmina, was a student at Sweet Briar College in Virginia; and Roy Cullen was asked by Mrs. Carter Glass, the president of the college, to address the students at their graduating exercises. He was then nearing sixty—a solidly built man, his raven black hair now streaked with iron gray; and the rugged mask of his deeply lined face had grown more gentle with the years.

> Education and my business—the oil business—have one thing in common. If they are to be of the greatest service to the most people, both must remain free . . . Do not misunderstand me. I am not opposed to proper regulation. There are those in all industry who need regulation. But it should be regulation of a free enterprise, in which politics should play no part. We are in a fight to defend Democracy. Let us not lose Democracy, in defending it. . . .

A few weeks later, in another address to the graduating students of the South Texas School of Law and Commerce, he said:

"A government of bureaus leads to national socialism . . . There can be no compromise with any threat to our freedom."

His growing distrust of politicians, coupled with his fear that war hysteria might plunge the nation into a virtual eclipse of its traditional concepts of freedom, persuaded him that some voice must be heard in the wilderness of war alarms and "home-front" scares.

And—at the start—it was a voice in the wilderness. Few people heard the warnings of the rugged Texas wildcatter; and except for those who knew him, his warnings were passed off as a natural complaint of a representative of the "Texas oil hierarchy." Why shouldn't an oil man, who had found millions of dollars in natural wealth, object to rigorous government controls?

Roy Cullen's attack was not against "government control," however. Like most oil operators, he recognized the need for industrial regulation . . . but not control that destroyed the right of private ownership.

In a message to the graduating class of Kinkaid School for Girls in Houston, where two Cullen girls had graduated, he addressed a challenge to the people of Texas:

> Are we about to lose our Bill of Rights? Are we about to lose our state rights? . . . We have had a so-called list of "must" legislation—and emergency after emergency—until we have formed the "emergency habit." Each new emergency calls for new bureaus, and these bureaus are usurping the powers of the courts. All the power and authority over our people is being concentrated in the national government-by-bureaus . . .

The country as a whole was paying little heed to those who were alarmed at the trend of "emergency laws" and "defense measures."

When war finally came, with the Japanese attack on Pearl Harbor, Roy Cullen turned his energies toward the support of civil defense and the rise of America's "air power." Frank Hawks had aroused his interest in an "Air Youth" movement before Hawks was killed in a plane crash in 1938; and now the oil man began to apply his efforts toward the development of this movement.

He helped organize a model airplane show to stimulate the "Air Youth" movement; and when someone suggested that Houston form an "Air Scout" troop, Roy Cullen put both money and energy into organizing a city-wide group of "Air Scouts"—the first in the country.

He stood beaming in front of thousands of cheering boys, and told them:

"It is necessary for our national defense that our young people become air-minded, and I am happy to see Houston leading the nation."

His energy was tireless; and as the flames of war roared across the Pacific, his activities increased. A campaign was launched to raise $36,000,000 in war bonds to build another cruiser *Houston,* after the city's namesake was sunk. Roy was on a trip to Florida when he telephoned Randolph Bryan, the same Houston banker who had told John Pearson of the Washburn Ranch to "let Roy Cullen have anything he wants —he's good for it."

"How is the bond drive coming along?" Roy asked.

"Not so hot," Bryan said.

"I'll tell you what I'll do," the oil man said. "You lend me a million dollars and I'll buy another million dollars' worth of bonds."

Bryan agreed. The bond drive took a spurt and went over the top.

Roy's interests did not stop with fund drives. Back in 1933

he had contributed a few thousand dollars to help the struggling Houston Symphony Orchestra, which was sinking financially with the depression. As a result, he had accepted several honorary positions and in 1942 he found himself President of the Symphony Society of Houston.

He announced that the Symphony Orchestra would get "in tune with the times" by playing martial music, entertaining servicemen and assisting in the sale of war bonds by public concerts. The idea caught on in Houston; and the Houston Symphony Orchestra, its transportation financed largely by Roy Cullen, traveled throughout Texas, staging concerts at Army camps.

His deep interest in the early development of character in young people led him to combine his wartime efforts in behalf of the Houston Symphony Orchestra with a "Wartime Youth Council" in a campaign to reduce juvenile delinquency by exposing the youth of the city to good music.

"I haven't the remotest idea that music can stop juvenile delinquency," he said. "But I am firmly convinced that music is the universal language of all mankind, and a medium for reaching every cross-section of the community."

He urged the churches of Houston to use their influence to bring underprivileged boys and girls of Houston into the concert hall as part of the drive to reduce juvenile delinquency.

The activities of the Symphony Orchestra in the war effort soared to a new high in sheer novelty when Houston's sporting fraternity persuaded the Symphony Society to sponsor a weird wrestling match, combining music and mayhem. "Wild Bill" Longson, then the world's wrestling champion, was matched with Louis Thesz, his leading challenger, in a title match in which they wrestled to the dulcet strains of the

Houston Symphony Orchestra, at which admission was paid in the purchase of war bonds.

Roy was dubious when the proposition was presented to him, as President of the Symphony Society, by the sports writers of the Houston newspapers; but he finally grinned, and agreed.

"War is war," he said. "Let's try it."

CHAPTER 18

"The people of Texas do not want a dictator!"

DURING THE first half of his life, Roy Cullen had been an independent voter, supporting men rather than parties. But in 1928 he made a complete break with the Democrats, traditional party of the South, and voted for Herbert Hoover . . . "I had two reasons—both of them good," he explained. "I admired Hoover, and I didn't admire Tammany Hall."

He was in Houston when the Democratic Convention nominated Governor Al Smith of New York in 1928, but he did not even look in on the convention—the most spectacular political event in Houston since the Bailey-Johnson debates.

Except for his one-man campaign against Franklin D. Roosevelt in Texas in 1932, and a few sporadic forays into Texas politics, Roy Cullen was merely a protagonist of "free enterprise and states' rights" in national politics—until Roosevelt's third term drew toward an end. Then the storm warnings went up.

He had helped elect W. Lee O'Daniel Governor of Texas in 1940 when the ex-flour salesman launched his political career; but this was not so much in deference to the O'Daniel personality, which Roy Cullen did not particularly endorse, but because "Pappy" O'Daniel had denounced "New Deal Socialism" and Roy Cullen was heartily in favor of any "voices in the wilderness" that would warn the nation against the incipient dangers of "government-by-bureaus."

In the 1940 national campaign for President, he methodically threw his support to Wendell L. Willkie as "the only man who can unseat the New Deal . . . and whom honest, God-fearing Democrats can elect in November!" He had not expected Willkie to win, and his judgment was vindicated. Roy Cullen had not regarded Willkie as a real representative of Republican opposition to the New Deal, but he was sure no other Republican candidate would have a chance against President Roosevelt, and he had supported him, personally and financially, as he had Governor Landon of Kansas four years before.

It was at the close of Roosevelt's third term that Roy Cullen—by now fully groomed in the art of political protagonism—decided the time had come for believers in traditional American "free enterprise" to make a determined stand.

The war had dominated the preliminary skirmishes of the candidates—President Roosevelt carrying into the campaign the banner of the incumbent war President, bearing the familiar legend: "Don't change horses in mid-stream!"

The term "rugged individualist" had been battered into disrepute by the regimentalists of the New Deal. Born and nurtured in a century of individualism, which had been the deep pride of Americans, it had become anathema. And yet no man lived during these years who bore more indelibly the stamp of the "rugged individualism" of America than Hugh Roy Cullen.

He had become a free agent when he was a boy in San Antonio; he had fought to maintain that freedom as a young man, hardly out of his teens, when he tackled the rough cotton traders of South Texas and Western Oklahoma. He had pulled up stakes in Oklahoma and taken his family to Houston because he believed in himself . . . and he had driven himself through two decades of hard, uncompromising work to win his position in the world.

And he now saw in the "welfare state" of Franklin Roosevelt a kind of "creeping socialism" that he believed would inevitably corrode and destroy the rugged qualities of initiative and free enterprise that had made America a great nation, if it were allowed to develop in the fallow soil of New Deal intellectualism.

In 1942, when he was in Washington, he had read a speech of President Roosevelt calling for greater executive powers of the President, made in an address to the Congress on Labor Day. Again utilizing the political fighting tricks he had learned in the Harbor Board fight in Houston, he bought a page ad in the Washington *Times-Herald,* quoting the critical comments of Senator Robert A. Taft on the President's speech.

> "A deliberate effort to discredit and nullify Congress . . . to induce the American people to accept the rule of a man-on-horseback—a dictator!" That is how Senator Taft yesterday characterized the President's Labor Day message to Congress and to the people!

He wound up with a typical Texas challenge to the members of Congress:

> The people of Texas do not want a dictator . . . And if you fail to pass proper laws to control a possible dictatorship—while

our brave boys are fighting to preserve democracy—then you should resign at once and permit patriotic men to take your place, so that our children may enjoy the blessings of freedom!

He mailed copies of the ad to the members of Congress with a note saying:

"The people of Texas have not had time to contact you on this serious matter; that is the reason I am using this unusual way of telling you our feelings."

Roy Cullen returned to Houston convinced more than ever that the United States faced as great an internal threat against its liberties, in the form of the thinly disguised political totalitarianism of the New Deal, as it did in the military threat of Germany and Japan.

He had advocated Wendell Willkie's candidacy in 1940, believing he was the only hope of the Republican party; but by the fall of 1943, when the Republican standard-bearer roared back into the field on the wings of "World Union," he wrote Willkie:

> In none of (your) planks have you proposed to liquidate the bureaucratic form of government we are now living under and return to the democratic form of government . . . In none have you covered the serious question of inflation . . . You offer nothing to labor, not even fatherly or brotherly advice . . . You do not have a plank covering our foreign policy . . . which would consider the precedent set by Jefferson, Monroe and Madison, whose diplomacy kept us out of war for practically a century . . .

Willkie visited Houston in his pre-election tour of the country, but never met Roy Cullen; and the newspapers picked up the growing feud between them. Willkie had written Cullen warmly acknowledging his campaign contributions for the 1940 elections; and he had sent an autographed copy of his book, *One World.* But now he ignored his erstwhile supporter. His refusal to answer the questions put to him by Roy Cullen dogged his tour, and Cullen poured salt into the wounds by releasing Willkie's letters to the newspapers.

Discouraged with Willkie's political reversal, Roy began to cast about for some new "white hope" to defeat Roosevelt and the New Deal; from the list of available Republicans he began to sift the potential candidates for the Republican nomination. He had hoped that Senator Taft of Ohio would make a good showing, since he regarded him as one of the most able and honest men in Congress. However, the primary returns in the spring of 1944 disillusioned him on the score of Taft's vote-getting ability.

"Taft is the best man we have," he told his friends in Houston. "But he can't win."

He turned his political binoculars on Tom Dewey of New York. Roy Cullen firmly believed that the key to the reversal of the New Deal tide was a sensible and realistic appraisal of the position of labor.

"Labor is the key to a Republican victory this fall," he wrote Dewey in January of 1944. He suggested that instead of regarding labor as an idiot child, to be pandered to if it seemed to behave well, and kicked in the back-side when it appeared to behave badly—labor should be regarded as part of America's economic team. The basic needs of labor should be a part of the Republican platform, as a matter of economic horse sense; and the excessive demands of labor should be rejected, just as the excessive demands of one partner in a business firm would be rejected by the other partners.

This belief in the partnership of labor with business—as an investor and therefore a beneficiary of the profit system—had long been deeply embedded in Roy Cullen's basic philosophy. In 1944, during the early stages of the Presidential campaign, he wrote to Dewey, explaining his plan under which working men would divert part of their wages to investing in the corporations for which they worked.

"The social revolution taking place in this country cannot be stopped until labor assumes a financial as well as moral responsibility," he said. "The only way this can be brought about is for labor to 'sit on the same side of the table' with capital."

He had picked up the germ of this idea in Norway and Sweden, when he visited those countries in the 1930's; working men in these countries had acquired an interest in the industries for which they worked, and Roy believed this relationship accounted for the lack of labor disputes in these countries. As stockholders, with a substantial voting interest, employees could participate with management in setting policies, including fixing wages and salaries.

"This would end the strike menace, which hurts both labor and capital," he pointed out to Dewey. The plan, he felt, would work in two ways: In addition to permitting working men, as stockholders, to have a voice in the fixing of wages, they would also have an interest in seeing to it that their company was not crippled or hamstrung economically by excessive payrolls and other concessions, often extracted by strikes forced on the employees themselves.

"After all," he said, "the chief difference between wage earners and executives in a company is one of degree. The president is an employee of the company, the same as a junior clerk. He seldom owns much stock. Under a system of universal stock ownership it should not take many employees to outvote him."

He suggested that Governor Dewey support this plan, as a means of reviving labor's former adherence to the Republican party, which traditionally had supported high tariffs "which protects the American laboring man."

Years later, Cullen said in a statement warning against proposed tariff reductions: "American labor faces an infinitely worse threat in the free-trade movement than in the evils which some labor leaders seem to see in the Taft-Hartley Law."

Governor Dewey wrote back:

> There is a good deal of merit to the proposal of stock ownership by employees of large corporations. A good many companies have made progress in this direction, but it has never been approached on a mass basis. Either this, or some other profit-sharing system, has always seemed to me to be an ultimate part of sound labor relations in the future.

The New Yorker's reply fell short of what Roy would have regarded as an enthusiastic response; it was neither constructive nor critical. Roy began to feel that Dewey would characteristically fail to take a position on any issue, if he could avoid it. He firmly believed that unless a more capable leader appeared, with vote-getting ability, the Republicans were doomed to another defeat.

Meanwhile, he continued to pepper away at the New Deal. One of his methods of annoying and harassing the New Deal in Texas was the organization of a political "splinter group" known as the "Texas Regulars," which sought to place a ticket at the Texas Democratic Convention at Austin in 1944 in opposition to the Roosevelt forces. The effort was abortive, and failed—as Cullen had predicted it would; but it created such high feeling among the Texas Democrats that several threats were made against Cullen.

A friend warned him: "If you don't stop fighting the New Deal in Texas, Roy, they'll carry you off in a stretcher."

"Let 'em try!" Cullen snapped, chewing furiously on his cigar. "I'll fight 'em harder!"

Roy Cullen had never advocated a third party as a political

faction; but he felt the time had come to raise the threat of a "third party" in the South in order to weld together the Democratic and Republican adherents who believed in "states' rights and freedom from bureaucratic control."

The "Texas Regulars" were formed as a splinter faction to try to force recognition by the Roosevelt-controlled state Democratic party of the fact that an extremely large number of Texas Democrats were not in sympathy with the New Deal-dominated Administration in Washington. They also hoped that a "third-party" drive might conceivably gather enough electoral votes in the South to hold the balance of power in the Electoral College and throw the election into the House of Representatives.

"We're shooting at the moon," Cullen told E. E. Townes, one of the leaders of the "Texas Regulars" movement. "We won't get anywhere—but we may throw a scare into 'em."

By this time Roy Cullen's political philosophy had crystallized into a hard core; he believed the future of America depended on destroying the political power of the New Deal. Although he had no intention of entering the political arena personally, he believed it to be the obligation of every American to take part in the political affairs of the country. He had seen Texas grow . . . in his own lifetime, and—in the memory of men he had known—during the lifetime of his father and grandfather. He had helped in that growth in a very material way; and he felt that the economic and political strength of Texas was being dissipated by politicians . . . and in a similar measure, the strength of the nation.

"The men who made this country great—the men who worked and fought to create a country of free men, with free institutions—have abdicated in favor of politicians," he told a group of the "Texas Regulars." And to Governor

Dewey of New York, the Republican Presidential candidate, and his running mate, Governor Bricker of Ohio, he wired after their nomination:

> Each of you promised the kind of freedom our boys are fighting and dying for . . . But you failed to tell the American people that the Democratic party . . . has become ill with political sickness, the philosophy that the way to create wealth is to destroy wealth . . .

In his fight to carry out the "third-party" threat, Cullen waded into the Democratic strongholds in Harris County, where Houston is located. He made plans to attend the Democratic County Convention—even though he was a Republican—to try to present the "third-party" argument. Word was sent to him that he would be "thrown out of the hall" if he showed up.

He called Captain Frank Hamer, a former Texas Ranger who was famous throughout the state.

"The Roosevelt boys say they're going to throw me out of the place if I show up tonight. Want to come with me?"

"Sure!" Hamer said. He and Cullen took seats in the middle of the hall, and three rough-looking characters moved into seats near the pair. Hamer slid over until he was in front of the trio.

There was no violence that night. But many of Roy Cullen's close friends warned him that his fight to break the grip of the Roosevelt faction in Texas was stirring bitter animosity, and that his personal safety was involved.

"Good!" he said. "That means they're worried."

Two weeks before the election he issued a statement to the press again warning against the bureaucratic New Deal's invasion of individual rights. "For twelve long years the voters have permitted the President and his ever-growing army of bureaucrats . . . to rule over them, their families, their worldly possessions . . . even their innermost desires . . ." But even then, he knew the task was hopeless for the moment.

When the election returns came in, with another Roosevelt victory, Roy Cullen chewed halfway through a cigar before he turned to the newspapermen who had asked him for a statement, and growled:

"Just say we're starting now to work on the 1948 campaign!"

Roy Cullen's interest in politics had not absorbed all his attentions . . . nor those of his family. He still stood firmly at the helm of Quintana Petroleum; and much of his time was occupied with his growing interest in the welfare of the youth of America—an activity to which he had begun to devote himself with his usual enthusiasm at the start of the war.

His second daughter, Agnes—now Mrs. Isaac Arnold—had launched a drive to assist the Girl Scouts in developing a camp near Houston, providing a 300-acre camp site for them. Roy had long ago instilled in his children an understanding of the meaning of charity.

"Don't buy expensive clothes for yourself," he always told them. "Buy what you need, and if you have more money than you need, use it to make other people look as well as you do—not to make you look better than other people."

The simple sense of human charity, learned years ago from Louise Cullen, had guided Roy; and now it guided his children. The generosity of his daughters—Agnes, Margaret and Wilhelmina—started their father on what was probably the most astonishing series of philanthropies on record anywhere in the world.

Each of the three daughters had contributed ten thousand dollars to a fund that was being raised to build a home for the Baylor School of Medicine in Houston. These contributions—matched by an equal amount from their father—attracted the interest of Bill Blanton, the manager of the Houston Chamber of Commerce, who had taken over a personal responsibility for Houston's moral as well as economic welfare.

Blanton was interested in the Gonzales Warm Springs Foundation for Infantile Paralysis—an organization seeking to build a hospital for children who were victims of polio, at Gonzales, Texas. Dr. Ross Booth had planted the idea in Blanton's mind, with a simple request for thirty-five thousand dollars.

"If we could get that much, we could build a small hospital," he said. "I believe we could go on from there and build a wonderful institution for the treatment of polio."

Blanton had noted the contributions of the Cullen clan—father and daughters—to the Baylor College of Medicine. So he trotted over to Roy Cullen's office with an armful of papers and plans on the Gonzales Warm Springs project.

He dumped the pile of papers on Cullen's desk.

"Here are the plans for the new Warm Springs Hospital," he announced cheerfully.

Cullen gave him a bleak look.

"Has this got anything to do with Mr. Roosevelt?"

"Oh, no! This is for Texas. I'd say the Texas Warm Springs is almost a competitor of Mr. Roosevelt's Warm Springs. It may be better than his Warm Springs for curing infantile paralysis."

"All right, Bill . . . ask Dr. Booth to come and show me his plans."

Dr. Booth arrived the next morning. He started to outline the project, and the need for an initial fund of thirty-five thousand dollars, when Cullen pressed a buzzer on his desk.

"Is that what the building will cost?" he asked.

"Yes, but we wouldn't need that much at the start," the doctor said. Cullen turned to the young lady who had come into his office, in response to the buzzer.

"Have a check made out for thirty-five thousand dollars to—" He turned to Dr. Booth. "Who should it be made out to?"

"Gonzales Warm Springs Foundation," the doctor said.

Cullen nodded to the girl.

"Gonzales Warm Springs Foundation."

John Scott, who had brought Dr. Oberholtzer to visit Roy Cullen seven years before, became chairman of the Children's Hospital Fund. A meeting was called, attended by many of Houston's most important citizens—from the viewpoint of their philanthropic potential. Jesse Jones, who had been Roy Cullen's old adversary in the Harbor Board fight, was among those present.

The discussion of the need for the new hospital had gone on for some time, when John Scott suddenly interrupted the flow of conversation.

"We've had a lot of nice talks," he said. "We've heard a lot about Gonzales Warm Springs. But this meeting was called to raise some money for a worthy cause. I would like to hear from Brother Jones or Brother Cullen."

For a few seconds there was quiet in the room. Then Roy Cullen stood up.

"I'll open the pot for fifty thousand," he said.

Later each of Roy Cullen's younger daughters—Margaret and Wilhelmina—gave enough money to build two buildings at the Gonzales Hospital, the Margaret Cullen and the Wilhelmina Cullen Buildings.

CHAPTER 19

"I'm going to give Memorial Hospital a little over a million dollars"

THE PHILOSOPHY of that "noble philanthropist," James Whitcomb Riley's "Jim"—who "loaned a critter a dollar and borrowed a dime"—had a profound effect upon the lives of Roy and Lillie Cullen.

"Both Lillie and I are pretty selfish about our giving," he told members of the Texas Hospital Association in March of 1947, in Houston's Music Hall. "We want to see our money spent, so we can enjoy the spending. A lot of our friends are much less selfish than we are—they are willing to let their heirs or trustees distribute their money after they are dead and gone, when they won't even get the kick out of giving it away."

Many men of wealth look upon bequests as a kind of posthumous vindication—perhaps a proof to their detractors, after they are dead, that they were not as bad as they were painted. No doubt a good many of these benefactors indulge in a kind of anticipatory relish, a premature satisfaction at the grudging credit that will go around when it is learned, after the philanthropists' demise, that they had given so many millions to this hospital, or that foundation.

Roy Cullen was not of this kind. He had few illusions about wealth in itself: it was hard to come by, and it was of no use to anyone unless something was done with it. His philosophy of giving was closely bound up with his philosophy of living. And over the years he has given away about 93 per cent of his fortune.

"Giving away money is no particular credit to me," he said. "Most of it came out of the ground—and while I found the oil in the ground, I didn't put it there. I've got a lot more than Lillie and I and our children and grandchildren can use. I don't think I deserve any great credit for using it to help people. It's easier for me to give a million dollars now than it was to give five dollars to the Salvation Army twenty-five years ago."

As a matter of fact, Roy Cullen's first organized charity was a five-dollar check made out to the Salvation Army—and the check bounced.

"I didn't know my bank account was so low," he explained ruefully. "I had plenty of credit in those days—to buy cotton with—but I didn't have much cash."

Shortly after New Year's Day in 1943, Roy Cullen was chatting with Robert Jolly, superintendent of Houston's Baptist Memorial Hospital. Jolly had been a psalm-singing evangelist in his early days, before he became director of the hospital; and Roy Cullen, always a good hand for singing, had joined with him on many evenings, reviving the memories of old songs of the sawdust trail. On this occasion, Jolly was singing a familiar kind of "blues."

"I wish more people in Houston had the same idea about giving money while they are still alive and can see the good it does—the way you and Lillie are doing. There's old Bob Welch—a bachelor, got lots of money, and keeps it!"

Roy's face settled into a mask—a kind of "poker face" he always assumed when he was thinking deeply.

"Tell you what I'll do, Bob. I'll write Bob Welch a letter; but first you write me one, so I can send it along. Maybe we can explode a little dynamite under his pocketbook."

A few days later he wrote a letter to Welch—a wealthy Houstonian who had made a fortune in oil and sulphur:

> I am enclosing a letter addressed to me from Robert Jolly; also a page of some interesting facts concerning the Memorial Hospital. The bonded debt, as you will see, is $576,000, which I would gladly pay off if I had the ready cash, for I feel sure the thrill of doing such a wonderful thing would add a few years to my life. I haven't any stocks or bonds with the exception of about a million and a half in government bonds, and this is just about the amount I owe.
>
> Most wealthy men leave great sums to worthy causes at their death, but I am more selfish than they, for it is my desire to spend all the money I possibly can during my life, so that I may get a selfish pleasure out of spending it. I probably am possessed with more ego than many men who leave their fortunes to good causes, for I feel I can spend my money to better advantage than someone else can, after I pass on.
>
> There is not a man in Houston more capable of doing his own thinking than you, and I would be the last one to try to change your way of thinking, so I am just presenting the facts in these letters and giving you a quick glance at my philosophy of life.

A few days later Cullen received a note from Jolly: "Just a few days after I wrote you, Bob Welch became a patient at the hospital . . . I sincerely hope and pray that your letter will have the desired effect."

Whether the letter had the "desired effect" Roy Cullen never knew; but when Bob Welch died a decade later, in his will, which left most of his fortune to chemical research, there was a provision for several permanent hospital beds.

One evening, about two years later, Roy and Lillie sat in the big living room of their home in River Oaks. Roy watched the last light of the sun fade from the reflection pool beyond the windows, and the soft shadows recede across the lawn; and suddenly he turned to Lillie.

"Honey, we've got the children all taken care of," he said. "And the grandchildren, too . . . There is a lot of money coming in from the wells that we don't need. Let's give it to the University of Houston."

Lillie nodded, her deep blue eyes looking thoughtfully at Roy. She knew how deeply the future of the growing University, with its thousands of students whose education had been made possible by the Cullen family endowments, had become engraved in Roy's heart. Finally she said:

"Yes, Roy . . . I think that's a good thing. But what about the hospitals?"

He looked at her, slightly puzzled.

"We've given to the hospitals," he said. "Agnes and Wilhelmina and Margaret have all given money, too, Lillie."

"I know . . . but I've talked to some of the people in the hospitals, and they need money, Roy. They need new buildings and more hospital beds."

Roy remembered his talks with Bob Jolly, and the letter to Bob Welch . . .

The next day, at his office, Roy asked his secretary to get Bob Jolly on the telephone.

"Bob," he said, over the phone, "you remember telling me your hospital needed some money?"

Jolly laughed.

"Of course, Roy . . . hospitals always need money."

"Well, I'm going to give the Memorial Hospital a little over a million dollars, Bob."

"A little over a million—" There was a long silence at the other end of the phone. Then Jolly's voice said: "I'd better come right over, Roy."

Cullen next called Marion Law, president of the First National Bank. He had known Law since he first came to Houston; and he knew that he was a director of the Memorial Hospital. He asked Law to come over to his office.

At that time the Memorial Hospital was housed in a gray building near the central business district of Houston. The building and facilities were old, and the hospital staff was inadequate; there were not enough physicians or trained nurses, and not enough room for the patients to receive adequate care. Jolly had labored to keep the institution at a high level, in spite of its inadequate space and inadequate funds.

Law arrived at Cullen's office, and without any preliminaries, Roy said:

"Marion, I'm going to give Memorial Hospital a million dollars."

Law had known Roy Cullen when he first came to Houston, a struggling young man in his early thirties trying to make a living in the cotton business. He had advanced money to Cullen for his cotton-buying operations, and had arranged personal loans to enable him to pay off household bills of his growing family.

Now Law—in his seventies—saw the deeply seamed face of the man he had known more than thirty years crinkle into a smile, and at the same time Roy's eyes filled with tears.

"It's a wonderful feeling, Marion—to be able to do this. Lillie and I are awfully happy at this opportunity to do some real good."

There were no strings attached to the gift. It was to be made out of oil payments, with the bank advancing the money to the hospital. When Jolly arrived, carrying a bundle of plans for the new hospital building, he looked as if he also were ready to cry.

"It's the most wonderful thing that has ever happened to the hospital—and to me," he told Cullen. "God bless you and Lillie for it, Roy!"

Roy had already decided upon a similar donation for the Hermann Hospital, one of the largest in Houston and one of the great medical institutions of the Southwest. Jim Anderson had often told Roy that Hermann Hospital needed money; so he called Anderson on the phone and told him that a check for "a million plus" would be forthcoming. The plus was an additional $156,000, just to "round off the payments in an even number of years."

Bill Blanton, who had interested Roy in the Warm Springs Hospital for Children at Gonzales, Texas, was engaged in a strenuous effort to raise funds for the Methodist Hospital, a small, undernourished institution which had been struggling along on inadequate money. The Methodists wanted to build a new hospital.

Roy Cullen telephoned Blanton.

"Can you come over to my office, Bill?" he asked. "I'd like to give you a million dollars for the Methodist Hospital . . ."

Blanton, a small man whose head hardly came above Cullen's shoulder, walked into Cullen's office a few minutes later. He looked at Cullen's face, wrinkled in a smile. Then he shook his head slowly.

"You do things in the damnedest way, Roy . . ."

As far as anyone knew, the Episcopal Church was the only church in Houston that had no plans for a hospital. But the next day Bishop Clinton S. Quin set the record straight on that.

The Bishop, a tall, genial man, with an open face and a

benign smile, called on Roy Cullen with a bundle of plans under his arm. He had written a note to Roy, congratulating him on "the magnificent work you and Mrs. Cullen have done and are doing, in your benefactions to mankind . . ."

Roy had read the letter, and he smiled when the Bishop came into his office.

"I didn't know the Episcopal Church was planning to build a hospital," he said.

The Bishop also smiled.

"Just a dream . . . one we hope will come true some day." He unrolled the sheaf of plans.

Bishop Quin left with the fourth "million plus" gift in two days—and Roy Cullen had accomplished an all-time record in philanthropy. In less than forty-eight hours he had given more than four and a half million dollars to four separate hospitals—in personal donations by his wife and himself, with no strings on any of the bequests. The money was to be used to "build new hospital buildings" and for any other purposes the hospital directors saw fit.

Out of these funds Hermann Hospital announced it would apply the Cullen donation to a four-and-a-half-million-dollar expansion program; Methodist Hospital, an old, small institution, was to be completely rebuilt on new land; Memorial Hospital planned to increase its bed capacity and expand its nursing school and nurses' home; and the Episcopal Church immediately launched plans to build its own hospital.

The Memorial Hospital nurses' home was built on ground donated from another source. At the ground-breaking ceremonies, Roy announced that he and Mrs. Cullen wanted to add to their donation the cost of the land, which had been given to the hospital by Mrs. J. W. Neal.

"The building is named for Lillie and myself—and we feel we ought to give the land, too," he explained. Cullen's check for seventy thousand dollars in payment for the land was transferred to the hospital funds as Mrs. Neal's donation.

Roy had not lost interest in Houston's educational problems, and a short time later it was announced that he had given one hundred thousand dollars to a Houston College for Negroes—an institution that was transferred later to the University of Texas. And he continued to pour additional funds into the University of Houston, contributing to the erection of a science building and adding to the big Ezekiel Cullen Memorial, the central building on the campus.

At the end of the war, in 1945, two additional members were added to the "Cullen family"—Captain Douglas B. Marshall and Captain Corbin Robertson, both of the Army Air Forces. In ceremonies—just a week apart—that flooded the "big white house" with guests, Captain Marshall married Margaret and Captain Robertson married Wilhelmina, the "baby" of the family. The two girls were contrasts in appearance and personality: Margaret, a tall, calm, blonde girl with her mother's deep blue eyes; and Wilhelmina, dark-haired and gray-eyed, with an energetic manner that was like a feminine replica of her father. Both were beautiful brides, and the scores of friends that gathered agreed that the cup of Roy and Lillie Cullen was now overflowing.

"Why don't you retire, Roy?" one of the guests asked. The old wildcatter laughed, and shook his shaggy head. He was slightly stooped—more from the habit of striding through brush and mud than from any lack of posture; and his big hands gave him a bearlike appearance.

"The longer a man lives, the more things he learns," he said, his gray eyes twinkling. "Ten years ago I'd never have known much about these hospitals that Lillie and I are helping out . . . The more things you know about, the more you got to do."

There was a ring of sober conviction in what he said, in spite of his smile. Roy Cullen had plunged into the business of giving away money with the same energy and rugged determination that he had gone into cotton buying nearly fifty years before, and later into oil and politics.

His political life was as active as his philanthropies. He had settled himself into a role of a perpetual thorn in the side of the New Deal—and later the "Fair Deal"—policies in Washington. Sitting behind the wide, brown desk in his Houston office—now in the new City National Bank Building—he peered at all sections of the country from his Houston office, and wherever he saw a flank of the opposition exposed, he shot a barbed message at it.

In the early days of World War II he had stood almost alone in Texas in his opposition to the foreign doctrines that he believed were creeping into the Government at Washington . . . some perhaps motivated by sincere intentions, but most of them poisonous to the doctrine of free enterprise expressed in the American Bill of Rights. On July 31, 1942, he had written Jesse Jones, then Secretary of Commerce:

> Sooner or later a strongly centralized government draws vicious and unscrupulous men, who prey upon its citizens. You know I have no political ambitions and you also know that I am not thinking of any financial gain. Lillie and I have given away more than we have received for the past ten years. I am solely thinking of the future of our children and grandchildren. . . .

And, with a typical Cullen flourish, he ended the letter with: "This letter will probably do no good, but I feel it my duty to write you of the existing conditions."

Jones replied within a week:

> I believe we will be able to survive the period through which we are going, without destroying our form of government and the thing most dear to us—freedom. Undoubtedly the whole world situation is about as bad as it could be and we will be fortunate to come out of it with anything like a sound economy.

This was in August, 1942. In April of 1945, one of those unforeseen events occurred which sometimes change the course of history. Franklin Roosevelt died; and Harry Truman succeeded him as President of the United States.

The previous summer Roy Cullen had persuaded the "Texas Regulars" who were delegates to the Democratic Convention in Chicago to throw their support to Truman as Roosevelt's running mate, and although the effort had been more an "anti-Wallace" drive than it was "pro-Truman," he felt they might now look to the new President for some support of their political views. Shortly after Truman took office, Cullen wrote to him:

> We are all very happy to have you as President. . . . I say this, although my family and I probably furnished more money than any other family in the state for the Dewey campaign last year . . .

By the end of the year, Roy Cullen's illusions of the betterment of conditions in Washington under the Truman regime began to fade. The Senate had ratified the participation of the United States in the United Nations Organization, and Roy viewed this with grave concern. In a speech in December, of 1945, before the Sons of the American Revolution in Houston, he said:

"I am of the opinion that our great country is decaying politically—so fast that it is very doubtful if we can continue as a democracy much longer, unless we retrace our steps . . ."

He believed the action of the Senate, ratifying the United Nations covenant, in effect took the power to declare war away from the Senate and placed it in the hands of the President.

> I do not believe the Constitution of the United States permits our Senate to delegate such power to one man . . . I am sure those Americans who are responsible for our part in this world movement are sincere in their efforts, but in my opinion it is the most dangerous movement this country has ever embarked upon. How can we enter into a treaty of contract with nations whose philosophy has always been foreign—and still is foreign—to the philosophy of the American people?
>
> The ink was scarcely dry on the treaty signed by the United Nations in San Francisco when they started breaking their agreements. Both England and Russia are now in the act of taking over the smaller nations and it is a sad commentary when our boys on these foreign soils are dying to perpetuate an imperialism . . . which we Americans hate and repudiate.

He turned his guns again on the "creeping socialism" in Washington, saying:

> In 1935 in Germany I saw Germans goose-stepping to the forest with shovels and picks; and in 1937 I saw those same men marching with guns . . . The situation in Germany at that time was very similar to conditions that exist in America today.

He recalled that President Truman, only a few days previously, had advocated "a bill to regiment doctors, nurses and the entire medical profession—a plan of socialized medicine." He warned that the same regimentation would occur in other phases of life, "including labor."

> Labor here is blindly following foreign agitators, who head powerful political organizations in Washington . . . It is my honest opinion that if these men succeed in their efforts to consolidate labor, it will end the working man's freedom in this country. The so-called labor leaders will have so much power that they will control not only the unions, but our Government as well . . . the power to put working men in and out of unions at will, demanding greater and greater portions of the individual

income; and we will become serfs in an organization that can create the same conditions here that existed in Germany under Hitler in 1937.

Two years later Britain had passed into the hands of a Socialist Government, and Roy Cullen again repeated his warning, this time in an address before the Houston Surgical Society at the Baylor School of Medicine.

"The Dark Ages can very easily return to this earth," he said. "The President has asked us to deny our own needs, and perhaps bankrupt our country, to help countries of Europe and Asia, whose philosophy of government is utterly alien to our own, and whose intentions in many cases is to destroy our form of government . . ."

As the nation headed toward another election year, Roy Cullen began to focus his attention on what he believed was the most critical time in the history of the country: the decision as to whether America would follow the pattern of individual freedom—the rugged courage of men who had carved a nation out of the wilderness and the wide plains, or whether it would gravitate back to the sterile authoritarianism of European political ideals . . . governments of masters and serfs.

For fifteen years the country seemed to have been skidding down a toboggan that ran contrary to everything he had believed about America. The great question in Roy Cullen's mind was: When will it stop?

CHAPTER 20

"I had faith in people—and in myself"

FOR FIFTEEN YEARS—from 1932 to 1947—Roy Cullen had been directing scattered and intermittent artillery fire at the entrenchments of "creeping socialism" in Washington. This was not a passing phase of his life, nor was it a crusade. It was born of the hard realities of his own life, as he had lived it . . . the creed of "rugged individualism."

From the days when he sallied forth as a young man into the wild lands of Western Oklahoma, determined to wrest a good livelihood from the cotton business, until he picked up his family and moved to Houston, Roy Cullen had learned about "rugged individualism" in a hard school. And the lessons he learned then never left him.

"Faith . . ." Again and again he turned back to this axiom: "I had faith in people—in my fellow-men—and in myself."

He believed in the individual rights of men, and he had fought to defend those rights as the occasion arose. He could recall the words his mother had spoken, when he was a boy in San Antonio: "Don't ever give an insult to anyone, Roy—and don't ever take an insult from anyone . . ."

It seemed to him—as he moved through the massive corridors of life, driven forward by immediate hopes and ambitions, by struggles and tragedies and heartbreaking failures —that the victories men won in life came from qualities of courage and persistence. And when he faced the ominous clouds of the future that were gathering on world horizons, he believed that the same rugged principles of individual courage and individual faith, that a man needed to apply to his own life, should also be applied to governments . . .

And so from his desk at the offices of Quintana in Houston, he pored over papers and letters and newspaper reports; and whenever he saw from under his gray, shaggy brows a place where the forces of regimented "creeping socialism" were gaining headway, he opened fire.

As election year of 1948 swung into view, he began to realize, however, that the time had come for more than "intermittent fire." If the advocates of "creeping socialism"—foreign and domestic—were to be stopped, they must be stopped before they were so well entrenched that no amount of artillery fire from the hinterlands could dislodge them. And ultimately, if they gained absolute power, all firing would be stopped—as it had been in Germany and Russia.

Meanwhile, he had an opportunity to sharpen his shooting eye in a local political embroglio which, in a sense, whetted his appetite for the national battle impending in 1948. The issue arose over the establishment of a paper pulp mill on the outskirts of Houston. The odors from the mill, wafted in on an easterly wind, smote Roy Cullen's nostrils early one sunny day in the summer of 1947. His political gorge rose with his outraged olfactory sense, and he promptly addressed himself to this new menace to the City of Houston.

"I have closed most of my office windows, during these hot summer days," he told his friends at the Houston Club, "to keep out the horrible odors of the paper mill. If I believed in Hell, I would say the odors of the paper mill and those that steam out of the cracks in Hell must be very similar."

Such odors, he decided, must be injurious to both plant and animal life.

"The fumes give off an acid," he said, "that turns my camellias yellow—and my camellias are twelve miles from the paper mill!"

Shortly after the first invasion of odoriferous "smog" from the paper mill, it was reported that another similar mill was to be built near the suburb of Pasadena on the eastern outskirts of the city—and an easterly wind also would blow these fumes in billowing clouds of nauseous yellow right across the heart of the city, and over the campus of the University of Houston.

This aroused Roy Cullen to a fighting pitch. He had just purchased a tract of land, costing about $130,000, which he had deeded to the University of Houston for enlargement of the campus. The land lay along Calhoun Road, and he noted that a proposed new city zoning plan, set up by the City Zoning Commission, showed a 4000-foot strip of land along Calhoun across from the new university land had been designated as available for "new industry."

He checked with the weather bureau, and found that prevailing winds would blow industrial odors right smack across the campus. A new paper mill in this vicinity, he decided, "could conceivably destroy the University of Houston."

Roy decided to launch a campaign, and using his old, familiar weapon, he wrote letters to the Houston *Post* and the *Chronicle.* The letters—reminiscent of the days when Ezekiel Cullen had opened his rhetorical fire on "that abominable place—that graveyard of men—the City of Houston"—drew headlines in both newspapers.

"I have done all in my power to help make this city a fine place in which to live," Cullen wrote. "But if we cannot cure the nuisance caused by the paper mill, and stop other nuisances from coming to our city, I am going to move to a place where I can find clean air to breathe. I have not come to this conclusion in haste, but have done so only after having given it much thought."

The citizens of Houston suddenly awoke to the sobering realization that the man who had done much to build the hospitals in Houston and to build the University of Houston might move elsewhere . . . And the issue became even more complex when a new phase of the controversy over the zoning laws cropped up. It was alleged that Jesse Jones and some other large property owners were well protected in their downtown holdings, but that the east flank of the University of Houston was not protected at all—in fact, it was fully exposed to the establishment of "nuisance industries."

Cullen got a map and checked off all the pieces of land owned by Jesse Jones. Then he compared these locations with the plan outlined by the City Zoning Commission. The results were illuminating. He recalled the events leading up to the Harbor Board fight thirty-five years before: when he had waded into his first altercation with Jesse Jones over the waterfront land owned by the I. & G. N. Railroad—upon which Jones, a director of the I. & G. N. and Chairman of the Harbor Board, had planned to build.

As a result of Cullen's attack on the zoning plans set up by the Commission, a public hearing was held in the City Council in August of 1947; and early the following year the citizens of Houston voted on a referendum seeking to repeal the zoning ordinances.

Roy Cullen sailed into the fight as he had years before when the Harbor Board issue came up in a city referendum. He had never lost a referendum to Jesse Jones, and he was determined not to lose this one . . . particularly as his beloved University of Houston was involved.

"It is another form of regimentation," he declared, in his first battle cry—a statement to the Houston *Post*. "It opens another avenue for bad politics. Keep the responsibility for running this city with the Mayor and City Council; and if they need more laws to protect homes from public or private nuisances, let them be adopted . . ."

He protested that the ordinance gave the proposed zoning bureaus "more power over the individual than any government should have over its citizens"; and added: "This very condition has led to most of the ills of regimentation in the totalitarian governments of Europe."

Two days before the voting was due on the zoning-law referendum, he unloosed another blast—this time directed squarely at Jesse Jones' newspaper, the Houston *Chronicle:*

> Yesterday's *Chronicle* carried a dozen stories in support of zoning, and not one in opposition to zoning. That means Mr. Jones is just interested in showing only one side of zoning—his side. I don't like that sort of policy in a newspaper, and I don't think other citizens like it. I believe the people of Houston should hear both sides of any question that might affect their lives.

And then he turned the full force of the barrage on Jones himself, charging that he had "been away (from Houston) most of the time for the last twenty-five years" and was now trying to run the city.

The story of the feud between Roy Cullen and Jesse Jones

was blazoned across the country; and Jones himself published a statement in the Houston *Chronicle* expressing regret at Roy Cullen's attitude "because some of us differ with him" on a civic issue. Roy had even threatened to resign from various Houston organizations—including the Board of Regents of the University and the Board of Directors of the Medical Center—and although this drew some acid comments from his opponents in the zoning fight, the people of Houston backed him again, defeating the zoning ordinance two to one.

Meanwhile, Roy Cullen had been building up fire power on the national front. In the spring of 1947 he had invited Representative Joe Martin of Massachusetts, then Speaker of the House and a Presidential possibility, to visit Houston. Two other congressmen—Leo Allen of Illinois and Frank Boykin of Alabama—came to Houston with Martin.

Martin made a hit in Democratic Texas. Cullen, who introduced Martin at a huge dinner at the Rice Hotel, used the occasion to direct his fire upon the "World Union" idea which Harold Stassen, the perpetual candidate from Minnesota, had been agitating.

A few months later—on January 22, 1948—Cullen again lashed at Stassen and the "World Union" idea in an address to about twelve hundred Methodists who had gathered to thank him and Mrs. Cullen for their donation to the new Methodist Hospital.

"I had decided that I would confine my remarks to the early life of Mrs. Cullen and myself, which might be of interest . . . But something of compelling force has caused me to change my plans. I must forget my memory lane."

The matter of "compelling force" was an article in the

Houston *Post* which was headlined: "Texas' World Federalists Convene."

Naturally I was very much interested to learn who started the "World Federalists," and as luck would have it, I found the answer—in the Houston *Post* of January 21. It stated that Cord Meyer, Jr., of New York City, was president . . . and that he was the author of a book entitled *Peace or Anarchy*. I learned from this book that he served as aide to Commander Harold E. Stassen at the conference that formed the United Nations Charter in San Francisco.

He quoted a letter which he had written to President Truman concerning Stassen in 1945, deploring the appointment of the Minnesotan as a member of the United Nations Conference.

He referred to Stassen's advocacy of the "foreign court" in which the Minnesotan had said:

> Let me also make it clear that I propose that the agency set up in this particular field will have world-wide jurisdiction, and that no nation shall be permitted to fly an airplane in international flight except under jurisdiction of this agency.

Cullen snorted.

> If this were put into effect, then we would not be permitted to fly a plane to Canada or Mexico without permission of the foreign court.
>
> Mr. Stassen is willing to create a world police force . . . an international Gestapo, subject to directions of a "foreign court." This "foreign court" will be created and dominated by a majority of the nations on this earth; and the United States would be a very small minority, with about 5 percent of the voting power. It is natural to suppose that such a "foreign court" would control the wealth of this country . . . and if we should refuse to accede to its demands, we should have to fight the rest of the world.

Since Stassen is running for the nomination for President of the United States, on the Republican party ticket, it appears to me as if this is a concerted action to further Mr. Stassen's interests in his political adventure.

Then, turning his guns again on the "World Federation" movement, he declared:

If the time ever comes when we have a World President and a World Court and a World Army, the first important business before the Court will be: Who owns the wealth of the world? And you may rest assured that the Court, being composed of a majority of nations of socialistic and communistic inclinations, will order a division of wealth, including all the gold buried in the mountains of Kentucky!

He traced the "World Federation" movement back to Wendell Willkie, and flipped over some pages of Willkie's book, *One World,* which he had brought to the meeting. He read:

Finally, everywhere I went in the Middle East, I found a kind of technological backwardness, along with poverty and squalor. The reason was that they were in truth returning to biblical times, where little had changed in two thousand years.

Cullen then asked: "Do we want to take food out of the mouths of our children and clothes from their backs, to care for these Asiatics, who have not changed their ways in two thousand years?"

Shortly before this the "Marshall Plan" had been announced, and Cullen assailed this as "a handmaiden of World Union." He noted that more than five billion dollars was being sent to European countries within the scope of the Plan.

Every banker and businessman of this nation knows that as long as this country has an indebtedness of more than two hundred and fifty billion dollars, it is not in a secure position . . . The billions we are now contemplating sending to Europe this year should either go toward retiring the government indebtedness of this country or else be put into atomic bombs and long-range airplanes to protect this country.

When word came from Washington that Will Clayton, his old competitor in the Oklahoma cotton markets and now a staunch New Deal economic supporter, had joined the "World Union" forces agitating congressional sanction of American participation in some kind of "World Federation," Cullen began to bombard his congressional friends.

"I hope this will never happen," he wrote Joe Martin. "We have enough trouble, without looking for more."

While directing continuous long-range fire on the "World Union" forces in Washington, Roy still had a good deal of homework to do in Houston. He had been elected Chairman of the Board of Regents of the University of Houston in 1945 when it was created; and the following year he had jumped to the assistance of the Baylor School of Medicine, which had decided to establish the major part of its medical facilities in Houston.

Ray Dudley, a prominent Houston oil man and publisher of a magazine devoted to oil production, who was also a director of Baylor University at Waco, had come into Roy's office one day.

"You look unhappy, Ray," Cullen observed. "Heart trouble?"

Dudley shook his head. "No, Roy—a headache. An eight-hundred-thousand-dollar headache!"

Cullen's face settled into an expression of careful attention. Dudley explained that the Baylor School of Medicine had been moved to Houston, and the first building had been erected in the "Texas Medical Center." This was the building fund to which the three Cullen girls—Agnes, Margaret and Wilhelmina—had each given donations several years before, indirectly stirring up their father's interest in hospital development. At that time, the Cullen family had given $40,000 to be matched by $160,000 raised from other sources.

"We have a wonderful medical school," Dudley said. "But we're broke."

"How much do you need?"

"Just what I said—eight hundred thousand dollars."

"Over how many years?"

"We don't need it over any years, Roy—we need it now," Dudley said.

Cullen agreed to call this matter to the attention of the trustees of the Cullen Foundation, which he did, and they gave him the check for $800,000.

Two months later Dean Moursound, head of Baylor's Medical School, came into Cullen's office. He laid some papers on the desk. The Baylor School needed an additional $175,000 to cover the deficit on its building program at the medical center. Cullen promised to take up this too with the trustees of the Cullen Foundation, who agreed to give the amount needed.

Soon afterwards he made arrangements for additional money in the form of oil payments to go to the Baylor School, at the rate of about $100,000 annually—which would bring his total contributions to the medical school to more than two-and-a-half million dollars.

Toward the end of 1947 Roy and Lillie decided to set up a permanent method of contributing to the continued development and growth of the various institutions and organizations to which they had given money. At a meeting of the Texas Hospital Association in Houston's Music Hall on March 27, 1947, he was asked why he and Mrs. Cullen had given so much to hospitals.

"In our opinion, there is no more worthy cause than caring for people who are suffering—the sick and disabled, who often cannot help themselves," he said; and then added—with his inevitable barb at politicians: "Graft and pork barrels, and other kinds of leakage that occur when the Government spends our money, do not exist when we give directly to hospitals."

And then, with a twinkle in his eye, he said:

> I'm going to let you in on a little secret. Mrs. Cullen and I are now having our attorneys draw up papers to create a foundation in which we will put oil properties estimated to produce eventually some thirty to forty million barrels of oil, worth eighty million dollars or more. Neither Mrs. Cullen nor I will be trustees of those funds, but it is our hope that the trustees of the Foundation will use them principally to make the Texas Medical Center and the University of Houston the kind of institutions Texans will be proud of.

A few days later the Board of Directors of the Houston Chamber of Commerce called on Roy Cullen in a body, to express their appreciation for his fabulous donation.

Roy Cullen nodded, and again his face settled into the grave mask that they knew so well. It meant that he was thinking something over—and he was.

"Thanks for your kindness," he said. "But since I made that announcement, Lillie and I have been thinking this thing over, and we've changed our minds a little bit."

None of the delegation spoke.

"We've decided—after looking over our property—that we can double that figure," he said.

The members of the delegation heaved a concerted sigh.

"We're adding 10,768 acres of oil-bearing lands to the 7,743 acres we first intended to set aside for the Foundation," Roy went on. "The estimate of oil recoverable from these holdings will be worth—at present prices—one hundred and sixty million dollars."

The Cullen Foundation had been born, with two simple announcements. It was the largest charitable foundation in the South, and one of the largest in America—exceeded only by the Rockefeller and Ford Foundations. And it was without any shadow of doubt the largest amount of money ever given by any single family during the lifetime of the donors.

Roy Cullen shrugged off the praise that poured upon Lillie and himself in waves of telegrams and letters. More than two hundred thousand letters deluged the Cullen mail during the next few weeks . . . a good part of them requests for various kinds of financial aid, wrapped in the none-too-subtle phraseology of praise and flattery. He had to hire a staff of emergency clerks to read and file the mail. An English sportsman wanted money to organize an American football team in England, and he addressed the letter to "Hugh Roy Cullen, Texas Oil King, Somewhere in America."

One letter, written in pencil by a man in Arkansas, simply said:

"I read your ad in the paper where you are giving away some money. Please give me some."

Another man expressed sympathy for Cullen and enclosed a dime with a note that read:

"I'm sure the touches you have received have given you a headache. So here is the price of an aspirin."

The only limitations set up by the Cullen Foundation, aside from legal requirements, were that the donations from the funds be confined to Texas. The trustees of the Foundation would have sole discretion in the distribution of the money—and the first trustees named were Agnes, Margaret and Wilhelmina Cullen.

CHAPTER 21

"Tell Tom Dewey to change his tune . . ."

NINE YEARS after the dark, soggy day when Roy and Lillie Cullen had stood in the dripping rain, turning over the first ground for the Roy Gustav Cullen Memorial Building at the University of Houston, they broke ground for the Ezekiel Cullen Building.

This was more than a memorial to Ezekiel Cullen: It was a dedication of the University to the principles for which Roy Cullen's vigorous ancestor had stood in the early history of Texas . . . and principles to which Roy Cullen himself had dedicated his own interest in the foundation of education in Texas.

Ezekiel Cullen had reported in 1839 to the Third Congress of Texas, as chairman of the Education Committee to the House of Representatives, setting forth the need for a public school system in Texas. With various currents of immigration pouring into the embryo Republic—Yankees from the North; adventurous young bloods from Georgia and the Carolinas, like himself; and the resident population of

Mexicans and Indians and "Tejanos"—it had been vital that an effective school system be established.

The Republic must provide "such education as shall render the people competent for self-government; and for want of which they will be grovelling slaves of their mean and despicable passions, or the pliant tools of wily and ambitious demagogues."

In less mellifluous language, but with the same intense belief in a free and untrammelled educational system, Roy Cullen had voiced his personal feelings:

> You must remember that it takes more than buildings to make a great University. You must have a capable Board of Regents, and a great President and qualified members of the faculty . . . And above all you must have great vision, and a great student body. At the University of Houston I think we have them all.

In spite of his words, Roy Cullen viewed the future of education with grave doubts. It seemed to him that education was closely bound with the foundations of democracy and freedom, and the breakdown of traditional freedom in America, foreshadowed by the growth of government regimentation in Washington, was a prelude to the breakdown of the educational system.

Ezekiel Cullen's warning that a nation must have "such education as shall render the people competent for self-government" might easily be swept away in the tide of Federal control through aids to the national educational system, grants of subsidies to agricultural institutions, and the gradual absorbing of the free practice of medicine under a socialized system.

A year later—on St. Patrick's Day of 1949—Roy voiced these fears at the laying of the cornerstone of the magnificent new Ezekiel Cullen Building. He had listened to Federal

Judge J. C. Hutcheson, Jr., deliver the formal address, in which he said:

> As Texans, we are fortunate that in the educational system of our state, which he did so much to provide for a hundred years ago, Ezekiel Cullen's star is still blazing in the skies. As Houstonians, we are doubly blessed that in the devotion of Ezekiel Cullen's grandson to the University of Houston, a new star has blazed across the heavens . . .

Roy's shaggy head was thrust forward as he listened to the speaker. He was thinking of the new and strange problems that confronted education a century after his grandfather's time . . . problems that Ezekiel Cullen had recognized, and had hoped to avoid.

He took a small trowel and plastered the first dab of mortar on the cornerstone. Then he squared his shoulders, and looking at the students from under heavy brows, he said:

> It is conceivable that this could be the last major educational structure in this country to be financed with individual gifts . . . because the fantastic sums necessary to pay for all the socialistic programs advanced by the Administration in Washington—if they are adopted—will leave the taxpayer little money to give to education.

Roy Cullen's words were born of a growing fear that the entrenchment of "creeping socialism" in Washington was solidifying to an extent that might require years to uproot it. Long before the campaign of 1948 started, he had lost all his illusions about Harry Truman.

Two men stood out prominently in the Republican picture—Tom Dewey and Bob Taft. Roy Cullen would have liked to see Joe Martin in a stronger position: he admired the stocky Massachusetts congressman beyond any other Republican of his day, and he felt that only a deadlock between Taft and Dewey could bring the nomination to Martin.

He had once asked some of Senator Taft's supporters if they would throw their support to Martin, in the event it became apparent Taft could not be nominated; and the Senator's brother-in-law, Thomas W. Bowers, had replied cautiously:

"You may be sure that I, at least, and I have reason to believe, others of our friends, are not unsympathetic to the idea."

In April he received the assurance of Ben Tate, treasurer of the Taft campaign committee, that the Ohio senator would support Martin—if all hope were lost. But Roy recognized that the moment when "all hope is lost" for a politician is almost in infinity.

By this time Cullen's behind-the-scenes power in national politics was beginning to be understood. He had been firing short bursts of artillery for so many years that he had built up an indefinable but nonetheless effective group of political leaders, chiefly in Congress, who were loyal to him and to his ideals.

Many of these had been helped in their local campaigns by Roy Cullen's support. He had mailed thousands of pamphlets, reprints of magazine articles and excerpts from speeches . . . and had become, in effect, a one-man propaganda machine, operating out of his Texas office in support of "free enterprise"—and in opposition to anything that smacked of "creeping socialism."

When friends of General MacArthur—still in voluntary exile in Japan, where he was winding up the tenure of the Occupation—approached Roy for support for the General, he explained that he "greatly admired the General," particularly for the executive ability he had shown in governing

Japan. But he added that "it takes something more than that for the kind of President we need now."

He felt the only kind of man who would succeed in the broiling currents of Washington's political maelstrom would be a "political statesman," like Taft or Martin, who knew the ropes in the nation's capital.

"Personally," he wrote to the General's friends, "I would like to see General MacArthur in Forrestal's job, for it is going to be the vital pivot around which the salvation of this country could revolve."

He began quietly building political fences in Texas for Martin, feeling that his strength would be sufficient so that he could step into a deadlock between Taft and Dewey as the leading "dark horse" candidate. To Martin himself he wrote:

"As far as I know, you are not obligated to anyone in the world. If you are nominated and elected President, the only thing I will ask of you is that you make us a worthy President, which I know you would."

When the deadlock between Taft and Dewey failed to develop, and Dewey won the nomination at Philadelphia, Cullen and his "Texas Regulars" turned their eyes toward the splitting ranks of the Southern Democrats. A new political front had been opened below the Mason-Dixon line, in rebellion against Harry Truman and his "civil rights" program and out of this was growing a "Conservative Democrat" party, known as "States Rights Dixiecrats."

Roy Cullen never had any illusions about a "third party." He did not believe in "third-party" politics; but he felt that a cleavage of the conservative bloc of Southern Democrats might be the straw that would break the Democratic donkey's back.

The "Texas Regulars," who had tried to effect a "splinter party" break in the pro-Roosevelt Democratic faction in

Texas four years before, now agreed to drop quietly into the background. Cullen—no Democrat—nevertheless was a staunch "States-Rights" advocate, and he began to marshal the "third-party" forces in Texas.

In July of 1948, after the "Dixiecrat" convention in Birmingham had nominated J. Strom Thurmond, the Governor of South Carolina, Cullen called a meeting of fourteen influential Houstonians in his office in Houston.

He explained that he was firmly in favor of the "two-party" system, and that he felt a permanent "third party" would wreck the American political balance; but he believed such a movement was essential at this time, offering the "only hope of voting for a conservative Southern Democrat in this election."

"The political grafters in the North, together with Truman and his New Deal friends, have just about wrecked the Democratic party," he said. "If Texas and the Southern states go for Thurmond, we will be in a powerful trading position where we can insist upon a proper adjustment of conditions in Washington, and maybe it will eventually turn the Democratic party in the direction the Southern Democrats want to see it go."

Thurmond and his running mate, Governor Fielding Wright of Mississippi, were invited to come to Texas to make their acceptance speeches. In an uproarious rally at the Sam Houston Coliseum in Houston, to the tune of thousands of shrill rebel yells, Thurmond sounded the tocsin for the Southern "Democratic Revolt":

> We appeal to you to repudiate radicalism, the rampant disregard of constitutional government—as approved in Philadelphia by all three conventions—and join with us in defending the American way of life.

Since the Texas Democratic Convention had already tied the state electors to the Truman ticket, Cullen and the "Dixiecrats" faced the superhuman task of unseating the regular Democrats.

In spite of the almost hopeless odds, Cullen and his forces set out with dogged determination to force a break in the Democratic ranks. They believed Texas Democrats were tired of Harry Truman, and would back Thurmond if they could reverse the action of the May convention.

There was a legal precedent for this. A convention was to be held in September at Fort Worth, and they felt if a "non-binding" referendum could be offered the voters of the state, on the issue of reversing the May convention, they could go to the September convention with what would amount to a mandate.

Governor Beauford Jester and State Chairman Robert Calvert declined to put the matter to a vote. Cullen promptly organized three county referendums, and all were overwhelmingly in favor of Thurmond and the "Dixiecrats." They sent a wire to the Governor, reminding him that "States Righters" had been "a pillar of support" in his last election; and even threatened to drag out the veteran Lee "Pappy" O'Daniel, now a United States senator, who had announced his retirement, and run him against Jester in November.

O'Daniel had gone into semi-seclusion on his Texas farm; and declined to come out. Cullen was furious. He had supported O'Daniel in 1940 and in 1944. "Pass the Biscuits Pappy" was adamant, however; he said the country was "going to the dogs anyway" and he wanted no further part of politics.

Two years later, when O'Daniel decided to come out of

retirement and run for Governor again, Cullen told him: "You go ahead, Lee—and I'll fight you every foot of the way!"

The feud between the "Dixiecrats" and Governor Jester, who had been elected on a fairly conservative "States-Rights" platform, continued until the September convention. By this time Jester and Calvert had an iron grip on the party machinery. Calvert ruled that none of the delegates would be recognized until they had taken a "loyalty pledge" to support the national Democratic party ticket—which automatically barred the Thurmond "States Righters" and ended Roy Cullen's second revolt in Texas' Democratic politics.

After this abortive effort to "purify" the Democratic party in Texas, Roy turned his attention back again to the national election. He wrote Governor Dewey, the Republican candidate:

> It is the consensus of those with whom I have talked that it would be folly to have more than two parties in this country, so it will be our aim (in Texas) to try to eliminate those Democratic demagogues in many of our larger cities and purify the Democratic party in November.
>
> However, I am sure that just a few of us believe this is a possibility; so it would follow that these fine people of the South should join the Republican party. I think this, in all probability, could happen if the majority of the Southern people should at one time cast their votes against the nominee of the Democratic party.

Cullen by this time was riding both the "Conservative Democratic" donkey and the galloping G.O.P. elephant, while the campaign was in full stride. He devoted himself with equal energy to the business of swinging Democratic votes away from Truman in the South, and lending support to the Republican campaign elsewhere.

He made a short trip to New York, after a vacation in Canada; and saw several of his Republican friends, including Joe Martin and Harold Talbott, chairman of the Republican National Finance Committee. While he was there, he listened to two of Governor Dewey's speeches.

"For God's sake!" he implored Talbott, "tell Dewey to change his tune or he won't have a chance of winning! He's trying to box while Truman is swinging with both fists. If he doesn't climb off his pedestal and start fighting, he'll be on the floor in November."

The others laughed. Dewey was pretty much of a "shoo-in," and they did not regard the dire predictions of the shambling Texas oil man with much seriousness. The following January, two months after the election, Harold Talbott wrote to Roy Cullen:

> As you can imagine, I was in pretty close touch with all the phases of the (Dewey's) campaign and I am sure now that you are the only man I know who sized up the situation clearly. You were positive enough in your argument to make me see the dangers of the situation as they existed. I telephoned the Dewey train in Chicago to tell them of your thoughts, and sent copies of your letter to them. The tragedy is so great—to have had it in our hands and then to muff it.

While he was in New York, Cullen received word from Texas that the Thurmond campaign had bogged down, and he hastened home. Many of the "Conservative Democrat" bloc in the South had been persuaded by Old Guard Republicans that the best chance of defeating Truman lay in voting for Dewey. This, of course, was contrary to the strategy of Cullen and his "Dixiecrat" friends, who wanted to cement the "States-Rights" Democratic bloc into a powerful faction, capable of wielding political power.

He organized a "Dixiecrat rally" in Houston two weeks before Election Day.

"The Republican party cannot carry Texas for Dewey," he told them. "They know that, because Dewey's 'Civil Rights Bill' is in the Republican party platform. That is the reason Dewey hasn't made any speeches in Texas. I've talked with Republican leaders in New York, and they know that, too. They don't want to see Texas split its conservative vote between the Republicans and the States-Rights ticket—because that would carry the state for Truman."

As election approached, he used every form of public approach—speeches, statements to the press, letters to political leaders—warning that unless Texans were aware of the dangers they faced, "they may vote away their liberty next Tuesday."

On Election Day four Southern states went over to the "Dixiecrat" party; but Texas—where the movement was born—racked up its customary lopsided Democratic majority.

Roy Cullen salvaged one victory from the Republican disaster, however. During the pre-convention campaign, he had been asked by Tom Bowers, Senator Taft's brother-in-law, to assist in blocking Harold Stassen's support in the primaries.

Cullen had always been fearful of Stassen's "World Union" leanings, and he provided Taft with all the support he could muster in areas where the primary race was close.

A year after Dewey's defeat, Stassen visited Houston and saw Cullen. They discussed the election, and finally Stassen said:

"Roy, if I had beaten Taft in the primaries, and at the Convention, I would have been President of the United

States today, instead of Harry Truman. But just when I was going along fine, something happened to my delegates. I never knew what it was."

Cullen chuckled; and then he told him.

CHAPTER 22

"A rumor has come to me direct from Washington"

ROY CULLEN was not much given to brooding upon the past. The election of 1948 was over; and Harry Truman was still in the White House. The fight, as Roy saw it, was not one of "reactionary" forces against "progressive" forces, as the "New Deal-Fair Deal" political philosophers had tried to describe it; it was a fundamental question of whether the tradition of freedom and free enterprise in the United States was to be scrapped for a new kind of government—a "welfare state." If Americans accepted this new kind of government, they had to surrender democracy—because free institutions and bureaucratic regimentation could not exist in the same state.

At the anniversary celebration commemorating the victory at San Jacinto, standing under the white shaft that marked the battlefield of Texas' greatest victory, Roy Cullen threw out a challenge to Texans—and to Americans:

> Why did Texans declare their independence in 1836—and then go on to fight for it at the Alamo—at Goliad—at San Jacinto?

. . . Sometimes I wonder what the heroes of San Jacinto would think of Texas if they could return and see us—as we are today!

Standing bareheaded under the burning sky, with thousands of fellow-Houstonians gathered around, Roy shook his heavy mane of hair, and plunged into his subject with the vigor of an old war horse, now scarred with some rather momentous political defeats . . . and probably more than ever aware of the character of his enemies in Washington.

Suppose your grandfather or my grandfather should return to stay with us a while . . . what would they think? I've wondered what my grandfather, Ezekiel Cullen, would say after having Washington bureaucrats tell him how he must run his affairs, and collecting a tax every time he turned around—to support the extravagant, wasteful, bottle-feeding schemes.

After a few tastes of that, I wonder if our grandfathers wouldn't decide it was time for another Texas declaration of independence!

Roy Cullen was not a professional political speaker; but his words carried the ringing conviction of a man who believed what he was saying. He spoke in a low, even voice that was carried over the huge crowd by loud speakers. His voice at times trembled slightly with emotion; and the square, rugged set of his wide shoulders made a striking picture as he stood hatless under the blue Texas sky and fired his salvos from the historic Texas battlefield—aimed directly at Harry Truman in Washington.

It seems to me that the fire of independence that blazed so high in the hearts of early Texans has burned down to a low flicker. They were ready to fight for their individual rights and liberties, and resented any encroachment upon them. As an instance, which may seem extreme and far-fetched to our generation, my grandfather led a fight on the floor of the Texas House of Representatives against President Sam Houston's proposal to deliver his annual message to the Third Texas Congress in person.

We of this generation are so used to seeing Presidents try to run the legislative and judicial departments, as well as the executive, that such a thing as delivering a message in person is too trivial to notice. But Presidents had not got that far over the line in those days, and Grandfather Ezekiel contended that it was contrary to custom and an encroachment of the executive branch of the government on the legislative branch. He said:

"Let each move in his proper sphere, and perform the duties assigned by the Constitution and the laws."

He recalled the complaint of Texans before the Revolt against Mexico—that General Santa Ana had disregarded the constitutional rights under which Texas was colonized, and made himself a dictator.

Those rugged pioneers valued liberty as highly as they valued their lives. They were willing to fight for it—and if necessary to die for it . . . You may not have thought of it, but there is an odd parallel between the Texans of 1835 and the Texans of 1949.

When the early Texas colonists settled in Texas, they became legally Mexican citizens. They owed that Government the same loyalty that we owe our Government in Washington. And when Santa Ana set aside the Constitution of Mexico and assumed dictatorial powers—they rebelled . . . During the past fifteen years we have seen one constitutional guarantee after another flouted or ignored . . . New Deal laws and New Deal decisions have taken them away; the rights of the states have been taken away; and our Government is being moved piece by piece from the city hall, the county courthouses, the state capitol—into the bureaucratic beehives on the Potomac!

He then tossed out the first challenge in what was to become one of the pivotal issues of Texas' ultimate political cleavage from the Southern Democratic party—the "tidelands oil question."

The Supreme Court has held that the Federal Government is entitled to the submerged lands off the California coast, and owns all the oil beneath the waters. This decision is contrary to law and all the previous rulings of the courts, which have held that the states own their tidelands. Now the Attorney General of the United States, that great and loyal Texan, Tom Clark, has filed suit in the Supreme Court to take the tidelands away from his native state . . . In doing this, he dishonors the solemn, specific agreement made by the Congress of the United States with our forefathers of the Republic of Texas, expressly reserving the tidelands to the Lone Star State.

A few weeks after the speech at San Jacinto, a compromise on the tidelands issue was offered in Washington, under which the Government would withdraw its suit on condition that it have control of the leasing of offshore lands and that a major share of the income from these oil reserves accrue to the national Government.

This drew a bitter blast from Roy Cullen, who took the position that no compromise of principle was possible. Either Texas owned the tidelands, or she did not own them; and if she did, then why should she share them with the Federal Government?

Cullen wired Price Daniel, Attorney General of Texas, who was in Washington fighting the tidelands oil case for Texas:

I urge you to do everything possible to break down the tidelands compromise. Those urging it are evidently doing it for political purposes, and are disloyal to the state of Texas.

If we sacrifice a fundamental principle in this manner, there will be nothing to stop the Federal Government from taking over the oil business and other businesses, just as is being done in England. We must stop here if we are to turn off the road that is now leading us to a socialistic state.

He sent a copy of his telegram to every member of Congress; and then he began his own investigation of the tidelands question, to determine the actual value of the tidelands oil deposits. His own experience—with Quintana—was rather curious; there had been almost no recovery of oil in the operations his drillers had undertaken, and he had a hunch there would be no real recovery of oil.

If this proved true, he would have a bombshell to drop into the dispute that would set the Federal Government back on its heels—and establish the true issue as he saw it: Did the states still have the basic rights guaranteed under the Constitution and the agreements of Congress; or were those rights being sapped and vitiated by the Federal Government?

"The real issue is not the value of the tidelands oil deposits," he wrote to his friends in Washington; "it is whether our socialistic national Government has reached a point where it feels it can ignore and flout the historic rights of the states, and thus destroy our constitutional form of government."

Roy Cullen never took his eye from the ultimate target of his attacks, which was "creeping socialism"; and in the fall of 1949 he swung his guns on a new sign of this in the person of Leland Olds, who had been appointed by President Truman to a third term as head of the Federal Power Commission.

Using his now-familiar artillery—a Western Union telegram—he wired twenty-two friends in the Senate:

> Leland Olds has admitted before a Congressional Committee that he does not believe in the profit system, and would establish "social responsibility" in place of the profit motive. This is conclusive proof that he does not believe in our form of government, and he should be rejected by the Senate.

When Olds' confirmation came up before the Senate, only fifteen votes were marshalled in his favor; and Roy Cullen, breathing fire as he assailed the "inner sanctum of the New Deal-Fair Deal politburo" in Washington, launched a "purge" on these fifteen senators.

He wired Joe Martin: "We must defeat these fifteen senators!" This was the beginning of a "grass roots" campaign in which the graying Texas oil man—now gathering momentum in his personal campaign to unseat Harry Truman and the "New Deal-Fair Deal Democrats" from Washington—sought to "bring the vital question of 'creeping socialism' vs. the 'free enterprise system' before the American people."

He said to friends in Houston:

"We have reached a turning point where all the arguments and persuasion in the world will not affect the bureaucrats in Washington. Only one force can stop the advance of these foreign-born theories of government—and that is the American people!"

The "grass roots" campaign was basically an effort to force what Roy Cullen believed was the fundamental national issue—socialism vs. free enterprise—before the electorate in every state.

He drew up a list of all candidates for Congress—the House and the Senate—in the 1950 mid-term elections; and he began systematically to inject the issue into each campaign. This was done by the simple strategy of supporting the candidate who supported "free enterprise," regardless of his partisan affiliations.

"I guess I'm supporting almost as many Democrats as Republicans," he told friends in Houston. "A lot of them may not expect my support, and some of 'em may not want it—but if they believe in our American system of constitutional government and the free enterprise system, they're going to get it."

He had reprints of speeches, presenting the "free enterprise" viewpoint, distributed in various areas of the country. He sent wires and letters to people in districts where the candidates were squarely opposed on this issue, seeking to focus attention upon the issue. He corresponded with many of the candidates—some of whom had hardly heard of Hugh Roy Cullen—offering encouragement and help to those who were fighting "the blight of creeping socialism in Washington."

The results were spectacular. The flood tide of political and economic literature—pamphlets, reprints of speeches, letters, telegrams—began to pour into various states from the seventeenth floor of the City National Bank Building in Houston, where the Quintana offices were located. Thousands of pounds of pamphlets were mailed; photostats of telegrams were prepared and sent off to key areas; congressmen were bombarded with telegrams and letters, advising them of the issues being laid before their constituents, and demanding that they take a position on these issues.

Probably never before in American political history did a single man undertake such a widely spread national campaign—with no personal political objective except "to see the best men elected."

This had been Roy Cullen's goal in politics since the early days in Oklahoma, when he wrote Governor Haskell: "All I want you to do is be a good governor." This had been his guiding axiom in the election of every man he had ever backed. And it was his guiding principle in what was to become the most important political adventure of his life.

Even his political foes, who accused him of misguided

interference in political affairs—who had cried that "discovering an oil well doesn't necessarily qualify a man to be political godfather to an entire nation"—had to admit that Roy Cullen's political motives were never obscure or ulterior.

"As long as I am an American," he said, "I intend to use my God-given right to fight for the things I believe made America strong, and to defend my country against the foreign 'isms' and the European and Asiatic political systems that I believe will make us weak, and ultimately destroy us.

"That is my creed, and as long as I have strength to carry it out, I will continue to carry on the fight!"

The "things that made America strong," in his view, were: a free people, who had built the "highest living standards in the world" through hard work and the courage of free enterprise; and tariff walls which could protect the country against economic invasion from other countries, where there was neither freedom nor high standards of living.

It was in the spring of 1949, when he was launching his "grass roots" campaign, that Roy Cullen received a letter from a man who was to become the spearhead of his fight against "creeping socialism." The letter had nothing to do with politics. It was a more or less routine request for a contribution for educational funds. The letter read:

Dear Mr. Cullen:

Chancellor Chase of New York University, President Conant of Harvard, President Day of Cornell, President Seymour of Yale, President Stassen of the University of Pennsylvania, and I, in behalf of Columbia University, have, together with an outstanding group of men in the professional and business world, given much thought and careful study to the serious financial crisis confronting the medical schools throughout the country today. This body has requested me to address a letter to you.

The letter explained that "substantial financial support" must be made available for these medical schools if they were to survive, and invited Roy Cullen to serve as a Trustee of a National Fund for Medical Schools. It was not the text of the letter which chiefly interested Roy Cullen; it was the signature: "Dwight D. Eisenhower."

He replied immediately, explaining that it would be a "physical impossibility" for him to serve on the board of trustees of the National Fund, and enclosing a booklet prepared by the University of Houston "which shows some of the work I am doing for hospitals."

This was on March 14, 1949. On July 13 of the same year, Roy Cullen wrote to General Eisenhower, recalling their earlier exchange of letters and mentioning some of the work that had been accomplished at the Texas Medical Center.

> But this is not what I want to talk to you about. I want to talk to you about the University of Houston. I take great pride not only in the University, but in the fact that I helped build it . . . I am extending to you an invitation to deliver the commencement address at the University of Houston next spring, on June 5, 1950, at 7:00 P.M. I sincerely hope you can accept.

The letter also extended an invitation for General and Mrs. Eisenhower "to stay at our home. We have wonderful bass fishing at our ranch, which is about one hour, forty minutes from Houston. If you like bass fishing, we might spend several days at the ranch."

This letter got much the same treatment General Eisenhower's letter had received: a polite rejection. "Most certainly I should be delighted to accept your invitation, were that at all possible," he wrote. "Unfortunately, commencement period at Columbia coincides with that at the University of Houston . . . Under the circumstances I have no alternative but to decline."

However, General Eisenhower expressed his keen interest in Roy Cullen's activities in behalf of the Texas Medical Center, and added:

"Should I have an opportunity at any time to visit the Southwest, I hope I shall be able to talk things over with you."

Roy Cullen's interest in General Eisenhower was not confined to the desire to have him address the student body of the University of Houston. He had more knowledge of the Kansan than General Eisenhower might have supposed; and long before this he had considered him as possible Presidential timber.

So on August 24 he wrote, with characteristic candor:

> A rumor has come to me direct from Washington that there is a possibility that you might accept the Republican nomination for President, if it is offered you. I hope this is true, because we are badly in need of a President who appreciates the democratic form of government. From all your statements made to the press, you do believe in the government created by our Constitution and the Bill of Rights.
>
> If the rumor that I received is true, I would like to have you visit Houston at an appropriate time, some time between now and next spring, and make an address to the prominent men of the state of Texas. I know they would do you great honor, as they did ex-Speaker of the House, Joseph W. Martin, when he visited Houston May 16, 1947.

General Eisenhower was away in Colorado when Cullen's letter arrived, and it was several weeks catching up with him. But he telephoned his office at Columbia University, dictating a reply to Cullen in which he explained he had "no definite plans currently for a trip to Texas" but "hoped to get down that way sometime during the academic year."

Roy filed away the correspondence for future reference; and early in October decided to go to New York. He jotted a short note to General Eisenhower:

"Mrs. Cullen and I will arrive in New York on October 18th . . . We would enjoy seeing you while we are there."

On the eighteenth when Roy and Lillie arrived in New York, there was an invitation to them to have dinner with the General and Mrs. Eisenhower at their residence on Morningside Drive, near the campus of Columbia University.

The first meeting between General Eisenhower and Roy Cullen, at the residence of the President of Columbia University in New Yoık, was something less than momentous. George S. Allen, the self-styled "friend of Presidents," was at the dinner, and the subjects of conversation were restricted.

During the dinner, Allen did most of the talking until—by what Roy Cullen described as a "happy accident"—his false teeth became dislodged from their moorings, and he found his fluency greatly impaired.

Roy returned to Houston with one definite outcome of the meeting with General "Ike." He had promised to come to Houston to address the annual meeting of the Houston Chamber of Commerce on December 7.

CHAPTER 23

"You can be nominated if you refuse to talk politics"

GENERAL EISENHOWER arrived in Houston on December 7, 1949—the anniversary of the bombing of Pearl Harbor. Houston took him to its bosom, lavishing typical Texas hospitality on the wartime commander of the European invasion forces.

The General established headquarters at the Rice Hotel. A luncheon in honor of General and Mrs. Eisenhower was given at the Cullen home on River Oaks Boulevard. The luncheon was attended by prominent Houstonians, and Roy Cullen had no opportunity to pose the question that was closest to his heart: Would General Eisenhower run for President on the Republican ticket?

That evening General Eisenhower was scheduled to address twenty thousand people at the huge Houston Coliseum. Reporters had bombarded him with questions, mostly about his political plans; and the General had replied amiably:

"I have no political ambitions."

But he added, with a twinkle in his eye: "That doesn't mean I have to keep my mouth shut."

Roy Cullen watched him closely during the dinner before General Eisenhower's speech, studying him carefully, and listening to his comments. After the General spoke, he turned toward Roy and said: "I have a pleasant duty to perform."

Roy had been awarded a medal by the Freedom Foundation at Valley Forge, Pennsylvania, and had been unable to receive it personally. General Eisenhower, who had received the same honor, had been asked by the Foundation to deliver the award in person to Roy Cullen during his visit to Houston.

Roy arose and received the medal. He turned toward the General, and thanked him for his "kind words."

"If I have done anything worth while in life—I attribute it to being surrounded all my life by fine and inspiring people," he said. "Our country is in a critical condition, and it is good to know that we have men, like our distinguished guest, who will help us solve the many problems our country is facing today . . ."

The next day the General's schedule was tightly packed;

and Roy Cullen did not see him again. But he had an impression, from the few talks that he had with Eisenhower, that he might respond to a call in the service of his country, in spite of his lack of "political ambitions" . . . if the country really wanted him.

"He hasn't said he would be a candidate," he told his friends. "But he also hasn't said he wouldn't."

The General left Houston, stopping for a half hour to look over the University of Houston campus on his way by automobile to Galveston. After he returned to New York he wrote Cullen a friendly letter, beginning with "Dear Roy:"

> You may have heard that on the way out of Houston to take the road to Galveston, I had the opportunity to visit the University of Houston campus, in company with Dr. Oberholzer. Some of the others protested bitterly against my stealing the time for the expedition, but I was so interested in what you were doing there that I disregarded their well-meant advice, and as a result I had a most enjoyable half hour . . . I truly congratulate you on the progress made.
>
> Of course, as I have told you, I hope to interest you also in Columbia University . . . One of the basic reasons for the existence of such a national institution is to prepare our young people for effective citizenship in a free country. Columbia stands for free competitive enterprise.
>
> The next time that I may be fortunate enough to have an opportunity for a long talk with you and Mrs. Cullen, I hope to lay before you in some detail my hopes and aspirations for the future of this great institution . . . I am convinced that, regardless of particular political affiliation, one of our tasks today is to revive in all of us an acute respect for the values that must be preserved if America is to retain its position of leadership in the world, and continue as the land of individual liberty and opportunity.

As the campaigns for the congressional elections of 1950 warmed up, Roy Cullen warmed up with them. He believed the election of conservative candidates, dedicated to the basic principles of "free enterprise," was necessary, regardless of party affiliations; and he opened up a one-man campaign probably unparalleled in American politics. He was convinced the mid-term elections were crucial—as important in the overall battle to prevent "creeping socialism" from overrunning the country as the Presidential elections would be two years later.

If the "New Deal-Fair Deal" tide could be stopped in the congressional campaigns, through a "grass roots" revolt in 1950, it would pave the way for a complete change in 1952.

This was not a new kind of campaign for Roy Cullen. He merely stepped up the scope and volume of his personal efforts. He flooded the country with books, pamphlets, reprints of speeches and editorial comments that expressed the viewpoints he supported. Roy had started this practice back in 1936, when he became convinced the "Roosevelt Revolution" was threatening the fabric and framework of American constitutional government. He continued distributing literature with varying intensity through the campaigns of 1940, 1944 and 1948; and now he was prepared to throw the full force of his one-man crusade behind every election where the conflict of "free enterprise" and "creeping socialism" was evident.

Few men have had the time, inclination and resources to devote themselves so intensely to the interests of government; and it is doubtful if any other American ever threw himself so wholly into the political arena with no personal political ambitions whatever. Roy Cullen had never sought a political office, and never held one. He carried on his campaign singlehanded, as an independent citizen, with no political attachments except his unwavering convictions that the

"New Deal-Fair Deal" philosophy spelled ultimate disaster to American freedom.

He used existing political organizations for the distribution of printed material he sent out, when they were available; and when they were not available, he simply mailed out the material himself.

"I have always had faith in people—not in a few people, but in all the people," he explained to those who wondered at his tireless activity in the political field. "Unfortunately, there is a lot of information people ought to have that they do not have . . . I feel that if the people are given light, they will find the way."

He often compared his activities to those of a life-insurance company, which spends great sums of money counselling people in matters of health and the prevention of disease—believing that a healthy people means a healthy life-insurance business.

Many of the candidates he supported had never met him; and few of them had solicited his help. "The individual candidate isn't important . . . It's what he stands for, and his record in fighting for it, that counts."

He was far more interested in the people who were doing the voting, believing that if the people were well informed, they would take care of electing the right candidates.

In one instance, after reading the book, *I Chose Freedom,* written by a Russian refugee named Kravchenko, he mailed a check for $25,000 to the publisher, Charles Scribner's Sons, and asked that copies of the book be distributed to libraries and schools. The only information the libraries had as to the source of the book was a note from the publisher that it was sent "with the compliments of a believer in American freedom, who hopes this book will have the widest possible reading by American citizens."

A few years later the author, Kravchenko, wrote another book, *I Chose Justice,* dealing with a libel suit filed against him by Communists in Paris who objected to things said in the first book. Whitney Darrow, of Scribner's, sent Roy Cullen a set of galley proofs, asking him to read the proofs and tell them what he thought of the second book.

Cullen read the proofs, and wrote Darrow: "The story of the libel suit is fine, but I think the man is a socialist." There was no check accompanying the letter.

He often mailed out reprints of his own speeches, when he felt the subject was something that might plant seeds in fertile grounds; and in one instance he sent out thousands of copies of an address he made to the Baylor School of Medicine in which he advised the graduates of the medical school to join in the battle to stop the Government's proposed program of "socialized medicine" which, he said, would "change our entire way of life."

"The only thing that will check this creeping blight," he said, "is the concerted action of freedom-loving Americans at the ballot box . . . to elect men who will stand up for our form of government and our way of life . . ."

As the 1950 campaign wore on, he developed a voluminous correspondence with individual political leaders—congressmen, candidates, and with friends and acquaintances in districts where critical campaigns were under way.

In the summer of 1950 the outbreak of war in Korea cast an ominous pall over the nation; and Cullen seized upon this as a further indication of the faulty political steering of the ship of state by the Truman Administration. He was resting at White Sulphur Springs in Virginia when the news was flashed over the wires; and when President Truman ordered American troops into the "police action," Roy wired his congressional friends en masse:

I believe the people are opposed to this Administration's inept handling of our foreign affairs, and will register their protests at the polls in November. It is my suggestion that you consider making the battle cry in the coming campaign the fact that the Democrats have involved us in two World Wars and are now on the verge of getting us into a third one.

When the Chinese Red Army entered the war with the North Koreans in the big offensive of 1951, he wired President Truman to "take our boys out of Korea before they are all slaughtered or captured."

He poured his fire at the United Nations, insisting that the United Nations and the American State Department had permitted the Kremlin to "select the battleground where it could supply millions of Chinese, Koreans and Tartars to fight for the next hundred years without hurting Russia itself."

He wired congressional leaders again:

We have spread forty billion dollars over Asia and Europe, with the result that the peoples of those areas hate us more now than they did before . . . Get our soldiers out of Korea, get rid of the Marshall Plan, and let's spend every dollar we can afford to spend on armaments to protect this country.

In a letter to Governor Allan Shivers of Texas, an old friend, he wrote:

"Our country is in a hell of a boat, and I don't know how we can get out of it—unless we impeach Truman and throw out Dean Acheson and General Marshall!"

As the Korean situation wore on, growing more confused and vague as to American policy and the ultimate outcome of the "police action," he decided to canvass the country to get a cross-section of American opinion. First he turned his attention to the educational field. He wrote teachers and college professors all over the country, asking for their views on the Korean affair. He found the vast majority of educators sincerely opposed to the Korean War. When Senator Lyndon Johnson, Texas' Democratic senator, was reported in news dispatches as being in favor of centralizing wartime powers in the President, Roy wired a strenuous protest.

"Your attitude is a big disappointment," he said, "because the President has already put politics above principle . . . This will take our nation farther down the road to socialism and rob us of more of our liberties which have given America the highest standard of living on earth."

He sent copies of his telegram to other senators, and got many sympathetic replies. Senator Homer Capehart of Indiana wrote: "You have stated facts. I believe the people are opposed to the inept handling of foreign affairs by this Administration and will register their protest in the fall of 1952." Senator Kenneth Wherry of Nebraska wrote: "It is my fervent prayer that you are right in your forecast that the American public will register their protest against the bungled foreign policy when they vote in November . . ."

Shortly before the elections of 1950, Roy invited John T. Flynn, who had written *The Road Ahead*—a bitter denunciation of the political philosophy of the Roosevelt-Truman-Acheson triumvirate—to visit Houston. Flynn's books had been mailed out to hundreds of thousands of Americans by Cullen. Introducing Flynn to the Houstonians at a dinner he had arranged for him, Cullen said:

"This book may be one of the principal weapons we have in our fight to prevent the converting of our Government into a welfare state . . . and lessening the tragedy of our country, helping to prevent it from going down the road toward socialism."

The November elections showed the impact of Roy Cullen's "one-man campaign" to "bring light to the voters of

America." In more than fifty congressional campaigns, where the campaigns had been close and critical, the candidates to whom he gave his long-distance support had been victorious; and twelve senatorial candidates he had backed won their seats.

The week after the elections, Dwight Eisenhower again visited Houston—this time at Roy Cullen's invitation to speak at the University of Houston and Rice Institute.

On November 9, 1950, after an address at the Texas Agricultural and Mechanical College he came to Houston. This time the General's schedule was more relaxed. He was scheduled to attend a party given in his honor by an old friend, L. F. McCollum, and then he went home with Roy Cullen to spend the night.

After dinner, the two sat in the spacious "living room" of the Cullen home. The General, tired from a day of activity and travel, was completely relaxed. Roy took in every detail of expression . . . the warm, friendly smile; the keen blue eyes; the genial good humor in the General's round, rugged countenance.

After a few preliminary comments, Roy leaned forward, his shock of gray hair framing his face, his expression suddenly quite serious.

"General, you told us once you had no political ambitions —and I think everyone who knows you believes you."

Eisenhower nodded. Roy leaned further forward to emphasize his next words:

"I'm glad to hear that—because it isn't ambition that makes the kind of President we need today. It's honesty and faith . . . faith in America, and in the things that made America strong."

Through Roy Cullen's mind were running the thoughts that he had expressed the year before at the Coliseum, when the General had presented him with the medal of the Freedom Foundation: "If I have done anything worth while in life, I attribute it to being surrounded all my life by fine and inspiring people."

Now, as he watched the General's reactions in the flickering expression of his eyes, the sudden quirk of his smile, Roy felt that the real core of his own philosophy lay in something his mother had told him years ago: "Roy, fine character means more than anything else in life."

The future of America might lie in this man . . . and Roy wanted to be sure in his own mind how solidly he stood within the creed he believed in—the creed of character, straightforwardness, and a rugged honesty that was so sorely needed by the nation at this time.

Roy had long felt that the country was losing a kind of faith that was inherent in its early growth—faith in character, faith in the individual honesty of men, faith in the people themselves! What America needed, more than anything else, was a restoration of the kind of iron courage that had guided Americans through the hard years of pioneering. The country needed a leader—and the question foremost in his mind was: Is this man the leader?

He had met the General several times, but this was the first time they had sat together alone—in the words of an old Arab expression, "between four eyes." He studied General Eisenhower's face, the genial humor in the clear blue eyes, the kindness and human understanding etched in the lines of his face.

For several minutes they remained silent—the broad-shouldered Texan whose life had been a hard, blunt battle to make his own ideals stand up in a raw country, and whose sole "political ambition" was to see a leader worthy of American traditions; and across from him, separated by a few feet, the man whose calm will and judgment had guided the armed might of the free world, and led it to victory in the greatest war in history . . . the man who had then told his own people he had "no political ambitions."

Finally Roy leaned forward again, his great hands swinging idly between his knees, his eyes peering keenly from under his massive brows; and he said:

"General, the people of this country want you as their next President. I can assure you of this . . . I spend a lot of time writing letters to people. I talk with a lot of people from both sides of the tracks. I think I've got a fair idea what most of the people think. They're sick of politicians in Washington."

Eisenhower nodded.

"I'm not going to ask you whether you want to be President . . . because you've already answered that. You've said you have no political ambitions. But there is one thing I can tell you: You can be nominated and elected if you refuse to talk politics with anyone. Remain just what you are, a soldier."

Roy spoke seriously and earnestly; and the General seemed to consider his remarks thoughtfully. They talked at length, until it was nearly midnight; and finally the General said:

"I have no wish to run . . . as I told you. I've had all the honors I want or need, and I would wish—if I had the choice—to bow out of the picture. But if the Republican party doesn't trot out someone who can beat Truman, then if they want me to run . . . I'll run."

The two rose and shook hands; and the next day the General left Houston. A month later Roy Cullen read in the news dispatches that President Truman had selected General Eisenhower to command the "international army" in Europe, under the North Atlantic Treaty Organization.

On December 12, Roy Cullen wired President Truman:

> The United States furnished the Commanding General, nearly all the armed forces, and most of the money for the war in Korea. And now, after being overpowered by the Chinese Reds, many people are blaming us and General MacArthur for starting the war. If our country should be so foolish as to send General Eisenhower or any other American general to act as commander-in-chief of the armed forces in Europe, we will assume a responsibility which we are not able physically or financially to carry through . . . It is time for you and Congress to think about our country's interests first.

He received no reply. The next day he wired:

> The United Nations prevented our army from bombing Manchuria, which cost the lives of thousands of our boys. Our Government now proposes to duplicate that great mistake we made in Korea, by sending one of our generals to act as commander-in-chief of the armed forces in Europe, where we would have the same handicap that we have had in Korea.

He received a polite note from a member of the President's staff, assuring him that Mr. Truman appreciated his views and would give them "careful consideration."

Roy did not expect an answer from the President; but he sent copies of his wires, as usual, to congressional leaders, where he felt they would have some influence.

Then he wrote a letter to General Eisenhower, who was still at Columbia:

> I do not want you, nor any other American general, to be commander-in-chief of the Army in Europe, for the United Nations would probably crucify you, as it did General MacArthur.
>
> I want you to stay here and keep in a position where we can elect you President of the United States, and where you can play an important role in helping to save our country.

CHAPTER 24

"The issue is greater than any man"

GENERAL EISENHOWER left for his European job early in 1951; and in the spring of 1951 General Douglas MacArthur returned from Japan, summarily fired by President Truman in the midst of the Korean War. These two events focused sharply in the mind of Roy Cullen the absolute urgency of developing a nominee for the Republican ticket in 1952 that could not fail—as Dewey had failed three years before.

General Eisenhower, in a tactfully worded reply to Roy's letter on his assignment to the North Atlantic Treaty Organization, had written:

> Except for my very earnest conviction that the future of our way of life demands successful establishment of collective security in a free world, nothing could have induced me to take such an onerous task . . . I feel that every person who can boast American citizenship must do his utmost in these days of tension and bewilderment to help preserve and sustain our nation and our system.

Cullen read the letter carefully. It presented certain aspects of General Eisenhower's philosophy with which he was not in complete agreement; nevertheless, he had complete faith in the General's sincerity . . . and on that evening when the two had talked late into the night at Roy Cullen's home in Houston, Eisenhower had left a deep impression on the Texan.

He felt that the Republican candidate would be chosen from three men—Eisenhower, MacArthur and Senator Robert A. Taft. Roy had some definite views on all three: He admired General MacArthur, but he was not certain that his experience in military leadership would qualify him in the rough-and-tumble political arena in Washington; he liked and admired Senator Taft, but did not think he could draw enough votes to win; and he regarded Eisenhower as the least positive in his political approach, but perhaps the most effective vote-getter of the three.

In March, 1951, he wrote General Eisenhower, who was then in Europe, addressing him as "Dear Ike:"

> I am aware that you are in France, but I am writing you at Columbia hoping my letter will be forwarded to you. The Democrats, as you probably know, have wrecked the party and are now looking for a candidate and they often use your name as a possible candidate on the Democratic ticket. I feel certain that you would not accept the nomination on the Democratic ticket. I came to this belief due to the many things you have said to me . . .
>
> I feel certain that you will be offered the Republican nomination for President in 1952, and that you will be elected by a very great majority, because I believe that many Democrats as well as Republicans will support you . . . Up to now you have pleased the American people by refusing to discuss politics . . .

A month later he telephoned General Robert E. Wood, head of the Sears, Roebuck Company in Chicago—and a lifelong friend of General MacArthur. He asked Wood if he could arrange for the General to visit Houston and address a gathering there. The invitation was referred to General Mac-

Arthur's aide, General Courtney Whitney; and after some deliberation, Whitney telephoned Cullen in the middle of May that General MacArthur would like to visit Houston during the first week in June.

"I'm sorry," Cullen told Whitney. "If he comes then I won't be able to see him, because I've told my granddaughter I would attend her graduation exercises in New York on June 3."

Whitney coughed politely, and suggested that perhaps Cullen might forego his granddaughter's graduation in order to be in Houston when General MacArthur arrived.

"I admire General MacArthur very much," the oil man said, "but I wouldn't break my word to my granddaughter for a dozen MacArthurs."

After several more telephone conversations between Cullen and Whitney, it was decided that the General would arrive a week later—visiting the state capital at Austin on June 13 and Houston on June 14.

Hardly had the MacArthur visit been arranged than Cullen found himself knee-deep in a controversy over the visit with a fellow-Texan, Glenn McCarthy, keeper of the famed Shamrock Hotel. McCarthy had sent an invitation to General MacArthur to visit the Shamrock about the time Whitney had confirmed the date to Cullen; and a duplicate message was sent McCarthy.

The latter immediately assumed it was a reply to his invitation, and called the newspapers and announced that General MacArthur had accepted his invitation to visit Houston. The report said nothing of Cullen's negotiations; and everyone figured McCarthy was the host. So, when the time came to pick up the tab for the General's visit, a bill for $8,500 was presented to McCarthy.

The hotel man let out a howl, insisting that he had given

free lodgings for the General at the Shamrock, and he thought the city of Houston should foot the rest of the bill. Mayor Oscar Holcombe put it up to the City Council and that body voted to pay $2,500 on the basis of the publicity Houston had received.

By this time a report of the haggling reached Cullen, who was on his ranch. He promptly telephoned his office in Houston.

"This is embarrassing to Houston and to Texas," he said. "Find out how much the bill is—I'll pay it."

McCarthy and several others agreed to make up $3,500, and Roy Cullen paid the rest. It was on this occasion that Jesse Jones, who collected the money, wrote to Cullen: "You are the most generous man I have ever known."

After General MacArthur's swing through Texas, in which he addressed huge crowds at Austin, Houston, San Antonio, Dallas and Fort Worth, Roy wrote to General Eisenhower at his headquarters in Paris:

Dear Ike:

General MacArthur, his wife and son, and his aide, General Courtney Whitney, accepted my invitation to come to Texas . . . It is safe to say that 95 percent of the people in Texas feel that the President did a great injustice to General MacArthur. I was in New York City from June 4th to 9th to see my granddaughter graduate from the Masters School at Dobbs Ferry. While in New York I was with the MacArthurs and the Whitneys constantly, and I am of the firm conviction that MacArthur does not intend to get into politics. This was confirmed to me by ex-President Herbert Hoover . . .

I am fairly well acquainted with the Republican Presidential timber such as yourself, Taft, Stassen, Duff and Joe Martin, and will be better acquainted with a dark horse—Everett McKinley Dirksen—who will be a guest in my home tomorrow night. We must nominate the right man for President in 1952, for if we fail our country will be in jeopardy.

He detailed a thumb-nail sketch of the various aspirants:

> ... Taft is very capable ... but we would have a house divided and that would be bad. Joe Martin would make us a great President, but somehow he cannot get the publicity needed to elect a President. Stassen has not matured mentally and is widely disliked by the conservative element of our country. Duff is an unknown quantity. I cross-questioned him for one and a half hours, and when I got through, I didn't know whether he is a conservative or a liberal ...

He enclosed a clipping showing a Gallup Poll survey, "which shows that both the Democrats and Republicans would like to make you President of the United States." He wound up with a word of caution:

"I think it would be best for you to continue as you have done, and let the people make your case . . ."

After General MacArthur's visit, Cullen had decided the way to survey the Presidential aspirants on the Republican side was to see them in action—so he invited Senator Dirksen of Illinois to come to Houston. He had helped elect Dirksen in the senatorial race in Illinois ten years before, and he had great admiration for his character and ability.

"I consider Senator Dirksen a courageous, patriotic citizen, and a man of highest integrity," he said. "No one can tell who will get the Republican nomination for President in 1952 at this time—and Senator Dirksen is a dark horse. Right now he isn't too dark."

He talked it over with the Senator, suggesting that he should keep in line for the Vice-Presidential nomination. Dirksen agreed that the Presidential nomination was fairly remote; and he had always had a deep respect for Roy Cullen's political insight.

Meanwhile, Cullen received word that George S. Allen, the former friend of Presidents Roosevelt and Truman, was now in Paris, wooing General Eisenhower. He remembered Allen's conversation the night he and Lillie had been dinner guests at the Eisenhower home in New York. He had developed a deep antipathy toward Allen at that time; and now his suspicions were aroused.

He promptly wrote another letter to Eisenhower, commenting on Dirksen's visit—in which he described the Illinois senator as "sincere and very patriotic" and noted that he "has contempt for Truman and his bunch of socialists in Washington." And then, perhaps thinking of George Allen, he added: "Now the trouble is to push aside the professional politicians so that we can get you nominated on the Republican ticket."

General Eisenhower had studiously refrained from any communication that might be interpreted as an acceptance of Roy Cullen's thesis that he would be the Republican candidate. On June 26 he wrote from Supreme Allied Headquarters in Paris:

> Thank you for your letter. You have a knack of packing your communications brimful of interesting subjects . . . As you have suggested, I never comment, in my replies, on certain phases of your messages.

In the concluding paragraph of his letter, the General wrote:

> I feel that every single person who can boast of American citizenship must do his utmost in these days of tension and bewilderment to help preserve and sustain our nation and our system. Every man must work in the field for which he is best fitted, and every man owes it to himself to try to understand the great issues of the day. This applies with particular force to the Communist threat which combines external pressure and aggression with internal subversion, bribery and corruption. Their weapons are lies and deceit, and we have to make certain

that the truth of the great American drama and system is kept constantly before the world.

Shortly afterward Roy had occasion to write the General again, and this time he brought up the matter of George Allen with complete candor:

> You are acting wisely and much good is coming of it, but the press has stated that George S. Allen is taking the lead in promoting your cause for the Presidency, which is not so good. Also Dewey (Governor Dewey of New York) is building political fences at your expense, but I don't think this will do you much harm, for you are attending to your knitting, and the American people know this.

Roy also advised General Eisenhower of a rather momentous event—which he tossed off quite casually. He wrote:

"I recently purchased controlling interest in the Liberty Network to keep it out of bad hands. This is the second largest network in the country, and soon will be probably the largest."

The purchase of the "Liberty Network" was one of the most surprising moves in Roy Cullen's career. He had received information from John Flynn that that chain of radio stations was for sale, with the suggestion that certain "left-wing" interests were maneuvering to acquire it. The "network"—which was not a network, but an affiliation of radio stations—had been established in 1947 by an exuberant young man from Dallas, named Gordon McLendon. He had graduated from Yale shortly before the war; and in 1942 had joined the Navy. One of his wartime duties was broadcasting; and he became so enamored of the future of the broadcasting business that when he got out of the Navy at the end of the war, he decided to start a broadcasting system.

His first effort was to link together a small group of radio stations, for the purpose of broadcasting baseball games. The broadcasts struck a popular note; and from 1948 to 1951 the group of affiliated stations mushroomed into a fairly large chain of independent stations covering thirty-eight states, with more than four hundred broadcasting outlets. It was the country's second largest network, although the individual stations were still independently owned.

The idea of a network based on affiliation of individual radio stations was full of complications. McLendon found himself in deep financial waters with his chain, and he decided to sell a controlling interest to bail himself out. Flynn found out about it; and the report was circulated that a group of "left wingers" with financial backing was dickering for the network. Flynn then went to Cullen.

Roy Cullen had no interest in radio broadcasting; but the prospect of a powerful network falling into the hands of "creeping socialists" alarmed him; and there was also the reverse possibility—that the network might be used to counteract these forces, and perhaps reawaken the nation to the need of preserving the free institutions of America.

"Tell him to come down and talk with me," Cullen said. "We may work out something."

McLendon came down to Houston. He was a young man of thirty, ambitious and active, but without adequate financial backing or the business experience needed to chart the "Liberty Network" through the early stages of development. He thought a million dollars might save him.

Cullen questioned him at considerable length. If McLendon had accomplished what he had done in two years, without financial backing . . . the network must have enormous possibilities. McLendon offered him 51 percent interest in the broadcasting chain for a million dollars.

"All right," Cullen said. "I'll take it."

His lawyers and accountants suggested that he wait for

an audit of the company's books, but Roy was impressed with young McLendon. "I'm not betting on the books—I'm betting on this young man," he said.

Roy's interest in the "Liberty Network" went a lot deeper than merely buying a chain of radio stations to broadcast his own views, or the views of any one political group.

"America grew on our freedom," he told his friends. "Freedom of religion—freedom of speech—and freedom of the press. I think it's about time some radio stations gave us a chance to let this system work."

He invited diverse schools of thought—right, left and center—to expound their views. He conceived of a gigantic "American forum of the air" in which all views on current topics could be presented, and the American people could make up their mind which views to follow.

He was particularly interested in using this to promote the several sides of labor issues. Roy firmly believed that an exposition of his own theory of working men investing in corporations which employed them would bring a common understanding of the way in which economic factors affected both management and labor.

For many years organized labor in Texas had recognized him as a staunch supporter of fair labor practices, even making him an honorary member of the American Federation of Labor. On August 5, 1949, the *Labor Messenger,* official organ of the Houston Labor Council and the American Federation of Labor in that city, published a tribute to him in an editorial, which said:

> To some people it may seem out of character for a labor paper to toss orchids at a fabulously rich man. A moment's thought should convince them that . . . in this instance, it is an appropriate gesture.

The editorial listed Roy Cullen's many gifts to hospitals and institutions which directly and indirectly benefited working people; and it continued:

> The average Houstonian thinks of these gifts in terms of direct benefits . . . If there were no other benefits, it would put Mr. Cullen in a special place in the hearts of his followers. But the indirect benefits are even greater . . . When he gives a million dollars for a building, he is creating work for labor and business for industry and commerce . . .

It was this philosophy of common interests which Roy Cullen felt should be expounded; and he extended an invitation to labor representatives to use the "Liberty Network." John T. Flynn also used it, presenting the economic and political viewpoints he had expressed in *The Road Ahead.*

However, financial troubles continued to burden the radio chain, even with Roy Cullen's stimulus. The baseball broadcasts began to cut down attendance at minor-league baseball games, and the major leagues refused to permit their continuance. This dried up the lifeblood of advertising, which sustained the broadcasts; and on May 14, 1952—about a year after Roy Cullen became a partner in the enterprise—McLendon announced that the system was suspending indefinitely.

Several weeks before Roy Cullen had regretfully concluded his connection with the chain, offering to return his shares of stock to McLendon. "As long as my name is connected with anything, I want to give it full attention," he explained. "I couldn't do that with the Liberty Broadcasting System . . . there were too many complications."

Meanwhile, he had begun to concentrate on the approaching Presidential campaign of 1952, which he felt was the most crucial in the history of the country since the election of Franklin Roosevelt in 1932.

Roy Cullen had assayed the political possibilities of General Eisenhower and General MacArthur; but Bob Taft was still an uncertain factor, and very much in the race. Early in 1951, Ben Tate, Taft's manager, had written to Cullen advising him that he had heard "from quite a reliable source that the Dewey crowd is managing the Eisenhower campaign, and they have recently become very active." The note added: "I think the General is in bad company."

Roy Cullen thought so, too. In one of his earlier letters to General Eisenhower, he had said:

> Winthrop Aldrich visited Houston a short time ago and told me he was in favor of having Dewey nominate you at the National Convention, and I informed Aldrich that would be a very bad thing to do, and I hope you feel as I do.

This was written in March of 1951, a few weeks after Cullen had received the tip from Ben Tate. At the same time, he wrote to Senator Taft: "I am backing you and ex-President Hoover on your stand against sending troops to Europe . . . In my opinion, Governor Dewey and Harold Stassen are muddying the Republican political waters."

In the summer of that year—July 26, 1951—approximately a year before the Republican Convention in Chicago, Roy Cullen addressed a joint letter to Generals MacArthur and Eisenhower, and to Senator Taft. After referring to the acute Korean War situation and the "great danger" to the country, he said:

> It will be necessary to elect a President by a large majority, so he will have the power to restore our government to its democratic principles. The people of our country honor you gentlemen above all others as possible candidates for the Republican nomination for President . . . The reason I am writing you three

gentlemen is that I am going to back and support to the best of my ability the one who happens to be the strongest candidate for the nomination of the Republican party at the time of the primaries.

On November 17 he wrote Taft that General Eisenhower "has the advantage in the polls" but added that he was surrounded by "some unattractive people." As a case in point, he mentioned George S. Allen. Two days later he received a letter from Ben Tate: "I assume you have decided that you are not for Bob (Taft). I hope I am wrong, and so does Bob."

Cullen wrote to Tate on December 1st: "It is my opinion, and I have said this to you before, that Taft cannot carry one of the Southern states. The issue is much greater than any man, or group of men."

This correspondence assumed considerable significance the following spring when Senator Taft's political supporters in Texas carried out what was referred to as "the Texas steal." It was this effort to capture the Texas delegation at the Republican Convention that swung the final outcome.

Roy Cullen, sitting in his offices in the City National Bank Building, engineered the revolt of the Texas Republicans which paved the way for the victory of Dwight Eisenhower in Chicago in July, and ultimately for the landslide victory at the national elections in November of 1952.

EZEKIEL W CULLEN
BUILDING

CHAPTER 25

"It's not the value of the oil— it's the value of our freedom"

On JULY 3, 1951, Roy Cullen was seventy years of age. He had given forty of those seventy years in unstinting service to the city of Houston—never as a political office holder, but as a plain citizen, who wanted to see his city grow. He had fought for the development of the Ship Channel, which made Houston one of the world's great ports. He had founded a university and built it almost singlehanded. He had endowed hospitals and made possible the Texas Medical Center and the Baylor School of Medicine in Houston. He had given to the Boy Scouts, the Y.M.C.A. and the Y.W.C.A., the Art Museum and the Symphony. And he had fought for good government—in his city, his state and his country.

Forty years before Roy Cullen had looked at a map of the Mississippi Valley, and had decided Houston was the natural outlet of the most productive river basin in the world. Now he was able to assay the results of his decision.

On September 22, 1951, Roy stood with Lillie, bareheaded under cloudy skies that had dripped rain all afternoon, and looked at the faces of sixty thousand Houstonians who had come to pay a signal honor to the couple who had embarked nearly a half century before on a partnership of love and respect in the big frame house of Gustav Cranz in Schulenberg, some ninety miles to the west.

The celebration of "Cullen Day" had been a spontaneous expression of public gratitude, beginning with a suggestion from the president of the Houston Chamber of Commerce, Colonel W. B. Bates. The University of Houston football team was scheduled to play its first "homecoming" game against Baylor University on Saturday night, and Colonel Bates thought it would be an excellent occasion for the people of Houston to show a measure of appreciation for the things Roy and Lillie Cullen had done for the University and for the city.

The students of the University of Houston immediately took up the suggestion and prepared a huge scroll, with the signatures of several thousand students, expressing their gratitude toward the two who had virtually created the University. The Mayor of Houston declared a day of tribute to "the Cullens."

Governor Allan Shivers seized on the opportunity to declare a state-wide "Cullen Day" as a tribute to the couple for their "excellent record of Christian stewardship"; and Mayor Oscar Holcombe followed with a proclamation of "Cullen Day" for the city of Houston.

Early in the day Roy had ridden through the streets of Houston at the head of a parade organized in his honor; and although sporadic rain had interrupted his attendance at several other functions, rain stopped just before game time, and Roy and Lillie—the former suffering from a bad cold and bundled up to protect himself against the weather—arrived at the field and joined Governor Shivers.

The University of Houston team, resplendent in new

white jerseys, was not a match for the powerful Baylor Bears, but as half-time drew near the crowds began to forget the one-sided game and push toward the south end of the big stadium, where an improvised reviewing stand had been erected.

Governor Shivers, a tall, squarely built man, looked down at the seamed face of the old wildcatter, his hand on Roy Cullen's shoulder as he stood beside him.

> America is the only country in the world where Roy and Lillie Cullen could have lived the kind of lives they have led . . . and made their lives such a success and contributed as they have toward making this a better world to live in. We can all feel that because they have passed our way, the world is a finer place for us all.

The crowd was waiting for Roy to rise; but before he stood up, a girl—Anseth Peel, a former patient at the Gonzales Warm Springs Hospital for Crippled Children—came up to the platform and presented to Roy and Lillie a strange-looking object. It was a bronze leg brace and a baby shoe, mounted on a wooden base . . . Both had been worn by a crippled child who had been cured at the hospital; and the shoe and brace had been encased in bronze, to be presented to the Cullens.

"This is a symbol from us," Miss Peel said. "We love you both."

Roy Cullen's face was working in an ill-disguised effort to keep back the tears; but now they streamed down his face. He clutched the bronze piece, and looked to Lillie for help. She smiled at him, and took the gift as he rose to thank the crowd.

Roy Cullen had faced quite a few crowds—from the rough days in Oklahoma to the great audience that had listened to him in the shadow of the San Jacinto Monument; but he had never before faced a vast number of people who had gathered purely to express their feeling of gratitude and love toward Lillie and himself for the things they had done.

The gray-walled stadium was a white theater under the blazing arc lights; and the green field, with its rectangular white stripes, lay dark and flat under the brightness of artificial daylight. A band stood at attention in mid-field. Roy Cullen stood, with Lillie beside him, grinning and waving his hand, uninhibited tears still streaming down his weathered face.

A squad of young cadets, in trim olive drab coats and polished boots—known as the "Cullen Rifles"—flanked the speaker's stand, as honor guard.

"My heart is so full," he said, his voice choking. "No matter how much eloquence I might have, I could not express our gratitude in words. Mrs. Cullen and I can truly call this moment the best in our lives. Now we can really appreciate the Twenty-third Psalm—'My cup runneth over.' God bless you all."

The crowd drowned his words with a roar; and Lillie, now standing beside him, looked at the rugged face of the man she had followed into Oklahoma when it was a raw, untamed territory . . . and down to Houston when laborers were still dredging the Ship Channel into the heart of the city.

"We've tried to help everyone, regardless of their creed or color," Roy went on, in a half-choked tone, when the thunder died down. "We have tried to devote our efforts and our means to help bring education and health and happiness to people. We have always believed—as my grandfather Ezekiel Cullen believed—that only an educated and enlightened people can remain free.

"And now we have reached the time of fulfillment and contentment."

The short speech was unrehearsed; and just as Roy Cullen's deep emotions had expressed themselves naturally and simply in his remarks about the "education and health" of a free people, his equally deep distrust of those forces which were directed at the destruction of these things welled to the surface of his thoughts.

> I cannot close without telling you people that I have been fighting the things that are trying to destroy what we have—the freedom we enjoy as Americans—the kind of freedom my grandfather believed in. I have been fighting them . . . and as long as any breath remains in me, I will keep on fighting them!

In spite of his intense preoccupation with the national campaign of 1952, and with his philanthropies, Roy had not permitted the affairs of Quintana Petroleum to lapse. His three sons-in-law—Ike Arnold, who had been with Quintana from the start; and Corbin Robertson and Douglas Marshall, who had married Wilhelmina and Margaret shortly after the war ended—fitted well into the organization. Ike Arnold was an engineer who had taught at the University of Buffalo shortly after graduating from Rensselaer; and he had guided Quintana's engineering staff with a deft hand for twenty years.

The younger members of the clan—Robertson and Marshall—were alumni of Minnesota and Northwestern, respectively; and they quickly absorbed the "feel" of the oil business. A fourth member—Roy Henry Cullen, the eldest son of Roy Gustave and Katherine—joined the group in the early 1950's.

Roy Cullen had long looked toward the West to extend his oil domain—in West Texas, and on into Colorado and Wyoming. He decided late in the 1940's to send Corbin Robinson and Douglas Marshall, both of whom were now experienced field men, out to block up acreage in the Rocky Mountain areas, continuing the trail Roy had started on, out in West Texas, thirty years before.

Roy believed there were huge oil deposits in the Northwest United States. Years before, Wallace Pratt had made a report to Humble expressing doubt that much oil would be found in the colder latitudes; and Roy had taken exception to this theory. Roy wrote Will Farish, then president of Humble, that oil could be found "all the way to the Arctic Circle." Since then actual discoveries of oil deposits within the Arctic Circle have borne out his prediction.

The geology of the Rocky Mountains area intrigued Roy, and aroused his wildcatter's instinct. In the ages when the earth was million of years younger, much of its surface was covered by seas and shallow bays, which were later filled by the erosion of the uplands and the mountains. Petroleum deposits must have been formed by the decomposing and carbonizing of plant life and marine life that flourished alternately as the land lay below and above the level of the sea. This oil must have collected in the shallower floor of the ancient seas, in soft sand traps where the folding of the stratified layers of soil would have created traps for the liquid minerals.

In Wyoming and Montana he believed there were such areas—huge basins where the land had been washed down and built up many times; and he felt that a search for oil in these areas would produce great new sources of petroleum production.

And so he sent his sons-in-law and his grandson on forays into this area, with seismograph crews; and by the early 1950's he had leased more land in this area than he held in all of Texas. The "black gold rush" of 1949 had already started into Colorado and Wyoming—exactly a century after the California "Forty-niners"; and this had confirmed Roy's conviction that oil would be found there. He now saw an empire of oil for Quintana perhaps greater than those he had developed at the Thompson and O'Connor fields.

Much of the activities in this area were what is known as "behive" prospecting. Crews of geologists, with seismographs and magnetometers, swarm over the land, charting and defining the structural trends. Scouts roam the new country, looking for likely places to drill; and lease traders jockey for holdings, buying and selling leases, often under joint drilling agreements.

"There is oil in that country—lots of it," Cullen told his men. "We'll keep on until we find it."

Meanwhile, he continued to keep a weather eye on the political scene, which was rapidly moving toward the critical campaign of 1952. He had followed up his "joint letter" to Generals MacArthur and Eisenhower, and Senator Taft, in which he promised his support to "the strongest candidate" at the time of the primaries, with a short note to General Eisenhower, enclosing a copy of a letter he had written to General MacArthur in New York:

> I wrote this letter (to General MacArthur) hoping to get a "yes" or "no" reply, for no one knows what you are going to do about the political situation, and it is necessary in my opinion for the Republican party to nominate you or General MacArthur . . .
>
> I find that a large majority of veterans would prefer to have you run for President rather than General MacArthur, and from the polls of the country it looks as if you are the choice of the people throughout the United States.
>
> In my last letter to you I told you I thought it would be well for you to make an announcement sometime before the end of the year, if you thought it was in your line of duty to do so. I sincerely hope that President Truman will give you the "go

sign" so you can make the announcement to the American people.

This was early in November, 1951. A few weeks later he wrote again to General Eisenhower, referring to his joint letter to the two generals and Senator Taft; and he added: "There is no question but what you show the most strength throughout the United States." He referred to a poll of Southern states which gave Eisenhower 54 percent of the vote; but even more important, President Truman, in a comparative test with Senator Taft, had received 48 percent of the poll votes, against 35 percent for the Ohioan.

"I respect Senator Taft very highly," Cullen wrote, "and no doubt he would make a good President; but it would be dangerous to nominate him for the Republican candidate, for we might lose."

He expressed concern at General Eisenhower's continued silence on the most urgent question in the minds of the American people, which was: Would the General be a candidate? And at the end of his letter, Roy said:

"If I could learn from you through the grapevine just about the time you expect to arrive in this country, and at that time if you are prepared to make an announcement, it might be of value . . . I could get different organizations tuned up."

General Eisenhower replied with a short personal note, in which he said:

> I find myself in a strange position for one whose name is figuring prominently in such news. The fact is I am so busy here . . . that I am completely and constantly preoccupied with our current problems here. Addressing myself to one of your specific questions, it is clear that there is no possibility of my predicting with any accuracy when SHAPE (Supreme Headquarters Allied

Powers in Europe) affairs will be in such condition that I could of my own volition ask for relief from this assignment.

Cullen was distressed at the situation. Of his three "principal candidates," he had written Taft off as a man who could not get enough votes to win, even if he got the nomination; General MacArthur seemed unable to decide whether he was a candidate or a Taft supporter; and General Eisenhower, he felt, was so busy in Europe he might slip out of the picture.

He decided it was time to play a few preliminary hands, and he telephoned Harold Stassen, who had always been a close friend, although Roy had regarded him as "emotionally a socialist." He wrote to General Eisenhower of this conversation:

> I persuaded Stassen to put his hat in the ring with the idea of controlling certain electoral votes in the Northwest; and I asked Dan Gainey, who was Harold Stassen's campaign manager in the last Presidential election, to open offices and start working for Harold. After discussing the matter over the phone with Stassen, he has decided to visit you in Europe to discuss certain matters with you . . . I asked Harold Stassen to get in the Presidential race to stop Taft, whom I admire very much, but who would run a very poor race if nominated for President by the Republican party.

While Roy was trying to put the pins in a row on the Republican side, he did not neglect the activities of the "creeping socialists" in Washington. A telegram from John Steelman, one of President Truman's aides, inviting him to a White House conference of businessmen and Government officials "to discuss problems facing the country," provided an opening for one of Roy's broadsides on Administration policies.

He advised Steelman that his physician had ordered him not to take any extensive trip, and that he would be unable to attend the meeting; but he had a few suggestions "for extricating the nation from the perilous plight into which the Administration's disastrous course has plunged us."

One of these suggestions was to put a restraining hand upon the "Communist fifth columnists who are running around the country," many of them presumably "plotting more treason against the United States." He said the first step in this direction might be to curb the United Nations which provided "a base of operations and a sounding board for propaganda, without restraint."

Concerning the Administration's foreign policy, he wrote:

> Instead of knocking ourselves out fighting Reds wherever "good old Joe" Stalin may decide to set them upon us, why don't we reverse the charges and try playing his game? Why not spend some of our money and effort in arming and equipping the anti-Communists who are in a great majority in the countries now under Soviet heel and thumb? With weapons and supplies . . . I think we could induce some of the so-called satellite peoples to turn on their enslavers and . . . put Russia on the defensive, as we are now . . .
>
> We might have more effect against the Chinese Communists, at less cost of American lives, by supporting Chiang Kai-shek's trained Formosa army and his huge guerilla following on the mainland, and by arming Japan.

He never learned whether his suggestions were discussed at the meeting, since his letter was never answered.

The political forces which Roy Cullen had been welding together since the 1950 congressional elections—in which he had assisted candidates, regardless of party affiliations, who were fighting the "New Deal-Fair Deal crowd" in Washington—had now begun to gather into a swelling tide.

The strength of this political force began to be apparent when the so-called "Tidelands Bill' confirming state ownership of tideland oil resources came up for action in the Senate. The Administration tried to "shelve" the bill by bringing up the Hawaii statehood measure in its place on the Senate calendar.

Roy Cullen had never believed the tidelands were an important source of oil. Years before, Quintana Petroleum and Humble had found a submerged oil deposit in Lavaca Bay, southwest of Houston about halfway along the Gulf Coast toward Corpus Christi, and spent almost two million dollars on geophysical reports and in drilling holes, with one small producer—about twenty-five barrels a day. But Roy felt the principle of state control of the tidelands was more important than the amount of oil involved.

Governor Shivers, a Democrat, telephoned one Saturday morning to advise Roy that the Administration forces in the Senate had sidetracked the Tidelands Bill. Roy was not in the office, but Corbin Robertson received the call and immediately contacted him at the Cullen ranch, about fifty miles from Houston.

Shivers told Cullen: "Roy, they're trying to shelve the Tidelands Bill by taking up Hawaiian statehood ahead of it. If they do that, we can kiss our legislation goodbye for this year . . . and it looks as if that's what will happen unless you can get your Republican friends to help."

Cullen said he would see what could be done. He telegraphed Senator Dirksen of Illinois, and several other senators, and explained what was happening. Dirksen phoned the following morning: "The Tidelands Bill is going back on the calendar."

The issue, which had been confined to the states involved —California, Texas and Louisiana—suddenly became of national interest, during and after the campaign. A Washington columnist charged that the vote in the Senate was due to the influence of "Texas oilmen Roy Cullen and Sid Richardson." It was not until after the election that Roy Cullen laid the ghost of "Texas oil influence" to rest when he wrote to Eisenhower:

> The Magnolia Oil Company, a subsidiary of Socony Vacuum, spent twenty-eight million dollars on leases, geophysical work, and drilling wells in the tidelands along the Texas and Louisiana coasts. They offered me half interest in all their tidelands holdings—not for cash, but for the consideration that I would match dollars with them in future operations. I turned down this offer . . . In my opinion oil cannot be produced economically from the tidelands . . .
>
> When the history of the tidelands is written, it will show that gasoline can be produced from coal, oil shale, and possibly from the sawdust that is now going to waste at sawmills, at a cost much less than it can be produced from the tidelands . . . Now if Congress will take time to call before it oil men who are familiar with the tidelands, I am sure they will confirm my statements.

Roy Cullen had entered the tidelands fight for one reason: He believed the effort of the Federal Government to control the Texas tidelands was a basic violation of the agreements entered into between the United States and Texas when the Republic of Texas joined the Union.

"I don't care whether the tidelands oil is worth a billion dollars or a dollar," he said. "It is not a question of the value of the oil; it is a matter of the value of our freedom and the rights that have been guaranteed to us under the Constitution and under the Treaty of 1845, in which the United States Congress by resolution declared that Texas should retain her public lands."

And he repeated what he had said two years before to the graduating class of the Baylor School of Medicine, when he warned them against "the nationalization of the medical profession" by the "socialist Administration in Washington."

"If the Federal Government can take the tidelands from the states, they can take the coal lands, or the coastal fishing grounds, or the oil or gas lands, or the ports and inland waterways, or anything of value that the states may have . . ."

IKE
ARKANSAS
IKE
CONN
IKE
IKE
OREGON
FOR IKE
ARIZ
NEW MEXICO
NEVADA
IKE
ERMONT
WITH IKE
LAND
XAS
IKE
VOTE FOR BOB
TAFT
AINE
E
JOB
BOB
TAFT
AMERIC

CHAPTER 26

"These brazen tactics will result in a national scandal"

SENATOR TAFT visited Houston in March—three months before the Republican Convention in Chicago—and spent a busy day. He crowded into his schedule two speeches, a press conference, a public reception, and several private talks with Republican leaders in Texas.

Roy Cullen made no move to interrupt the Senator's plans or schedule; but about five o'clock in the afternoon Taft telephoned Cullen and asked him if he would drop over to his suite at the Rice Hotel for a chat.

When Cullen came into the room, the Senator was talking with a few friends; but he asked them to leave so he could talk with the oil man alone.

"How does it look to you, Roy?" he asked.

"It looks the way it did when I wrote you in November, Senator," Cullen said. His gray eyes looked steadily at the smiling man from Ohio. "I admire you, and I believe in you, Senator—but I don't think you can win, even if you are nominated."

Senator Taft blinked. His smile was tighter; and finally he said:

"At least you're frank about it, Roy."

"I know you wouldn't want me to be otherwise," Cullen said quietly.

Taft sat down, and his mouth straightened into a firm line. He explained, quietly and without rancor, that he had never lost a political election; he saw no reason to believe he would lose this one. In every race in which he had been entered as a nominee, his opponents had said he had no "vote appeal" . . . yet he had won. In his last race for re-election to the Senate, he had won by 430,000 votes, in spite of the most expensive opposition the labor crowd could muster. Didn't that disprove the theory that he could not win a popular election?

Roy slowly shook his head.

"You won't carry Texas, Senator—and that means you won't carry the South. You've got to have most of the Southern states to win."

The Senator arose and smiled. He extended his hand.

"We'll see, Roy," he said, as they shook hands.

Roy Cullen still believed the Republican nominee would be one of three candidates—Eisenhower, Taft or MacArthur. If Taft could marshal enough votes among the convention delegates to block Eisenhower, MacArthur might be the solution. For this reason, he disliked the public efforts General MacArthur had made in support of Senator Taft.

As the pre-convention fight among the Republican aspirants warmed up, he could see the approaching contest between Eisenhower and Taft as the most crucial in the history of the party. The Taft forces were pulling out every plug in their effort to stop the popular swing toward the Kansan. In one of his letters to General Eisenhower in Europe, Roy Cullen had written:

I am enclosing a clipping from the Houston *Post* . . . The last paragraph states that Senator Brewster is convinced you are an indispensable man in Europe. This is bad. If the politicians who are not for you can put the idea over to the American people that you must stay in Europe, they will succeed in putting you out of the race . . .

He kept up a running fire of comment at the General in Europe, advising him of the shifts of political opinion in the United States; and at one time after receiving a clipping from Roy Cullen in which a writer criticized the General for not coming back and entering the political fight, Eisenhower replied:

Thank you very much for sending along to me the article . . . I do not, of course, know the writer, but in his anxiety to direct at me a volume of criticism, I am moved to wonder whether he has ever heard of one simple word—"duty." I know of nothing easier than to stand on the sideline and shout advice to others.

During the evening General Eisenhower had spent at Roy Cullen's home in Houston, a few months before he left for Europe, the Texas oil man had urged the General to avoid "talking politics." He had argued that if the General stayed away from any political alliances, the American people would look to him—and to him alone—for leadership.

Now, as the campaign roared toward the summer of election year, he wrote the General again:

Much water has gone over the dam since you and I had a heart-to-heart talk in my home some twenty-eight months ago. I told you then and I have written you often that if you would refuse to talk politics to anyone that the people of this country would nominate you and elect you President . . . Since the New Hampshire and Minnesota primaries and the backing away of Taft from New Jersey, that same old crowd that followed Roosevelt, Willkie, Dewey and Truman, all looking for an easy winner and prestige, are all lining up behind you.

Ike, I have a high regard for your patriotism, intellect and your great spirit of friendship, but I am just wondering whether anyone can successfully combat this lot of political leeches.

On February 18, 1952, Cullen—who was taking a short rest in Phoenix, Arizona—had met Harold Stassen; and after a long discussion, he frankly told the Minnesotan:

"Harold, to my way of thinking you are mentally a conservative, but at heart you are a socialist—and I can't go along with you."

In spite of his feeling that Stassen was "at heart a socialist," Roy knew the Minnesotan had a strong following and he felt his support might be the means of halting the progress of Senator Taft; so he had suggested that he "put his hat in the ring to slow down Taft."

Stassen had put his hat in the ring with such emphasis that Roy now began to wonder about it; and he wrote General Eisenhower:

He (Stassen) has done many things recently of which I do not approve, the last being that of telling the voters of Wisconsin that he is going to give you half of his electoral votes in that state. To my way of thinking, this is a pure steal for Stassen. I also know that he has approached General Marshall. In other words, he is working both sides of the street . . .

In another letter to the General, he wrote: "It is doubtful which way Stassen will act at the convention."

Meanwhile, Senator Taft's campaign, under the astute direction of Ben Tate, was consolidating his strength in areas where the outcome was fairly certain, and deftly avoiding a show of strength against Eisenhower in the political battleground where Eisenhower had shown strength.

The campaign moved toward the early summer . . . and into Texas. It was here that Roy Cullen had felt the issue would come to a head—and where his pre-campaign pledge, to "support to the best of my ability the one who happens to be the strongest candidate for the nomination of the Republican party at the time of the primaries," would be carried out.

Roy remembered the 1948 campaign, in which the "Dixiecrat" splinter party had sought vainly to break the regular Democratic grip on the state; and as the primary election drew near, he cautioned conservative Democrats in Texas—many of whom were as close to him politically as the Republicans—not to "jump the fence" too fast, or Governor Allan Shivers would be a sacrificial victim.

Shivers had led the Texas fight against the renomination of President Truman, and had fought the "Fair Deal" program; and Roy Cullen believed that in a direct choice between a "Fair Deal" Democrat and General Eisenhower, he could swing the Governor with his powerful political following toward Eisenhower.

As the critical primary election day approached, the number of Texans who paid their poll taxes—a requirement for voting in that state—increased sharply; and it was evident that powerful political undercurrents were gaining force.

Senator Taft's political sponsor in Texas was Henry Zweifel of Fort Worth, a shrewd political organizer and leader of the "regular Republican" faction in Texas. Zweifel blandly announced that Democrats would be welcomed into Republican ranks, and might even take part in Republican precinct meetings, without doing violence to their individual consciences. The numbers who flocked to Republican meetings startled even veteran politicos; for the first time since Reconstruction days in Texas, there were more people at Republican meetings than at the Democratic gatherings.

This aroused the suspicions of Zweifel and the regular Republicans, most of whom were behind Senator Taft; and their suspicions became sharper when the Taft forces began to be outvoted at nearly every precinct meeting. It was quite evident that a Republican "ground swell" had started in Texas—but it was for Eisenhower, not for Taft.

The political battleground of Texas, for the first time in the hundred-year history of the state, was no longer a contest for the Democratic nomination; it became a fight for the Republican nomination.

Zweifel ordered "rump sessions" of the precinct meetings, and Taft delegates were elected at most of these. This procedure was repeated at county elections; and as the State Convention drew near, it became apparent that two sets of delegates would show up. Roy Cullen wired Senator Taft that the "people of Texas are shocked" and warned him against permitting his henchmen in the state to "ride roughshod over the will of the majority of the State Convention."

He referred to the "steamroller tactics" of Senator Taft's illustrious father, William Howard Taft, whose political henchmen had blocked Colonel Theodore Roosevelt in 1921, and thrown the election to Woodrow Wilson. "We do not want history to repeat itself in 1952," Cullen said.

He asked the Senator to reply to his message, explaining his attitude toward the Texas primary maneuverings; and when Taft failed to reply, he released his telegram to the Houston *Post,* which published it on Sunday, May 28.

The electoral mechanics in the state of Texas are not materially different from those elsewhere in the country. The precinct and county voting determines the party representation at the State Convention, which in turn elects and instructs the delegates to the National Convention, where they adopt the party platform and select the party candidates.

However, the prospect of two different sets of delegates posed a question of seating the accredited delegates—and the accrediting authority was the State Executive Committee.

This group was a holdover from the previous convention . . . which had been almost solidly for Taft.

Thus the decision would rest in the hands of the State Executive Committee, dominated by Zweifel and controlled by the Taft organization. That organization had already extended its long arm from the Ohio Senator's headquarters in the East into Texas, advising the state committeemen as the campaign progressed.

These matters were freely reported in the Texas newspapers; and just before the State Convention was scheduled to assemble at Mineral Wells, a Houston reporter, Ben Kaplan, telephoned Roy Cullen that the Executive Committee planned to seat an entire list of Taft delegates, in effect ruling out the voting at the regular precinct and county elections.

"There won't be any fight on the Convention floor," the newspaperman told Cullen, "because there will only be one side voting."

"If they do that," Cullen warned, "it will be a disgrace to the state of Texas . . . It will be a national scandal."

The Executive Committee's decision to throw out the Eisenhower delegates was based on the assumption that they had been elected by Democrats, who had invaded precinct and county meetings, rather than Republicans.

General Eisenhower's supporters tried to block the Taft maneuver with a compromise, fearing that the "Texas primary scandal" would affect the Republican cause adversely; but Zweifel's best offer was to give General Eisenhower eight of the state's thirty-eight Republican delegates, leaving thirty for Senator Taft, and this was rejected.

The published reports of the elections showed that 736 Eisenhower delegates had been elected at Republican primary elections—out of a total of 1,060 in the state. Approximately an equal number of Taft delegates had been elected at "rump elections." These delegates all headed for Mineral Wells, where the State Republican Convention would decide on the delegation to represent Texas in Chicago.

Roy Cullen sent a final plea to Taft:

> If these brazen tactics are adopted at Mineral Wells, I honestly believe it will result in a national scandal . . . This telegram is sent in the spirit of friendship and humility, because I feel certain you will do all in your power to see that nothing is done at Mineral Wells to reflect upon your good name. Please let me know what action you plan to take.

Senator Taft took no action. The Convention met; and without much debate the Zweifel forces, in command from the start, ruled out every Eisenhower delegate on the grounds that they had been elected by Democrats. The Convention then selected thirty-five pro-Taft delegates to the National Convention in Chicago, and three remaining spots were handed to Eisenhower supporters.

The Eisenhower forces promptly held a "rump convention" and elected a full slate of pro-Eisenhower delegates—and the battle of Chicago was joined.

As Roy Cullen had warned in his telegram to Senator Taft, the proceedings at Mineral Wells quickly attained the proportions of a "national scandal." Even some ardent supporters of Senator Taft in Texas, who had not taken part in the political maneuverings, urged him to repudiate the election.

Roy Cullen's own family was split over the Taft-Eisenhower controversy. One of his sons-in-law, Corbin Robertson, was elected as a delegate by the Eisenhower "rump convention"; but his other two sons-in-law, Douglas Marshall and Ike Arnold, supported Taft. Marshall was elected as a delegate by the Taft faction; and both young men headed for

Chicago—assuring Roy Cullen that he would at least get first-hand reporting of the Convention.

Shortly before the Convention started in Chicago, B. Carroll Reece, Taft's "Southern manager," telephoned Cullen, asking him not to attack Taft until the Convention had an opportunity to pass on the delegations, because of the "unfortunate effect" it might have on the entire Republican campaign.

"If Bob Taft sanctions carrying out the Texas steal, I'll hit him harder than I've ever hit him yet," Cullen wired back.

On the day the Chicago convention opened, Roy Cullen issued a statement to the Houston newspapers. He recalled that a year ago he had told Senator Taft and the two Generals—MacArthur and Eisenhower—that he would support the one who "happens to be the strongest candidate" at convention time.

General MacArthur eliminated himself by declaring he was not a candidate, and by actively supporting Taft.

Senator Taft's failure to condemn the robbery of the delegates voted by his henchmen in Texas and other Southern states, and his attitude of aiding and abetting the rawest political deal I have ever witnessed, convinced me that he is not the right kind of man to be President of our country.

I have been on friendly terms with Senator Taft for a number of years. I donated freely to his previous campaigns for the Presidential nomination. I have been grievously disappointed in him.

Aside from that, I do not believe Senator Taft could be elected, even if he were nominated . . .

If a Republican is elected in November, it will have to be with the votes of several million Democrats, for the G.O.P. is short by several million of a majority. General Eisenhower can get these votes; the polls and the primaries have shown this.

If the political bosses ram Taft down our throats in Chicago, it will mean another Willkie-Dewey defeat, and I doubt that the Republican party can stand another one. The consequences likely would be a one-party system, which means a dictatorship.

The Eisenhower forces carried the banner of the "Texas steal" into the Convention, and the results are history. The first show of force on the seating of the Texas delegation lined up the opposing factions solidly between the pro-Taft and pro-Eisenhower groups, with the independent delegations, led by Warren of California, Fine of Pennsylvania and Stassen of Minnesota swinging the balance of power toward General Eisenhower.

Roy Cullen watched the Convention in the directors' room of his offices in Houston, munching on one cigar after another; and his face crinkled into a genial smile as he saw the vote roll up on the seating of the Texas delegation.

Taft's forces never recovered from that blow; when they lost Texas, they lost the nomination.

In the tumult of the Eisenhower victory, Roy Cullen wired congratulations to Eisenhower:

> Some two years ago while you were visiting my home I told you that the citizens of our great country would like to nominate and elect you President of the United States. I have repeated this statement to you many times in my letters to you while you were in Paris. It was my opinion that no one man nor group of men could stop you. The tale on the television today confirmed my belief. Lillie joins me in love and respect to you and Mamie.

General Eisenhower replied from Denver, where he had gone after the Convention:

Dear Lillie and Roy:

Mamie joins me in sincerest thanks for your heart-warming message received during the Convention in Chicago. We got a real lift from your wire, and it is certainly encouraging to know that warm friends are with us in the campaign ahead.

Best personal regards,

Sincerely,

Ike.

Roy Cullen
Houston
TEXAS
Roy Cullen
TEXAS

CHAPTER 27

"I have fought for nineteen years to save our form of government"

ROY CULLEN watched the first few weeks of the campaign from a hospital bed in Vancouver, B.C., and it was a galling experience to the old warrior. For nearly twenty years he had been fighting to drive the "New Deal-Fair Deal" from the White House; and now when victory seemed imminent, he was forced to observe the battle from the sidelines.

He had gone to British Columbia to visit Douglas Marshall and Margaret, at a mineral springs resort near Vancouver. On the way north he had been ill for a short time, but he scoffed at any suggestion that he was ill. When he arrived at the resort to join his children, the illness returned, and finally a physician from Vancouver told him he had serious kidney trouble.

Roy was taken to a hospital in Vancouver where an emergency operation was ordered. Meanwhile his lifelong friend and personal physician, Dr. H. J. Ehlers, flew to Vancouver; and with Dr. John McCaffrey, a young Canadian surgeon, the operation was performed.

For twenty-one days Roy had been unable to eat properly,

and the physicians had feared he would be unable to stand the shock of surgery. However, Roy Cullen had his own ideas about his physical condition.

While the physicians were discussing his ability to withstand the operation, he managed to aim his feet at one of the doctors, and almost sent him sprawling. This convinced them that the patient was in shape for surgery.

After the operation, Dr. Ehler and Dr. Ben Weems Turner, who had also flown up from Houston to attend the oil man, told Roy he would have to take a "complete rest."

This was a worse blow to Roy Cullen than the loss of his kidney. He had planned to get into the thick of the fight to elect General Eisenhower, and now—after two decades of fighting on a score of political fronts—he would have to sit idly by, twiddling his thumbs in obedience to his doctors' orders to "take it easy."

The party returned to Houston in a special plane, and Roy was like a caged bear when he arrived. However, Lillie—who had hardly left his side even for sleep since he had been stricken—saw to it that he followed instructions to take a complete rest.

Even from semi-retirement during his convalescence, Roy still kept his eyes on the national campaign. It had become evident to many Republicans that the General's campaign was bogging down. Roy watched the progress of the rival candidates—General Eisenhower and Governor Adlai Stevenson of Illinois—with growing anxiety. He recalled his repeated warnings to Eisenhower to "avoid politicians," and he was fearful that political alliances might defeat the Republican candidate.

Meanwhile, he had not overlooked the possibility that despite General Eisenhower's strong showing in the Republican primaries, he might stumble in the national campaign.

During the Democratic Convention in Chicago, Roy had wired Governor Shivers that if either Senator Russell of Georgia or Governor Stevenson of Illinois were nominated as the Democratic standard bearer, it was most important to "get the right running mate." He added: "If the international group led by Dewey and Aldrich control Eisenhower's campaign, good Texans may have to vote the Democratic ticket."

This betrayed a grave uncertainty in Roy's own mind as to the direction the Republican campaign might take. He had watched with growing misgivings the kind of men who had gathered around General Eisenhower; now as he watched the campaign on television at his home, his face still gaunt from the effects of the kidney ailment and the operation, he pondered over the possible shifts in the political currents.

The campaign was more than a political issue to Roy; it was a turning point for the country. Nearly ten years before —during the last months of World War II—he had written to Governor Beauford Jester of Texas: "The next few years will prove whether we will survive as a democracy, or whether we will become the pawns of political left-wingers and foreign theories of government." This was just before the campaign of 1946, in which Jester was elected Governor of Texas; later he wrote him again:

> Politicians, like poets, have great privileges; so you were in order when you left unsaid many things which would have cost you votes. But when you became Governor, you cannot with any degree of honor straddle any issue or go down the middle of the road when it has to do with a principle.

He now felt that much the same decision confronted General Eisenhower. If he let the same group surround him and advise him that had advised and influenced Dewey four years before, then the real issue would never be placed before the American people; and he was convinced that it was upon this issue—of individual freedom and individual rights against "creeping socialism"—that the nominees of the two parties must stand or fall.

On September 11, shortly after he returned from Vancouver, he wrote to General Eisenhower:

> Ike, as I have so often written you while you were abroad, the majority of the voters of this country are fond of you and would like to make you President, and the only thing that could defeat you would be some of the boys on your band wagon influencing you . . . You don't have to be a politician, but you are a soldier, and if elected you will place in your cabinet the top men in our country—top in experience and in integrity.
>
> I hope to recover in time to get into this political fight for you, because I feel I can reach many kinds of voters.

What disturbed Cullen most was General Eisenhower's failure to come forward with a strong, earnest statement on the basic questions raised by "New Deal-Fair Deal" policies. He was convinced that the trouble stemmed from the same thing that he had referred to in previous letters to the General: the influence of his campaign advisers and associates.

The General replied from his New York headquarters:

> Thank you for your encouraging letter. I particularly appreciate your constructive suggestions and your offer of assistance . . . I was sorry to learn about your serious operation in British Columbia and hope you are making a rapid recovery. Be sure to take good care of yourself and don't try to take on any additional obligations until you feel completely up to it.

Within a short time the Eisenhower campaign showed a sharp revision of tactics; and it was apparent the General had taken control of his own program. Roy Cullen was delighted with the change; and after the election, in which the Republican nominee piled up an unprecedented majority of more than 100,000 votes in Texas, he wired the President-elect:

> A large majority of the people of the United States have the same faith in you that I have, and they will stand behind you and Congress in curing the ills that now exist in our Government.

This was on November 5, 1952. Two weeks later he again wired Eisenhower:

> I am fully aware that the pork-barrel gang will give you a big working over. In view of this fact I am writing you a letter which may be of benefit to you. Personally, I have nothing to ask of you for myself, my family, nor any of my close friends; and I have no intention of trying to tell you who to appoint in your cabinet or how to handle the Korean tragedy.
>
> When President Roosevelt tore up the wonderful Democratic platform of 1932 and in 1933 started our country down the road to socialism, I then started fighting to help save our form of government. During all the nineteen years of my efforts I have worked with worthy political leaders of both parties . . . As I told you some two years ago while visiting my home and as I have repeated to you often in my letters while you were in Europe, the people wanted to nominate and elect you President. I informed you that many politicians trying to build their political fences were getting on your band wagon. I would give little heed to this pork-barrel gang.

The President-elect was busy building his cabinet, breaking precedent by announcing these appointments as they were chosen. Roy Cullen noted with satisfaction the men who were announced, and on November 21 he wired the General that he was "very gratified and happy over the appointments . . . and I think beyond a shadow of doubt that the people now have a leader they can trust and follow."

General Eisenhower wired back his thanks, adding: "I will

do my best to regard first of all the best interests of all of the American people. I am the same man I was before I became a candidate, and I have accepted the responsibilities of the Presidency with humble recognition of its obligations."

This was on November twenty-fifth. A week later Roy Cullen read the newspaper report that Eisenhower had named Martin Durkin, a New Deal Democrat, who had supported Governor Stevenson, as the new Secretary of Labor. The news was as shocking to Roy as it was unexpected. He felt that once again the advisers of the General were leading him astray. He wrote a long letter on December third, in which he said:

> I am worried over your last appointment of Martin F. Durkin to the position of Secretary of Labor. This may create trouble in Congress. It may give the Truman Democrats and the lukewarm Republicans an opportunity to criticize any of the legislation that you would want passed . . .

He was also disturbed about the appointment of Harold Stassen to head the Mutual Security Agency, which was then handling the purchase of critical materials throughout the world. He had telephoned Stassen, immediately after the appointment was announced, and had asked him point-blank whether he still held to the views of "world union" that he had advocated in his book, *Man Was Meant to Be Free,* published in 1943.

Cullen wrote Eisenhower:

> His reply was that the world had made so many changes since he put forth those ideas that he had fully changed his mind, and he knew his idea wouldn't work.
>
> I have known Harold Stassen for some time; I have had him in my home, and I am fond of him, but in some ways he is a most peculiar fellow. Last February Harold visited Lillie and me in Phoenix, Arizona, and after several hours spent with him I

told him that sometimes I am of the opinion that mentally he is a conservative but at heart he is a socialist.

General Eisenhower replied briefly to the comments on the Durkin appointment:

"I am grateful for your friendly interest and I appreciate your frankness. I am confident that events will soon dispel your apprehensions as to the appointments to which you refer."

Roy's apprehensions were not entirely dispelled; but on January 22, 1953, after the inauguration of General Eisenhower as the new President, he wrote with deep emotion:

> I have known you as a man and a soldier, and I believe you have the best opportunity to become the greatest President the United States has ever had. I am sure I shall not always agree in every detail with all your policies, but I know full well that fundamentally we have been in accord in the thoughts of what is ultimately best for our country. I know you will never willfully destroy the trust the people have placed in you, and my only fear is that you could be misdirected by those "little men" who have lost the prime quality of greatness and have become nothing more than politicians.

The inauguration of General Eisenhower as President might have marked the close of a twenty-year battle which Roy Cullen had been waging—sometimes with others, and at other times virtually alone—to restore a concept of American freedom as he had known it since he started as a young man in Texas and Oklahoma more than fifty years before.

He had passed the mark of "three score years and ten" which a man traditionally is allotted for his work on this earth; and again he might have retired to his "big white house" in Houston, satisfied that he had lived fully and well, and had done all that could be expected of any man.

But "retiring" was not in the Cullen vocabulary. He could

have retired after Blue Ridge, or Rabb's Ridge, and been comfortable and well fixed financially for the rest of his life, and for the lives of his children and grandchildren. Years ago he had told Lillie: "As long as folks live, they must keep on working . . . when you quit working you die—physically, or mentally."

If the fruits of the November victory were to last, other battles must be won. One of these was the status of the Republican party in Texas . . . which had swept Texas into the Republican column for the third time since Reconstruction days. The fact that Eisenhower had carried four Southern states—Texas, Tennessee, Virginia and Florida—was almost as significant to Roy as the outcome of the election nationally.

It meant that the time had arrived when a two-party system—the backbone of American democracy—might be established in the South. So he wrote a letter, and sent copies to eighty-nine members of Congress, urging the Republicans and conservative Democrats to join forces and "hold the bridgehead" gained in the 1952 election.

"It is time," he wrote, "to undertake a positive program for building up the Republican party in the South."

The key to the problem was patronage.

> By handling patronage wisely, the national Republican party can take a long step toward showing the people of the South they can come into the G.O.P. and not fear that they are merely joining up with a lot of patronage-hungry politicians who want to keep the party leadership small for various reasons.

He named a group of Texas Democrats—such as Allan Shivers and Wright Morrow, "and others like them in the Southern states"—who should be recognized by the Republicans on important political matters affecting the South.

> It is well to bear in mind that the only kind of Republicans we had in the South after the Civil War were carpetbaggers, and down through the years the situation changed very little until 1948. In that year the States' Rights Democrats succeeded in getting four states . . . to desert the (regular) Democratic party.
>
> In 1952 . . . some of the most prominent Democrats in Texas and the South supported the National Republican ticket because the Democratic party is now controlled by big-city machines, racketeers, minority groups and unscrupulous political bosses. It is no longer the party the South once belonged to. Therefore the time is now ripe to develop a two-party system in the South.

Replies to the letters came from all over the country, some of them cautiously reserving final judgment, but all those who replied—conservative Democrats as well as Republicans —urged Roy Cullen to "continue with your program."

The two pillars that he felt had made America strong were the "two-party system," which assured the final judgment of the American people; and the protective tariff which had served as a dyke against the onrushing tides of cheap labor in the world market. In March, 1953, replying to an invitation to meet with President Eisenhower and his Cabinet, sent by Sherman Adams, one of the principal advisers of the President, Cullen declined, but wrote:

> If we do away with our tariffs and have free trade with the world, it will wreck the financial structure of our country. I am sorry to say this is beginning to happen . . . Labor of all kinds and legitimate concerns have by hard work built a great market in this country of some three hundred and sixty billion dollars. This market belongs to the people who built it, and neither the President nor Congress has a right to give it away by flooding our market with merchandise made with the cheapest kind of labor, including slave labor.

Adams replied that the Administration did not contemplate efforts to knock down tariff walls "at this time," a modification which in no way relieved Roy Cullen's anxiety.

His concern mounted during the early months of the Eisenhower Administration when it became increasingly evident that the "international influence" was affecting the President's handling of the Korean situation. On June 25 he wired the President: "Our Government should not enter into a treaty with Korea, for their physical protection, for if this happens they will be everlastingly getting into trouble with some Asiatic nation knowing we will protect them."

The clash between the so-called "international group," which had supported the United Nations policies under President Truman and now sought to swing President Eisenhower in that direction, and the "Old Guard" Republican "isolationists" grew in tension as President Eisenhower headed toward completion of his first year in office.

Roy Cullen, watching every change in the political picture from his office in Houston, felt that the battle that had been waged so long and at so much cost to throw out the "New Deal-Fair Deal" faction would not be ended until the holdovers of this group had been removed from the Washington scene; and on December 14 he wrote the President, congratulating him on his address to the United Nations "on the atomic bomb." He said the speech was a "masterpiece," but added a word of caution:

> If Russia were to call our hand and we would have to enter into a contract with them regarding the pooling of atomic resources, we would then be in the same embarrassing position we are now in with relation to the peace treaty signed in Korea.

And then he plunged into the matter that was causing him great concern:

"Ike, I want to write you on a subject that is a thousand times more serious than our troubles in Korea." The subject was the so-called "Bricker Amendment."

The focal point of Roy Cullen's interest was what he had described as "the international influence." For twenty years he had watched the growing development of foreign theories of government creeping into the American political system. He had belabored a hostile Administration during this time with all the weapons at his command—telegrams, letters to congressmen, public speeches and published statements—in an effort to combat the inroads of "creeping socialism" and "one-worldism." Now, within a year after General Eisenhower had taken office, he saw the alien specter rearing its ugly head once more.

Late in 1952, while President Truman was still in office, Senator John Bricker of Ohio presented to the Congress a proposed constitutional amendment to correct the current reading that treaties were the "supreme law of the land," superseding the Constitution itself.

Roy Cullen sensed in the "Bricker Amendment" a great new bulwark of protection of American freedom against "internationalism" and "one-worldism," and he promptly launched a campaign to support it. The suggested amendment was designed to do two things: First, to make inoperative as "domestic law" any treaty which did not conform with the laws of Congress and the state legislatures; and second, to give Congress the power to "regulate" treaties and agreements which the President might make with foreign powers.

The proposed amendment, introduced into the Eighty-third Congress with the backing of (forty-five) members of the Senate, had been born on the tide of resentment against the Truman Administration's actions in Korea, and President Roosevelt's secret understandings at Yalta. What had started as a move to curb Democratic Presidential powers became an issue within the Republican party itself. The restraint upon the historic powers of the President to make treaties "with the advice and consent of the Senate" was regarded by the new President as a restriction upon his right to "conduct the foreign affairs of our country."

The actual effect was to bring before the nation the issue that Roy Cullen had wanted General Eisenhower to present in the campaign itself: the concept of American freedom and inherent rights, including the historic rights of the states, pitted against the advancing forces of "international influence" and "one-worldism." The fact that the issue was brought out a year after President Eisenhower had been elected was a new complication, since it involved the solidarity of the Republican party itself.

The lines of battle were drawn squarely between the "Old Guard" Republicans, who supported Senator Bricker, and the new coterie of advisers who surrounded the President; and Roy Cullen charged into this battle with flags flying.

"If wanting to protect this country against every foreign 'ism' and doctrine which can be made part of our own law by a treaty or agreement signed by the President—if that's being an isolationist, then I'm an isolationist!" he roared. "We built this country on American principles, and we fought to make those principles part of our kind of government. We don't want to see some treaty destroy what has been built."

He recalled the words he had spoken under the shadow of the monument at San Jacinto several years before: "I wonder if our grandfathers wouldn't decide it was time for another Texas declaration of independence. . . . Those rugged pioneers valued liberty as highly as they valued their lives. They are willing to fight for it, and if necessary die for it . . ."

Meanwhile, President Eisenhower and Senator Bricker were battling openly in Washington. The President had said:

"I am unalterably opposed to the Bricker Amendment . . . It would so restrict our conduct of foreign affairs that our country could not negotiate the agreements necessary to handling our business with the rest of the world . . . notice to our friends as well as our enemies abroad that our country intends to withdraw from its leadership in world affairs."

And Senator Bricker had replied: "The Amendment was approved by extremely able lawyers. The President is not a lawyer. His statement is utterly without foundation."

And from Houston, Roy Cullen fired his salvo—again in the medium of a telegram to the President:

> The people of the United States are becoming greatly alarmed over what is happening in Washington. Word has come to me from the North, South, East and West that the internationalists in New York are using all their influence, including "brain washing," to pressure our Administration; and lined up with these internationalists are the most radical members of Congress.
>
> If the Bricker Amendment is not passed, the Republican party is wrecked.
>
> In all my interviews and correspondence with you, I have continually warned you, since the first meeting long before you were nominated, about the unscrupulous influence that you would be subjected to if you were elected President.
>
> Ike, I hope you can overcome the situation. Because of the importance of this matter I am handing copies of this telegram to the press, which may be of assistance to you.

CHAPTER 28

"Home to me is where Lillie and the children are"

As THE TWENTIETH CENTURY passed into its second span of fifty years, the figure of Hugh Roy Cullen loomed larger and larger on the horizon of Texas. His oil wells were spread over the vast domain of the Lone Star State; but more important, he had assumed a kind of benevolent protectorate over the political affairs of his state and country. Claiming only the status of an ordinary citizen—and never a candidate for office—he used the scope of his vast personal contacts to create a kind of political momentum . . . the force of opinion of Mr. John Q. Public, in the person of Hugh Roy Cullen.

He wrote voluminously to congressmen and senators, to governors and members of the Cabinet; and he answered letters that came to him from every walk of life. By means of this constant flow of correspondence, he was more in touch with the political temper of the times, the ebb and flow of public opinion, than the professional politicians and editors of newspapers and magazines, whose business it was to know what people were thinking about.

Whether he was giving away money or personal opinions,

Roy Cullen operated with equal vigor and enthusiasm. By the time he had passed his seventieth year—in the first year of Dwight Eisenhower's Presidency—he had a correspondence file that reached every segment of public thought, and included thousands of personal and private opinions throughout the country. Men wrote to him who had never seen him; women, stirred by his human benefactions, wrote personal and deeply moving letters to him. Politicians from the North, as well as the South, sought his advice.

His friends and foes, political followers and political opponents, and the "little people" everywhere who knew him chiefly by what they read in the papers, were united on one point: Roy Cullen was one of the most generous Americans of all time. The healing balm of human feelings, that covers many a soreness of spirit, was his to an unusual degree, counterbalancing the quickness of his opinions.

His vast oil fortunes had given him perhaps more individual power than any other man in Texas—because it was a power controlled entirely by himself, and not dependent upon any political support or anyone's votes. Yet in the exercise of that power, he bridged the gap between the forces of high finance and the common man. The reason for this was quite simple: in all of his political forays, Roy Cullen was always on the side of the people.

"I know what the people are thinking about," he often said, "because I get letters from them. I get a lot more letters than anybody in politics."

This flood of letters has at times reached monumental proportions. A reporter for the Associated Press interviewed him, shortly after he had announced a donation of two and a quarter million dollars to the University of Houston, and wrote a story about the "human gusher from Texas" who gave away millions of dollars and opinions with equally impulsive generosity.

The response was overwhelming, and in some respects, startling. More than twenty thousand people wrote to Roy Cullen. Many were seeking donations—some personal, but most institutional. But the greatest proportion were merely showing a spontaneous human reaction to generosity. A priest wrote from a school in Minnesota:

"Will you and your wife visit us as our guests . . . We have prayerful hopes that you may be interested in our plans for a new library." Others sought assistance in establishing scholarships, and others sought contributions to the endowment of educational projects. But the vast majority wrote simply to tell the Texas oil man how glad they were to find a man who devoted himself so unstintingly to the service of mankind. From Ontario, Canada, a woman wrote: "I can't help thanking God for people like you . . ."

And from Calgary, Canada, another writer—also a woman—wrote: "Tell me, Mr. Cullen, are you for real?"

Most of the letters contained a religious note. One wrote: "May the Lord continue to bless you as you continue to serve Him." And this was in spite of the clear indication in the newspaper that Roy Cullen espoused no specific religion or creed, and that he had donated money without preference or favor to Protestants and Catholics, Jews and Christians.

Many of these letters contained strange points of view, yet all seemed to be responsive to the impulsive generosity of heart which the story portrayed. A seventy-two-year-old farmer in Connecticut wrote: "You seem to be noted for giving away your money and your opinions. Could you give me an opinion?" He wanted to know how he could live on Social Security payments of eighty dollars a month.

Many of the responses were deeply human and loving. An Air Force enlisted man in a Texas air base wrote: "Here I am writing to a person I have never seen . . . I would like to shake your hand." Many of the writers engaged in lengthy philosophical discourses, one writing a four-page letter on the atomic age, its perils and implications, and closing with the concise summary: "I still feel fine."

One man from Minnesota, a farmer, wrote skeptically that he "just couldn't believe all the things that have been said about you are true—or are they?" Roy replied to that letter, pointing out that "all human beings are subject to error, but on the whole, the story was accurate."

Another man from Minnesota suggested that Roy Cullen "looks so much like my father—which is gone—so I am asking you if you can see your way to call on me some time, if the weather gets nice, so I can see for myself."

Roy Cullen's explanation of his own philosophy of giving as "selfish"—the desire to enjoy the fruits of his benefactions while he was alive—struck varying chords. A man from a Bible school in Kansas wrote: "Many have never taken the opportunity to be 'selfish,' as you call it—and their cup never runs over." As an afterthought, he mentioned that if Roy Cullen wished to donate something to "a small Christian school" it would be acceptable.

A lady, also from Kansas, wrote: "Thank you, two people, for being 'selfish.' Who am I to dare to write to you? Just a farmer's wife. Ha!"

As Roy and Lillie Cullen moved toward the afternoon shadows of their lives, the scene around them acquired the rich glow of sunset. Their fifteen grandchildren and three great-grandchildren were a deep source of love to both; and although two—the sons of Lillie Cranz Portanova—were in Italy, the others were close to the Cullen hearth.

During the war years Roy began to build a home on his ranch—an expanse of several thousand acres about fifty miles northwest of Houston, near Columbus.

Wartime restrictions on building made it necessary to move a house onto the ranch, rather than to build there; and Roy decided to transfer a house he had built on the bayshore, twenty miles below Houston, out to his ranch at Columbus. He took his gardener and helper and two carpenters, and together they moved the country home at the bayshore piece by piece to the ranch, where it was rebuilt as a smaller ranch house.

On this rambling estate Roy found a place for relaxation; and often on week ends, or at other times when the pressure of work at the Quintana office subsided, he and Lillie would drive out for a few days of rest. The ranch house was not large—two bedrooms, each with a bath; an old-fashioned "sitting room" and a dining room and kitchen; but there was hot and cold running water, gas for heating and cooking, and good plumbing.

In the evenings the two—Roy and Lillie—would sit, talking over the affairs of the family, or playing dominoes. Both were early risers, and after Lillie had made breakfast, the two would sit together, looking out over the rolling timber lands of the 14,000-acre ranch where more than a thousand deer roam, together with some five hundred head of white-faced steers.

The ranch is about thirty miles from the little town of Schulenberg, where Roy and Lillie had met half a century before; and yet the two had come a long ways since that day —through the wild frontier days of Western Oklahoma; the hard struggle to make a living and a place for his family in the early days in Houston; the long rides across the broken tablelands of West Texas, hunting for oil . . . and now the afternoon of life, surrounded by their children, grandchildren and great-grandchildren.

"We've lived in a lot of different places," Roy often said, "but I guess home to me is where Lillie and the children are."

Although the "children" were all grown and married—with children of their own romping through their houses—the "big white house" on River Oaks Boulevard was always headquarters for the entire family. The mansion, built of Texas limestone, was far too large for two people, yet it seldom seemed that way, because there were always people in it—members of the family or old friends who dropped by to "sit and talk a spell."

The house and gardens are staffed with more than a dozen servants, yet there is never a sense of "too many servants." The luxury of the Cullen home is obvious, but not ostentatious; and the quiet grace which Lillie Cullen created in every room has lent to the home a simple, warm dignity and beauty which no interior decorator could have contrived.

Most of the week days are spent down at the Quintana office, where Roy sits with the Star Spangled Banner and the flag of Texas standing in opposite corners behind his desk. His sons-in-law, Ike Arnold, Corby Robertson and Doug Marshall, come in from time to time; and often Grandson Roy Henry drops in to talk over oil-drilling problems.

Maps and geological charts are spread out on the desk, and Roy sits with his shirtsleeves rolled up, pouring over the lines of earth structure. The old sense of "a nose for oil" is still very much in evidence; and after the members of the younger generation have worried over the problems, it is usually the final word of the gray old ex-wildcatter that makes the decision.

Between oil problems he is busy with problems of the

nation, dispatching a telegram or a letter to a senator or congressman, or perhaps a word of caution or advice to "Ike." Shortly after the President had addressed the United Nations on the future of atomic energy, late in 1953, Roy Cullen wrote him a letter congratulating him on the speech, and adding:

> Ike, I want to write you on a subject that is a thousand times more serious than our troubles in Korea. We came so nearly losing our form of government when three members of the Supreme Court held that Harry Truman had a right to take over the steel industry . . .

And the letter then launched into a vigorous appeal for the President to support the Bricker Amendment, urging him to confer with those who have the nation's welfare at heart, and winding up with a succinct admonition:

"Ike, I hope you will not wait, but will attend to this important matter immediately."

Since the early days of the Roosevelt tenure of office, when the political ideologies of the country were pretty well lined up to the right and left of center, Roy Cullen's position had been quite firmly established. He was well to the right; and he was a conservative. But above all, he was an American and a Texan.

As the years rolled on, his name had become famous in many places outside Texas, and particularly in the halls of Congress. Many owed their political fortunes to him, at least in part; and these and many others were his friends. He continued to pepper them with opinions and advice, tossing out quick and sometimes acrid comments on the conduct of public affairs. Yet even his sharpest comments were salted with good humor and the human kindness so natural to him.

The reporter who wrote the story that drew twenty thousand letters had remarked that Roy Cullen, whether "giving away money or opinions, is often unpredictable . . . He is by turns impulsive, sentimental, opinionated, gentle, sharp-tongued and folksy, and as tactful as a Texas steer stampeding through a glass works." But the writer added: "All the adjectives pale in favor of one word: generous."

And as Roy Cullen moved down toward the closing corridors of his span of life, he left on the state and nation his forefathers had helped to build the indelible imprint of the thing that had made America strong: faith in himself, and in people; and the rugged courage to make that faith stand up.

EGGENHOFER

CHAPTER 29

"This is fifty years of Texas history passing in review"

IT WAS late in the afternoon of December 29, 1953. The sunlight slanted through the window, glowing softly on the pale green walls of the big office on the seventeenth floor of the City National Bank Building in Houston. Roy Cullen sat at his big desk, his face etched in deep lines, drumming lightly on his desk with his finger tips. Two standards were against the wall—one with an American flag draped against the staff, and the other with the Lone Star flag of the Republic of Texas.

Roy was in a reminiscent mood. His grandson, Roy Henry Cullen, was sitting in a big easy chair against the wall; and Douglas Marshall, his son-in-law, had just come in with a gold cigarette lighter, with the words "50 golden years" engraved upon it.

"I know you don't want any presents, Dad—but here it is, anyway," he said.

Roy Cullen took the lighter.

"Thank you, Doug." He looked at the lighter, and

chuckled. "Lillie'll get this anyway—for one of the tables in the living room."

Across the flat city the white buildings of the Texas Medical Center stood like granite blocks against the shimmering haze of the afternoon sun. Beyond these shadowy shapes stretched the rolling plains of Texas . . . on toward Schulenberg, where he had courted Lillie, and where they were married; and beyond to San Antonio, where he had lived with his mother and his brother Dick, and the Beck children in the big square house on Frio Street . . . Dick Cullen was still living in San Antonio, but all the others were gone—Joe and Jim and Lucien Beck; his sisters, Louise and Daisy; and his mother, who had spent many of the closing years of her life in the Cullen home on Alabama and Austin.

The day had dawned bright and clear; and now the sun was sinking into the west.

"It's time to get home and help Lillie get the party started," he said suddenly.

It was the "Golden Wedding Anniversary" of Roy and Lillie Cullen.

That night they came from all over Texas, and from all over the country. Dr. John McCaffrey, who had operated on Roy Cullen in Vancouver the year before, flew down from Canada with his pretty wife, to be at the party. Old friends came from New York, Miami, San Francisco and Los Angeles . . .

During the day vast preparations had been made for the party, which was to mark a half-century of wedded life for Roy Cullen and the blue-eyed girl he had met and loved in the last year of the old century . . . and who had been at his side since they were married in Schulenberg on December 29, 1903.

To Houstonians, it was an opportunity to pay one more tribute to the couple who had given more to their city than anyone else . . . to the University of Houston, the Art Museum, the hospitals and medical school, the Boy Scouts and Girl Scouts, the Symphony Orchestra. There was hardly a cultural or educational or medical establishment in Houston that did not owe some of its existence to Roy and Lillie Cullen.

Within the Cullen home the tables were piled with food and delicacies—huge hams and roasts, and canapés, with vintage champagne, and a big buffet of smoked oysters in barbecue sauce.

From room to room, beginning with the long living room at the east end, and ending at the "sun room" on the west end, the interiors were decorated in yellow. There were yellow roses massed in arrangements of varying sizes and shapes, yellow chrysanthemums, gladiolas, carnations, and even gilded magnolia leaves. In the center of a round table, upon which food of all kinds had been heaped, was a huge bouquet of yellow tulips; and in the big dining room, glittering with the icy sheen of candelabras, was a huge five-tiered wedding cake at one end of the long table, and at the other end was laid out the golden trays and candlesticks that were part of the gold service presented to Lillie and Roy by the members of their family.

Perhaps the crowning touch in the atmosphere of magnificence were groups of candy orchids, delicately shaped and colored in shades of gold. And following the golden theme, yellow roses and orchids—also of candy—decorated the tall, white wedding cake.

There had been few events like this in the history of Houston—which was not without some measure of fame for its spectacular parties. But the "Golden Anniversary" of Roy and Lillie Cullen was more than a party. As one of the guests said, "This is fifty years of Texas history passing in review."

Roy Cullen stood inside the pillared portico of his home on River Oaks. Beside him, as the guests streamed in, was Lillie, in a blue "sea foam" dress. There was little formality about the greetings. The men slapped Roy on the back and kissed Lillie, and Roy kissed their wives. The guest list was a roll call of famous names in Texas—Jesse Jones; the Governor, Allan Shivers; and former Governor Will Hobby, with his wife, Oveta Culp Hobby, who had founded the Women's Army Corps. Wright Morrow was there; and Jim Abercrombie, the oil man who almost bet Roy fifty thousand dollars he wouldn't strike oil in his first well on the Washburn Ranch.

The gleaming chandeliers and the massive marble that lined the foyer lent an air of nineteenth-century magnificence to the scene; and on a huge dining table was laid out a golden tea service, with gold candelabras and trays, designed for the "Golden Anniversary." The rooms were a vivid mass of yellow flowers—chrysanthemums, yellow roses, gladiolas and ranunculi—with gold leaves laid on the table tops.

The decorations were only a setting, however. The spacious rooms soon became filled with chattering guests; and now and then the wriggling form of one of the Cullen grandchildren squirmed through the crowd. They were all there—daughters, sons-in-law and grandchildren—and even Roy Cullen's great-grandson, young Roy Cullen III, the son of Grandson Roy Henry. Only the eldest daughter, Lillie Cranz Portanova, and her two children who were in Italy, were unable to be there.

There had been few anniversary parties like it . . . A half a hundred members of the Cullen and Cranz families had gathered with hundreds of friends in the big home Roy had built. Lillie's relatives, Gus Cranz Jr., Mrs. G. E. Cranz Sr., John Foster Cranz and Mr. and Mrs. W. P. Cranz had come down from Fort Worth; other old friends had come from San Antonio and Schulenberg, including young Charlie Perlitz, the son of Annie Schuhmacher and Charles Perlitz, who had introduced Roy and Lillie. But most important of all, the children, grandchildren and great-grandchildren of Roy and Lillie were there . . . and this brought them the deepest happiness.

For five hours Roy had stood in the foyer, greeting guests and saying "Goodbye" to those who were leaving. At midnight he sat down on the lower step of the winding staircase. He had said "Good night" to all his grandchildren—Margaret's two boys, Hugh and Douglas Junior; and little Lillie Therese, and Beth, and Corbin Junior, the children of Wilhelmina. Mary Hugh Arnold, the daughter of Ike Arnold and Agnes, had been there with a young Houston physician, Dr. Russell Scott, Jr., glowing and happy . . .

Raymond "Buddy" Dickson, who had known Roy in the cotton-buying days in Oklahoma and in Houston, nudged him with his elbow, and said: "Remember, Roy, when you told me there were more people in the cotton business than there was cotton business—and pretty soon we'd have to start half soling each other's shoes?"

Roy grinned; there were many reminders on this night of those early days. There were also reminders of later years—when his family had been taken care of, his children and grandchildren provided for . . . and he and Lillie were able to start taking care of other people.

Bishop Frank Smith of the Methodist Church, a guest at the anniversary party, told of a remark Roy Cullen had made some years before, when the Bishop had thanked the oil man for his gift of a "million plus" to the Methodist Hospital. Roy had said: "I've always wanted to help people. My mother used to feed every tramp that came to the door when I was a boy, and I guess I was as eager to help people when I was poor as I am now—only I didn't have much to help them with. I've watched a lot of men getting rich—right here in Houston—and I've talked with a lot of them about what they were going to do with their money. Getting money never made people generous. It is my conviction that unless a man is generous to begin with, the richer he gets the tighter he gets."

Dean Manion of Notre Dame had sat one evening several years before in the same living room of the Cullen home, where the guests were now drifting about, and had asked Roy questions about his philosophy of life . . . and later Dean Manion had said:

"Roy Cullen freely declares his disbelief in any religious dogma; but he has the most profound belief in God I have ever encountered . . . He follows his moral conscience more carefully than many a monk in a monastery. The keynote of his life is faith—the faith that determination, truth and hard work would bring rewards of personal happiness and material prosperity."

Looking back over the years, Roy Cullen could see in the house filled with his family and friends on this night the tangible results of the days of his life. Here were old companions . . . Marion Law, the banker, who had known Roy when he had to borrow money from the bank to pay his rent; and Mrs. Law, who came to the anniversary party with her broken arm in a cast . . . Jim Elkins, a grizzled veteran of a half century of banking in Houston, who had seen oil fortunes come up like a gusher and burst like a bubble . . . the Hugh Montgomerys, the Cullens' landlord in the first house

Louise Cullen, Hugh Roy's mother.

Cicero Cullen,
Hugh Roy's father.

Left to right: Dick Cullen, Hugh Roy Cullen, at the time they were "kid-napped" by their father.

Mr. and Mrs. Gustave Cranz,
Lillie's parents.

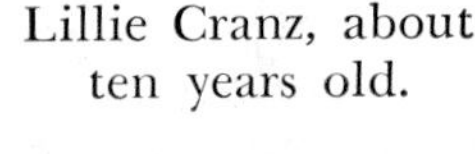

Lillie Cranz, about
ten years old.

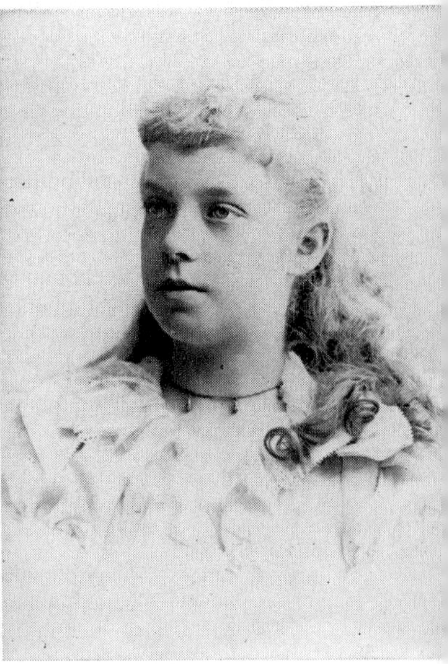

Ezekiel Cullen.

Lillie in her wedding dress, about 1905.

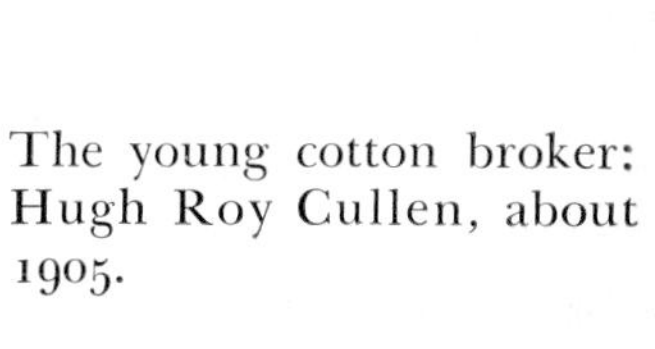

The young cotton broker: Hugh Roy Cullen, about 1905.

Roy Gustave Cullen.

Left to right: *(standing)* Jim Beck, Dick Cullen, Lucien Beck; *(seated, center)* Louise Cullen; *(seated, below)* Hugh Roy Cullen, Daisy Cullen. Picture taken at Mrs. Cullen's home in San Antonio.

Doctor of Science, University of Pittsburgh. Left to right: Dean E. A. Holbrook, Hugh Roy Cullen, Chancellor J. G. Bowman.

Margaret, Hugh Roy, Wilhelmina and Lillie, with Fred Lloyd at Walden Oaks, England, 1935.

Family holiday at the Greenbrier, White Sulphur. Rear seat: Wilhelmina and Hugh Roy; middle seat: Wilhelmina's daughter Beth, Lillie, and nurse; front seat: driver, Corbin Robertson, and Corbie, Jr.

The big white house.

The big white house from the air.

Houston Municipal Wharf, 1915.

Oil field near Houston, about 1920.

Spindletop, the first Texas well.

Drilling for oil—

—is a complex (and muddy) job.

Campus of the University of Houston.

The Roy Gustave Cullen Building
University of Houston

Ezekiel Cullen Building
University of Houston

Cullen Nurses Home
Baptist Memorial Hospital

The dormitory group at the
University of Houston

Cullen Family Building
St. Joseph's Catholic Hospital

The Lillie and Roy Cullen Building
Baylor University College of Medicine
Texas Medical Center

Golden Wedding Anniversary.

A word with a great-grandson, Golden Wedding Anniversary.

they had lived in when they came to Houston . . . and a host of others.

On the table were telegrams from many who could not come—John Flynn, whose *The Road Ahead* had been one of Roy Cullen's most powerful weapons in his fight for political freedom; Vice-President Richard Nixon; Carl Wente, president of the Bank of America in San Francisco; a warm letter from Mamie Eisenhower, and a telegram from the President; letters from Representative Joe Martin, Senator Dirksen, Leo Allen; a note from Paul Neff, president of the Missouri Pacific; Julie Penrose, owner of the Broadmoor in Colorado Springs, where Roy and Lillie had spent many days; and from Bob Harriss, whom he had known in his early days in Western Oklahoma; Senator Joe McCarthy, and his wife, Jean; and from Atif Benderlioglu, mayor of Ankara, Turkey.

Roy Cullen knew he had started with nothing but the bare things of life—a strong body, and a good mind . . . and the strong faith that had been passed down from forebears who came from Scotland and England and settled in America —in the Carolinas, Georgia, and finally in Texas.

Everything he had gotten in life had been built with his hands and his mind; and the courage and determination it had taken to build these things had come from something his mother had taught him . . . faith in himself, and faith in people.

And now Roy was able to look back over fifty years of his adult life—and to measure that faith against his own accomplishments. He could measure it in terms of things he believed in—not the oil he had dug out of the ground, but the things he had been able to do with the oil . . . for his family, his children, and grandchildren; and for the hospitals and the University of Houston; and for his country.

During the evening a Houston radio station had broadcast a message to the couple who had done so much for the city. Fred Nahas, the commentator, had said:

> Tonight, warmed by the love of their family and the cherished friends who are even now gathered at their home to do them honor on their Golden Anniversary, Roy Cullen and his lovely wife may well remember those golden moments a half century ago when their hopes and dreams were united in the sanctity of their marriage vows . . . And tonight, even as the twilight fades away and Mr. and Mrs. Cullen observe their anniversary among their family and friends, there are thousands of people in Houston and elsewhere who thank our Heavenly Father for this good and kindly man and wife, who have opened their hearts to all humanity . . .

EPILOGUE

"The riches extracted from the earth . . . they have given back"

THE FINAL PAGES of Roy Cullen's story must necessarily be blank. Most life stories are written at the close of a lifetime; but perhaps the philosophy Roy Cullen applied to his philanthropies may also be applied to his biography.

"All rich men leave their money to someone when they die," he said, "since they can't take it with them. If they bequeath it to charity or education or some worthy institutions, they may get a degree of satisfaction from anticipating the good they will do after they are gone.

"But why wait? Why not give it while you are alive and get the full enjoyment of seeing the good it does, day by day?"

And so perhaps the same reasoning may be applied to the story of Hugh Roy Cullen. If telling the story can serve a purpose today—if it will demonstrate how the qualities that Louise Cullen moulded in the character of her son more than a half century ago have found fulfillment in a life devoted to the service of his family, his home and his country, and in a sense to all of mankind—then, as Roy Cullen said of his philanthropies: Why wait?

There is something in the character of such a life that must appeal to all mankind. He spent his youth and his young manhood in a hard and often unrewarding struggle to make a home and establish a means of livelihood for himself and his family; and at the age of thirty he had achieved what would have been regarded as success by most young men of his day. He had a business and a home, and the good will of his friends and business associates. And yet he decided to abandon his career in the cotton business, because he did not believe it held the promise he expected—and wanted.

Years later, recounting that decision, he shook his head slowly and said: "I guess it took a lot of what folks would call a fool's courage—but it also took a lot of faith. I didn't do it hastily or without any reason; I looked over those maps and made a plan—and I was sure that plan would work because I believed in people, and in myself . . ."

The second quarter century of his life was spent in "proving up" on his faith . . . winning a home and security for the family he brought down from Oklahoma to Houston in 1911.

And Roy Cullen's third quarter of a century has been spent in carrying out what Governor Shivers called "an excellent record of Christian stewardship."

Through the fabric of his life is woven a consistent thread —not only in the development of his own character, but in the unflagging persistence with which he adhered to certain codes of living, inherited from his Scottish forebears, and nourished and strengthened by Louise Cullen.

Few men have fought as hard for what they have obtained; and, in the political arena, it is doubtful if any other man living today has given as much service without personal ambition or hope of reward.

He has been a thorn in the side of "New Deal-Fair Deal" politics; and not a few have denounced him as a "meddler" in public affairs. But he believes that "meddling" in public affairs is not only a privilege, but also the duty of a good citizen.

Roy Cullen has been for fifty years a "rugged individualist" —a fighter for American freedom as he understood the meaning of the word from his forefathers, who fought for freedom in the American Revolution and in the Texas Revolution.

His belief in freedom is more than a political conviction; it is a religion. And in religion itself, he has been a "rugged individualist." At a luncheon one day in Houston he sat beside Norman Vincent Peale, and told him:

"The trouble with most religions is that it is man-made. Many people who are quite intelligent seem to feel that their position in society requires that they embrace a particular brand of religion. They submerge their reasoning for dogma —and I suppose that kind of faith will get them to Heaven in the end. On the other hand, the crowning glory of God's creation—the thing that sets man apart from all other creatures—is the human intellect and the power of reason. I can't believe God would have endowed us with this gift, unless He intended for us to use it . . ."

On one occasion he was asked by a minister to come to his church; he wanted to express his gratitude to the oil man for his great contributions to hospitals in Houston. Roy went over to the church, and the minister asked him to kneel and pray.

"Why do I have to kneel?" Cullen asked. "Why can't I pray standing up?"

The minister was astonished.

Finally he said: "That's the way people pray, Mr. Cullen."

"It's not the way I pray," Roy said. "Look here . . . God made my feet as well as my knees, didn't He?" The minister nodded. "Well, I do most everything else on my feet, and I think it will be all right with Him if I pray on my feet."

Later he explained to friends: "I think the fundamental trouble with religion today is that our prayers are too much like petitions to get God on our side, and too little trying to get on His side. Many people wear the knees off their trousers asking God for favors, and they rarely do anything to merit the favors."

Although he has fought the "internationalist influence" in Washington, he is strangely lacking in provincial or racial prejudices. He has given more to the advancement of Negro education in Texas than any other man in the state; and a few years ago when he was invited to attend the National Conference of Christians and Jews, he wrote back:

> Replying to your letter I wish to say I have always been opposed to the "get-together" of the Christians and Jews, for the reason that I don't know of anyone who has separated them. The way I feel, Jews, Baptists, Catholics, Methodists and Episcopalians are all together to start with, and you don't have to have a meeting to get them together. If any Jews or Christians are apart, it is of their own making . . .

Roy Cullen has established himself as a perennial watchdog for American freedom; and each day in his Houston office, he scans the skies for signs of ominous clouds. When he sees any threatening phenomenon, he fires away—usually with a salvo of telegrams to senators and congressmen, who have learned to respect not only his sincerity, but his persistence.

But his activities are by no means confined to Texas and

Washington. His interests range far and wide—from philanthropic affairs, and his activities as Chairman of the Board of Regents of the University of Houston, to cultural organizations, the Government—and the vast network of oil wells that continue to pour millions of dollars into the coffers of Quintana Petroleum, a large part of which is poured back into the Medical Center, the University and the hospitals. In fact, he has given away 93 percent of his worldly goods.

And so the Cullen story goes on, with Roy Cullen striding through his seventies with the same vigor and zeal that he marched through his thirties during his early days in Houston. One of the most striking sketches of the career of Roy and Lillie Cullen was given by a young student from the University of Houston, Jack Valenti, who wrote:

> The riches that the Cullens have extracted from the earth, they have given back to their fellow-humans. All this they have done with simple directness and genuine tenderness; and with no thought of thanks, or the praise of other citizens, or public eulogies. Lillie and Roy Cullen want this world to be better when they leave it. This is Christian goodness at its height . . .

INDEX

Index

U

W

Y

Z